Dogs
Singing

A TRIBUTE ANTHOLOGY

Compiled & Edited by
JESSIE LENDENNIE

salmonpoetry

Published in 2010 by
Salmon Poetry Ltd.,
Cliffs of Moher, County Clare, Ireland

ISBN 978-1-907056-50-5

Compiled and edited by Jessie Lendennie

Cover artwork: *blue* by Margaret Nolan
(Email: margaretnolangraffiti@gmail.com)

Cover design & typesetting: Siobhán Hutson

Salmon Poetry receives funding from the Arts Council

for Zookie, her book

You keep on walking by . . . Why why why?

I have been like this for months and you keep walking by
You do not help me you just keep walking by
You do not see my hunger or thirst you just keep walking by
You do not see my pain you just keep walking by
When you do see me all you feel is disgust . . . Why why why
I come near you for help you chase me away . . . Why why why
My cancer tumors grow as does the pain, you ignore me . . . Why why why
You are many humans but are not humane . . . Why why why
Today my pain has gone as I am taken from this world, to the next,
for the first time in my life I was stroked and kissed as I slipped away
Why did I have to wait until my last minutes to feel love . . . Why why why

GILL DALLEY
Soi Dog Foundation, Phuket, Thailand
www.soidog.org

Dog Soul

In 1907 Dr Duncan MacDougall weighed six tubercular patients just before and just after their deaths and determined the average weight loss across the six as being 21 grammes.

This, the good Doctor decided, was the weight of the soul. 21 grammes.

He subsequently carried out similar experiments on 15 dogs and recorded no weight loss.

I have no idea what exactly the soul is or where it is or if it is but I know, instinctively, that Duncan MacDougall was wrong. If anything has a soul, it's a dog. It has a soul filled with love and loyalty and joy and the willingness to forget and forgive at the same time. It has a soul that smiles and says welcome. It has a soul that is grateful for small kindnesses. A soul that is free as it wanders the fields and mooches through the woods. It has a soul that says Friend to those who treat it with respect.

If Duncan MacDougall were really set on discovering things about the soul, he should have looked in the eyes of a dog and weighed its tail when its last breath was drawn.

JOHN MACKENNA

("Dog Soul" was broadcast on RTE Radio 1, 'A Living Word' 2nd November, 2010)

Contents

Foreword by the Editor   19
Introduction by Eileen Battersby   23

By...

Who'd be a dog?   Paula Meehan   29
The Hound of the Baskervilles   Neil Astley   30
Xochi's Tale   Maxine Kumin   31
The Bitch Protests Litter Murders   Bertha Rogers   32
César   Hélène Cardona   33
Dog Smart   Cynthia Schwartzberg Edlow   34
A Dog in California   Julian Gough   36
Come Back Soon   Jordan Taylor   39
Calvin's Story   Scott Edward Anderson   41
Fergus's Ode to Joy   Bette Lynch Husted   44
Ergo Sum   John Walsh   45

For...

Bridgette Was A Show Girl   Michael Heffernan   49
The Blood We Paid For   Thomas Lynch   50
January 19, Still Thawing, Breezy   Ted Kooser   51
Aubade   J.D. Smith   52
Lutherans   Larry O. Dean   53
To My Dog, With a Broken Leg   Larry O. Dean   54
For Prince   John Hildebidle   56
For Pine Goose the best dog in the history of the world   Sharon Young   57
Zookie   Jessie Lendennie   58
Izzy   Jessie Lendennie   59
Dog   Paul Genega   60
Zach   Desmond Gough   61
Zach Speaks   Devon McNamara   62
Spring Lament   Devon McNamara   64
Zach   Eleanor Cummins   66

Nobody Would Understand   Kate Newmann   67

For Both of Us, Beau   Joan Newmann   68

My dog Trotsky   William Wall   69

Cú na gCleas   Gréagóir Ó Dúill   70

Greta   Ben Howard   72

A Dog's Life   Maurice Harmon   73

Conbec   Maurice Harmon   75

Madraí na hÉireann   Laura Lundgren Smith   76

Dog Years   Gerard Smyth   78

Collie   Peter Fallon   79

Own   Peter Fallon   80

Walking In Snow On A Full Moon Night   Pam Uschuk   81

In Synch   Pam Uschuk   82

Howl For Edo   Ann Fox Chandonnet   83

Cat Person   Michèle Vassal   86

(for Juno)   Patrick Chapman   88

Dear Mickey   Peter van de Kamp   89

Bark   Peter van de Kamp   90

Mickey   Peter van de Kamp   92

The Dog is Disappointed in Me   Wendy Thornton   93

Curriculum   Adam Tavel   94

Ode to Noah Caterpillar Jackson, 1807-1880   Adam Tavel   95

Poem for My Daughter's Schnauzer   Nancy J. Thompson   98

Marker Of Our Lives   Katie O'Sullivan   99

Oliver   Julian Stannard   100

Still Life with Hound Dog   Michelle Valois   101

Doggerel for Emily   Richard Murphy   103

Night Watch   Mark Smith-Soto   104

Circumnavigator   Nessa O'Mahony   105

Elegy For A Basset Hound   Michael O'Loughlin   106

From One Old Dog to Another   William Pitt Root   108

Walking Story   William Pitt Root   110

Elegy for Apu   William Pitt Root   112

Minus Forty   Patricia Robertson   113

For Rimbaud (1965-1978)   Knute Skinner   114

Charlie   James Simmons   116

Tread Softly   Ben Simmons   119

Haunch   Anne Shaw   121

Meanwhile...   Breda Wall Ryan   122

chance of thunderstorms increasing overnight   Layne Russell   124

Freckles   Lex Runciman   125
Dog   Jacob Rakovan   126
For Pia   Irene McKinney   128
Welcoming a friend from the past   Seamus Cashman   130
Affection   George Petty   132
The Neighbour's Dog   John Perrault   133
Non-Dog   Harry Owen   134
Anubis In Oghery   Mary O'Malley   135
Cleo   Mary O'Malley   136
Eastwood   Chris Oke   137
Snowy in Candy Kitchen   James Desmond O'Hara   138
Threena   Tommy Frank O'Connor   139
Jake and the Last Day of Summer   Sheila Nickerson   141
With an Old Dog in the Autumn Woods   Sheila Nickerson   142
Circus Dog   Pete Mullineaux   143
Salty   Pete Mullineaux   144
Goldie   Mary Mullen   145
Clio   Noel Monahan   146
Canticle for a Samoyed   Karla Linn Merrifield   147
Yet   Alexa Mergen   148
The Wilder Dog and I   Alexa Mergen   149
Bran   Máighréad Medbh   150
Dire Consequences   Mary Madec   153
Trust   Cecilia McGovern   154
Cracked   Afric McGlinchey   155
Devotion   Bette Lynch Husted   156
Luckie Shows Up Seventy Years Later   Danuta E. Kosk-Kosicka   157
In Salamanca: Sinbad, the Dog   Danuta E. Kosk-Kosicka   158
Shelter   Jacqueline Kolosov   159
Local Spirit   Philip Kingston   161
Osgar   Deirdre Kearney   162
Hector   Conor Mark Kavanagh   163
The Truth About the Dog   Brad Johnson   164
A Bouquet of Ephemerals   Sabine Huynh   165
Maggie   Noël Hanlon   167
Dog   Noël Hanlon   169
Ringo   Gerard Hanberry   170
Whiskey in the Morning   Lisa Frank   172
Lassie   Gabriel Fitzmaurice   173
Sandy   Elaine Feeney   174

Death of a Love Junkie   Susie DeFord   178
Wrestling a Cerberus   Susie DeFord   180
Bulls of Pamplona   Susie DeFord   182
The Luckiest Dog in the World   Jack Brae Curtingstall   184
Nick   Nahshon Cook   185
Domestic   Thomas Cochran   187
Farm Dog's Comeback   Sarah Clancy   188
Another Ode to Joy   Kelly Cherry   190
Death of a Dog   Louise C. Callaghan   192
Paree   Sandra Bunting   193
Foggy Dew   Sandra Bunting   194
Old Dog   Brian Brett   195
Fetch   Pat Boran   196
Kilty Sue   Marck L. Beggs   197
Turn Left   Celeste Augé   198
Nick's Dog   Joan I. Siegel   199
The Blind & Deaf Dog Named Jack   Joan I. Siegel   200
Dog Outside a Grocery on Broadway   Joan I. Siegel   201
Dog   Joan I. Siegel   202
The Dog Kubla Dreams My Life   Anne Kennedy   203

About...

The Dog As Oracle   Patricia Monaghan   207
Above the Aquarius Mine, Ward, Colorado   William Matthews   209
The Drink Tryptich   Alicia Ostriker   210
Deer Walk Upon Our Mountains   Alicia Ostriker   211
Cheesy   Thomas Kabdebo   212
Walking The Dog   John Montague   213
Seven Dogs   Andrea Cohen   215
Eureka   Andrea Cohen   216
A Coonhound on Lieutenant's Island   Andrea Cohen   218
Food is For Me   Adam Wyeth   219
How To Like It   Stephen Dobyns   220
Widow and Dog   Maxine Kumin   222
The Apparition   Maxine Kumin   224
Seven Caveats in May   Maxine Kumin   225
The Dogs on the Rez Speak Lakota   Jean Kavanagh   227
The Dog   C.K. Williams   228

The Moon   Glenn Shea   230
I Keep Hearing How Life is Not a Bowl of Cherries   Gary Percesepe   231
Stuff of the Marriage   Gary Percesepe   232
Goya's Dog   Laura-Gray Street   233
Rat-Like Dogs and Tattooed Men   Rita Ann Higgins   238
Dog is Dog is Dog   Rita Ann Higgins   240
I Am Still Here   Renée Ashley   241
The Dogs   Renée Ashley   242
The Singing Bichon   Patrick Cotter   244
Bean na Leabhar / The Woman of the Books   Siobhán of Carna   246
Wilderness Legacy   Mary O'Donnell   248
Galician Watch-dog   Mary O'Donnell   249
Those two   Steven Ray Smith   250
Happy as I Believe Myself to Be   Amy Dryansky   251
Dog on Hind Legs   Amy Dryansky   252
The Space on the Floor Where the Dog Lay   Amy Dryansky   253
A Tale from Ovid   Sebastian Matthews   254
Night Pee   Sebastian Matthews   256
A Man is Only as Good …   Pat Boran   258
They Put Down Ronan's Neighbour's Dog   Susan Millar DuMars   259
Kerry Blue   Joseph Woods   260
Fire Poker   Scot Siegel   261
Thermodynamics   Scot Siegel   262
Seeing Eye   Kevin Simmonds   263
This is not a poem about dogs   Emily Wall   264
Dark Goddess   Anne Le Marquand Hartigan   265
The Bank Robber's Partner   Christopher Woods   267
Old Dog Watching the Sunset   Christopher Woods   268
Animal Memory   Laurelyn Whitt   269
A Dying Animal   David Wheatley   270
Three-Legged Dog   David Wheatley   271
Tranquillity   John Walsh   272
Seaward   Gordon Walmsley   273
Lame Dog   Micheal O'Siadhail   274
Dog Latin   Padraig O'Morain   275
Bullet Dog   Drucilla Wall   276
Building a Fire   Wendy Thornton   278
Dog on a Chain   Matthew Sweeney   279
The Dog   Matthew Sweeney   280
Bones   Matthew Sweeney   281

His Dog   Matthew Sweeney 282
Warrior Says People on 17th Street in Portland, Oregon,
   Are Dreaming of Dogs   Scott T. Starbuck 283
Dog Talk   Julian Stannard 284
My Dog   Joel R. Solonche 286
Policy   J.D. Smith 287
Dog in the Road   Knute Skinner 288
Street Dog Song   Dave Lordan 289
How to Keep a Setter   C.J. Sage 291
Memo from the Residents' Committee ref Dog Ownership
   Eileen Sheehan 292
midnight   Eileen Sheehan 294
The Bark of a Dog   John W. Sexton 295
The Dogs of Ourblood Road   John W. Sexton 297
Raftery's dog   Breda Wall Ryan 298
Wallace Stevens Welcomes John Crowe Ransom to Hartford
   Gibbons Ruark 300
Koan   Gabriel Rosenstock *(with translation by Michael Hartnett)* 301
Dogs in Passing Cars   James Silas Rogers 302
Dog and Squirrel   James Silas Rogers 303
Past Guessing   James Silas Rogers 304
The Beagle Factory   Billy Reynolds 305
Dog Gone   C. R. Resetarits 306
Dog and Girl   Bertha Rogers 307
Wild, Again   Bertha Rogers 308
Introduction to Teaching Nietszche   Barbara Regenspan 309
In the northern country   Jacob Rakovan 310
The Pound   Moira Rhoarke 311
Waning   Moira Rhoarke 312
I wish I believed in the soul   Alexis Quinlan 313
Sleeping With Your Dog   Susan Pilewski 314
Walking to Dublin   Richard Peabody 315
The Language of Hooligans   Harry Owen 316
Needing Puppies   James Desmond O'Hara 317
Haunted by Dead Dogs   Ron Houchin 318
Heaven Without Animals   Ron Houchin 319
Rituals   Ron Houchin 320
Trees register the dog   Les Murray 321
Two Dogs   Les Murray 322
I Will Be Gone...   Theo Dorgan 323

My Captain   Pete Mullineaux   324
The Stray Dog Café   Pete Mullineaux   325
I need the dog tonight   Susan Moorhead   326
July Twilight   Susan Moorhead   327
Concerns of the Old Dog   Susan Moorhead   328
Magione Umbria   Alan Jude Moore   329
I. The Ascension   Agi Mishol   330
Two Black Dogs   John Menaghan   332
On a Lavatory Wall   John Menaghan   333
About more   Kevin McLellan   334
Canine Haiku   Iggy McGovern   335
Rescue dog   Afric McGlinchey   336
False Start   Tom Mathews   337
A Moment of Woof   Caroline Lynch   338
Photographs with Poodles   Caroline Lynch   339
Dog Ideal,   Yahia Lababidi   342
Guidance   Jacqueline Kolosov   345
Even the Dogs Drink Beer Here   Noel King   346
Three Collies   Noel King   347
Le Chien Malade / A Sick Dog   Fred Johnston   348
The Wounded Dog Theory: My Dog Responds   Holly J. Hughes   351
After Watching a K-9 Assault Demonstration at Lackland AFB, 1967
    Adam Houle   352
Nomenclature   Adam Houle   353
Begging Home a Stray   Adam Houle   354
The Dog in the Crate   Diana Thurbon   355
Siam – A Thai Stray   Diana Thurbon   357
Or, Something   Amy Holman   358
Drawing Near   Amy Holman   359
Regime Change   Kevin Higgins   361
Nose Cone   Patrick Hicks   362
I didn't think I could be this kind of happy, my dear, ever again
    Richard W. Halperin   363
Our Cassie   Richard W. Halperin   364
The Lama's Dog   Desmond Gough   365
Words of Wisdom from My Master   Desmond Gough   366
queen-size bed...   Peter Joseph Gloviczki   367
Theogony   Philip Fried   368
Cocoon   Janice Fitzpatrick Simmons   369
Seven   John Fitzgerald   370

Dog   J.P. Dancing Bear   371
Man with Dog   J.P. Dancing Bear   372
Dog in the World   J.P. Dancing Bear   373
Regret   Dallas Crow   374
Separated   Dallas Crow   375
April   Nahshon Cook   376
Yowl   Susan Cohen   378
Lives Overlapped   Jennifer Clark   379
Old Cats   Sandra Bunting   380
Seventh son of a seventh son   Megan Buckley   381
In Duiche Iar   Eva Bourke   382
Winter Dogs   Drew Blanchard   384
from *The Manager*   Richard Berengarten   386
Still Life With Farmer With Hangover   Marck L. Beggs   388
This Lesson   Marck L. Beggs   390
Communication Skills   Paul Barclay   391
In a Pavement Café   Michael Augustin   392
Dog   Michael Augustin   393
Redbud & Pitbull   Scott Edward Anderson   394
A Dog Howls   Jane Blanchard   395
Dawdle and Scent   Aimée Sands   397
My Brother   Ilsa Thielan   398
Coyote   Simmons B. Buntin   399
3 Haiku   Anatoly Kudryadivsky   400
Refrain   Jacqueline Kolosov   401
Conversation and Its Discontents   Jeanne Wagner   403
Orla   Theodore Deppe   404
Shelter   Annie Deppe   405
Snapshot, Collioure   Annie Deppe   408
Top of the Morning   Larry O. Dean   409
Mr Scales Walks His Dog   Alexander Hutchison   411
A True Dog Story   Judith Barrington   413
Beating the Dog   Judith Barrington   414
A Life Of Pat The Scruff, Chapter 12   Eamonn Wall   416

Biographical Notes   417
Acknowledgements   455
Index of Authors   459
About the Editor   463
About the Cover Artist   463

Editor's Foreword

When my beloved Zookie (a Labrador/Border Collie cross) died in March, 2000, I wanted to publish a book of poetry about dogs in her memory. I had a great title in mind – *Dogs Singing: A Tribute Anthology* – but when I did a bit of research I found that an anthology of dog poems with a very similar title *Dog Music* was being published by a US publisher that year. Much of our distribution is in the US and two books of poetry about dogs, with similar titles, would definitely have come into conflict in that market (and the smaller publisher would have lost out.) I didn't want to change the title and I didn't want Zookie's book to be overlooked, so I decided to wait – and here it is 10 years later.

The 8th of March 2010 was the 10th anniversary of Zookie's death. On that day I made a donation to the Soi Dogs Foundation - www.soidog.org - in Phuket, Thailand, and received a poem in reply from one of the directors, John Dalley. It was written that day by his wife Gill. When I read the poem, I got the "YES" feeling that you get when an idea's time has come and I knew the circumstances were right for Zookie's *Dogs Singing*. I decided to donate royalties from sales of *Dogs Singing* to Soi Dogs and to Madra – www.madra.ie – a Connemara, Co. Galway, dog welfare group run by an old friend, Marina Fiddler, whose unfailing devotion to animal welfare is renowned.

Dogs Singing is divided into three sections: 'By' (a smaller section, since dogs are often reluctant to describe themselves as poets), 'For' and 'About'. The order of poems reflects the eclectic mix of style and intent.

Serendipity has graced the anthology since then; last April at the launch of the 2010 Cúirt International Festival of Literature in Galway,

I was introduced, by Galway City Arts Officer James Harrold, to the artist Margaret Nolan. While we were talking it entered my head to ask her if she had a painting of a dog and, after she and James exchanged surprised looks, she said "Sure... a large part of my work includes dogs". I was thrilled as Margaret took me through her exhibition at the City Museum that day, and through the Spanish Arch to show me the painting that was in the window of the old Museum. This was another "YES", with an added "WOW"! I couldn't believe it; here was *the* cover for *Dogs Singing*; totally perfect (I'm sure you'll agree, since you may have picked this book up because of it!). It's one of the most compelling portraits of a dog I've ever seen: BLUE. Margaret's dog. Our dog. The *Dogs Singing* Dog!

Meanwhile, the poems were coming in; and I was over the moon (delighted that is) with the range and quality of the work. We take dogs so much for granted; I imagine that most people don't think of dogs as suitable subjects for poetry. In fact, and I won't labour this (although I'd like to), it's exceedingly strange to me that despite our deep connection with, and dependence on, dogs, most cliches using the word 'Dog', or terms relating to dogs, are pejorative (one of the main ones being a word used for a woman one dislikes). Bad or 'unattractive' people are called 'dogs' and no one wants to be treated "like a dog". Given this, I was particularly pleased to see the phrase "die like a dog" being given a different and most positive meaning in Yahia Lababidi's poem "Dog Ideal".

Back to the genesis of *Dogs Singing* and its serendipitous growth: One morning I received an email featuring a poem selected by the former US Poet Laureate Ted Kooser for his 'American Life in Poetry' column for the Poetry Foundation. This particular day there was a poem, "The Blessing of the Old Woman, the Tulip, and the Dog", by Alicia Ostriker, which I loved. Hoping to contact her, I went to her website and found (unusual for prominent poets) her email address. She answered my request for poems... with poems! She also put me in touch with Maxine Kumin, who is (as her readers know) devoted to animals. Again, Maxine answered with poems. Later, Ted Kooser sent me his beautiful "January 19, Still Thawing, Breezy." (Another aside: People who *love* animals are generous, good, kind and humble; people who hurt animals are the opposite. Generalisation? Well, maybe, but born out by experience in my case, that's for sure. Good people treat dogs with love and respect, not as servants or ego boosters.)

I met fabulous poets whom I might never had met otherwise. I've come to think of the anthology as a massive, big-hearted, dog-respecting community.

Which isn't to say that all of the poems are feel-good, nice-doggie, sentimental fare. What I've aimed for is a full range of poems to highlight this seemingly simple, but deeply complex, relationship. There are funny poems, disturbing poems, heart-breaking poems, thoughtful poems, surprising poems, transcendental poems... you name it. All revolving around the central tenet of the special, challenging and satisfying relationship which calls for us all to be better than we are.

Special thanks to dog activists Gill and John Dalley of the Soi Dog Foundation and Marina Fiddler of Madra, and to each and every dog welfare group in existence. What would we be without you?

To Siobhán Hutson whose work on this book defines 'patience' and 'saint'.

To Eileen Battersby and Sharon Ní Bheoláin: Thank You beyond words for your support.

A special tribute to Izzy and Bella, neighbours on our lonely stretch of road. They were beautiful, silken creatures who loved running over the acres of peat bog. Tragically, horribly, they died from an unknown poison last June.

I have included my tribute to Zookie and I make no apologies for including poems for my gorgeous Zach (Zookie's companion, who died in 2005). Zookie was very much my girl, but Zach did spare time for his select fan club. His tributes were written by poets who knew and loved his irrepressible spirit: Desmond Gough, Devon McNamara and Eleanor Cummins. Sprinkled throughout are poems dedicated to me, which I include not out of ego, but out of gratitude for such kindness.

JESSIE LENDENNIE
Co. Clare, November 2010

Introduction

First love, enduring love; the witness, the stoic, the companion, the protector, the better part of us, the abiding presence, the warrior, the survivor, the guardian angel. Here is a big book of many poems, all inspired, devoted, motivated by a sacred bond that happens, the supreme privilege, that something far bigger than romance – a relationship with a dog. Dogs do sing; they also smile, socialise, engage and celebrate, mark a homecoming in proper style, even if it's only the return from the local grocery store; they sigh, but most of all they understand, they grieve, they mourn, they empathise, they remember, and they can tell the time better than any clock.

Many of the poets gathered here mark their experience with humour, a subversive tone emerges at times, almost a reluctance to admit that these special creatures stake their claims on our lives, yet some convey the longing that endures. In "Dog Years" Gerard Smyth recalls "our little dog who lived through the changes... / our terrier with grinding jaw, toothed grin,/who preferred to amble, never run." Her insistence "pawing me when/I was in the middle of a Berryman Dreamsong" captures that determination, a dog's need to be acknowledged, to belong. A dog can will a door to be opened by simply staring at it. Admittedly, some dogs are bossier than others; some expect that part of the sofa, that particular kitchen chair, the biggest pillow. Among my great dogs, the so aptly named Loveheart, believed in fully stretching out across the bed, leaving the human to curl up small and neat.

Brian Brett's "Old Dog" expresses the tactile genius that says more than words, those gestures and glances that only a dog can make. "Now she leans against my thigh –/trembling, full of pain/all hungry to live."

It is a short life, all too short, we look at the aged dog and recall the puppy of what seems like only yesterday. "Once she could catch/A season running and shake it by the neck" writes Ted Kooser in "January 19, Still Thawing, Breezy" "...but now they get away,/flashing their tails as they bound/over the hill." Young dog, old dog, they fill the world and then leave it so much emptier.

The voices of the poets are varied, not just in tone – Irish, American, European – as are their worlds, the US east coast to Asian streets, yet the dogs are constant, as is the love they incite. Annie Deppe in "Snapshot, Collioure", watches as an elderly couple from Barcelona arrive with their invalid dog to visit the grave of poet Antonio Machado:

"They're taking turns/pushing a baby buggy/with the raggedy spaniel stretched out within/*He's on ice*, they explain, as they flip back/the blanket. *His hips are shot,/but he does so love to see the world.* In "Cheesy", a poem of warmth, humour and eventually, a stark, fierce beauty, Hungarian poet Thomas Kabdebo, recalls the dog that entered his life when he was three and she could then "only" speak English "because her former owner/was the British consul in Budapest." Her world opened up, she became a hunting beagle and "collected pheasants, hares/wild ducks, found lost toys." She even "got married and/had six pups." Just when the smile is happily relaxed upon your face, the poet concludes: "Around us the war/reached its climax. The Soviets/entered our home, she barked,/they shot her dead./Her bark is locked in my memory."

In "Elegy for a Basset Hound", Michael O'Loughlin pays tribute to a singular character found on the autostrada, "wandering confidently/Like a nineteenth century English explorer." This self-possessed dog settled in life in an Amsterdam bookshop. It is a brilliant poem – McLoughlin balances humour with genuine feeling as he addresses the dog, his dog, revisiting the days when together they went to collect his child from school:

"You made a beeline through the crush/Of mothers and bicycles, to the class where/The children fought to touch your mighty ears/As you gambolled ponderously on giant paws/Like an ottoman pasha in his harem."

Elsewhere, in "The Bank Robber's Partner", Christopher Woods, describes the patience of the dog waiting "in the old green van/while the master is gone,/wearing a cat mask of all things." The robbery goes wrong and little does the dog know that the heist "was to get money for the hound's/operation to take the cancer away." In "An Old Dog Watching the Sunset" Woods writes of another dog, I'd like to think the same dog, now elderly having somehow battled that cancer, watching at day's end:

"Wizened but still alert,/His paws flat on the grass,/He watches the last light/Feels the rhythm of hours./Silence cloaks him/Like a Zen master."

Cecilia McGovern's "Trust", relives the agony of the final goodbye "– shock of your breath/loud and fast as/your heart gives out." Heart is a key word, dogs are heart, they infiltrate our consciousness, they subvert our rhetoric and teach us to feel, to observe more closely. Sabine Huynh sums up in "A Bouquet of Ephemerals", the wayward splendour of the journey that only a dog can take us on: "On your first day among us,/you ate my Barbie doll. I cried/when I saw the pink leg/sticking out of your mouth,/without knowing it would only be/a few years until I buried/that one-legged doll with you."

It is the ultimate joy, the ultimate love, the ultimate sorrow; it's the dog – your dog, my dog, our dogs, all dogs.

EILEEN BATTERSBY, dog lover

25

By...

Paula Meehan

Who'd be a dog?

Who'd be a dog, who'd be a poet's dog?
When we could be up the beach digging holes
sniffing holes, cooling the paws in the sea,

she's stuck to her iBook, worrying a line
'stars so clear have been dead for years...
stars so dead have been clear for years...'
She thinks she's it with her buttons, her plug.

It's bye-bye puppy, hello Microsoft Word;
it's laptop now where once it was lapdog.

We look so cosy, me curled at her toes,
the two of us here in the house on our own.
If she dropped down dead this instant who'd know?
Who's a good doggy then, eh? Who's the best girl?

Give or take a day or two, it'd be a week max,
before, craven with hunger, I'd start in to eat:

top o' the foodchain to you, my last mistress!
as I lick at her bare, her cooléd feet.

Neil Astley

The Hound of the Baskervilles

Master says obey, but I'll stand up
on my hind legs, though I sway like a drunk.
If I can't slip this leash, I'll see his eyes
bulging like a dog's, my jaw clamped round
his jerking arm: the fingers I once licked

I'll bite off, crunching knucklebones to taste
forbidden flesh beneath his salty skin.
I want to know the Moor. What held me back,
call it habit or the easy life, was
nothing to wilderness. I could have played

his pet, become the old retainer sprawled
across the hearth. But fire's in my eyes,
by torchlight they're red as coals. My mouth
glows sulphur-yellow, tongue lolling ahead
divining water, testing air for food.

I'm hungry but have kicked away the bowl
branded with his name for me. I'm hungry
as hell, for his damnation, not bondage
from tins, not meat the price of his abuse;
hungry to hunt down what I need, snatch it

on the hoof, hungry as the loyal poor
asking for change. I want another life.
He makes his answer with a gun: five shots
ring out in the dark, one grazes my ear.
He can't shoot straight. He's shaking like a leaf.

Closer, Master. Let me lick you again.
When I was a pup, he came to me at night.
He put it on my tongue. My clumsy teeth
flecked blood in drools of dangling cuckoo-spit.
One bullet left. *You feeling lucky, Master?*

Maxine Kumin

Xochi's Tale

Is it my fault I'm part rat terrier, part
the kind of dog who lives in a lady's lap?
I didn't ask to be bottom mutt in the pack
that runs untamed through the twisted trash-strewn streets
in Xochiapulcho, I didn't ask to be plucked
up by a pair of gringos. First, they took
away my manhood. No more sweet reek
of bitches, no hot pursuits, no garbage rot.
When they packed up to go back to the USA
I thought they'd cry, then dump me out, but no.
Macho mestizo, my entry papers say.
Who dines in style and sleeps the sleep of kings
ought dream no more of his rowdy half-starved days. . .
I dwell in heaven but without the wings.

Bertha Rogers

The Bitch Protests Litter Murders

When I was a singer of rain-dark songs,
I stood beneath important coats and gowns
and opened my throat, and the notes fell out,
and stroked those fabled jackets, sleek silks.

All the lights dimmed then, as though to hide
mayhem, and the suits and dresses fixed
their eyes on laden tables, and cried.

When I saw their tear-streaked faces;
heard their chiasmic moans, I spun on my
padded soles; escaped to righteous fields.

Teats leaking, womb aching, I disdained
their breached, lying grief,
even their own, howling offspring's –

I wept instead for my own kind, my doomed
daughters, gunny-sacked, drowned in the deeps,
by the farmer's calloused, practiced grasp.

Hélène Cardona

César

I've got to get that duck!
Hate the leash,
Get it off me…yes, see ya!
Gotta get that duck!
Now where did Hélène go?
Oh, she's far away, lost her for now.
Good, good…
There's that duck!
In the lake, love the water, love it!
Got a feather, got a feather,
All those feathers…
What's that? Oooh there she is…
She's going to be mad at me,
Shouldn't have done that…
Oh, there's another duck!
Did she see it?
She keeps calling me, what to do…
It's not as bad as rolling in cow dung, right?
Funny how much I like that too,
Though I can't stand cows,
I'll bark at them a mile away.

Cynthia Schwartzberg Edlow

Dog Smart

Hot day, dog inside.
Cold day, dog inside.
Peanut Butter treats, so why
change a thing?

Dog likes his people well enough.
Some would say his Lab-mutt-mix
loves fervently. Some, calculatedly
as a loan shark.

Still, dog won't fetch.
Man hollers, *Taz, get the ball.*
Taz side-glances: Hey now, you
had it, you threw it, I was nowhere
near you throwing it. Do the math Dad.
      Still, man calls – *Taz.*
                    Get that ball boy.
Hey engineer: I get that you get
that I do not get
the big scheme of things
you and the lady are preoccupied with.
I wish I could make it
easier for you. Pat me
on my silky brown head
and give us that jingle about gallantry.
                Just standing here
with the breeze
on our faces, starlings mewing in
the pecan trees, the hot dogs
plumping on the neighbour's grill
is boom times.
I leave all the big ideas

to the air birds. Why not?
Conversation is overrated.
For instance, here I'm yammering
when a simple whistle once in a blue
would be plenty.

Man says, *Hey Taz, let's sit outside,*
watch the sun go down. Taz approaches the patio steps:
No, inside it is. In is better than out, always pick in
if a choice is afforded you,

but the germane point here is while we're at it

I'm thinking about that
leftover ribeye.

Julian Gough

A Dog in California

It's hard to keep your balls in Beverly Hills
Got to take care who you mount
Make sure they want it
Some smile in panic
He can smell it, everything fake.

He's been a double agent so long, it's become second nature
A sleeper who's never had to wake.
California dreamer.
His second wife a screamer.

He buries his feelings so deep
That, even alone, he can't understand
Why he chewed up the other guy's iPhone
Glass in his mouth, metal, somebody's blood

His family bring him to see his shrink
He likes her, soft and pink. Years ago
She helped him with his phobias. His travel anxiety.
He greets her, rubs his cock and balls against her leg.

"Am I happy? Of course I'm happy, look at my stupid grin
I'm on fluoxetine, and something for my itch.
Great family, big pool, I'm rich.
Three days ago, I fucked Leonardo DiCaprio's bitch.
I'm up for a major, *major* role in the remake
Of Lassie Come Home, in 3D
Am I happy? Look into my eyes. Don't fall in
What do you see?"

(A spasm of anxiety. Why? Like he cares what she thinks.)

"You really want to know? I see black
Forests in there, the Russian steppe
The corpses of Wehrmacht officers
Napoleon's soldiers,
The prostitutes who follow armies all the way to Moscow
And halfway back."

...

Everybody agrees
A holiday, get away from the stress of the city, yes
Forests and trees, a lake.
Driving there, he wagged his long
Tongue out the window, hoped
They weren't making a
Terrible mistake.

He felt OK till nightfall, then slept.

He wakes up for the first time in forest.
Hears the timber wolves, high in the hills.
He gets up. Walks away from his family
Under moonlight that seems unusually bright.
Suits his eyes better than streetlight.

He stops, to shit silicon chips
From the TV remote. Alarm clocks. Three iPhones. An X-Box.

He trots silently through shadows.
Across moonlit clearings.
The swimming pool seems very far away
The blue shimmer, the chlorine
Much further away than the moon
Which calls his name
How did it know his name?
His cover is blown.
He can never go back
He howls
For all he has lost.

Stops, stands there, astonished by the sound.
Howls for all he has found.
These forests are full of bones
Genes don't disappear
They just don't get expressed

And now he runs
He's blurring back into his ancestors now
Indian dog
Back further
He's crossing the Bering Straight, just before
That land bridge fell
And he could never go back

He crosses the steppes
And now he's
A German guy's dog
In a French cave,
Holding down a woman.

Fifty thousand years before Germany
Fifty thousand years before France
Fifty thousand years before the invention of love
Her grunt is the first voice, his name the first word
He stares into her mouth.

A double agent, between the wolves and the people
About to make his first choice.
She's soft.
    Pink.
        Delicious.
He heads south
Outrunning a wall of ice
A thousand, two thousand, three thousand miles wide,
And a mile high
Scrubbing Europe clean, down to the rock,
You can never go back.

Jordan Taylor

Come Back Soon

Run fast, play hard
All day.
Good Dog.

Bark loud, call cat
All night.
Bad Dog.

Sleeping at your feet,
Lying on your bed,
Kisses in the morning
Before goodbye
All day.

Run fast, play hard
When you come home.
Good Dog.

You find the mess
I made.
Bad Dog.

Sleeping at your feet,
Watching now and waiting.
One day like another.
Missing you
All day.

Run fast, play hard
Less than before.
Bad Dog.

You need me beside you
But push me away.
Bad Dog.

Home now.
Car time.
Wind in nose and ears,
Loud barks, fast tail
All the way.

Strange smells, strange sounds.
Someone new
Takes lead.

You walk
Out of sight.
Bad Dog.

Strange smells, strange sounds.
Alone without you
Beside me.
Come back soon.
I still love you.

Scott Edward Anderson

Calvin's Story

"Make it stop, make it stop,"
was all I was thinking;
my eyes closed, some
bully biting my body, limbs,
tearing flesh and hair.
Boys pinned me to the pavement,
each one holding a leg, holding,
me down on my back.
Another boy – so there were five?
– pressing the bully into me
head lashing at anything
it could grab with canines.
I'm surprised I didn't black out.
Then, I remember a scuffle.
I was almost unconscious,
drifting in an out.
Two men freed my limbs,
but still I couldn't move.
One chased the boys
while the other lifted me,
cradled me, into a van.
I'll never forget the smell
– camphor, maybe, almost
lavender, medicinal.
The gentle one dabbed my
wounds with a wet cloth,
stroked me slowly, dabbed
– there was a lot of blood;
were there sirens? I don't
remember sirens. (Should
there have been sirens?)
The next thing I remember
is being on a cold, metal

table – a nurse or doctor
looking me over – another
shaking her head. The first
mumbles something (all I hear
is 'dog,' that word they have
for us), then I'm sure she said,
"This one's a keeper, let's give
him a second chance."
I wake in a crate, damp towel
beneath me, head swirling.
I must be in the 'pound,'
there are others barking.
(I wish they would be quiet,
my head hurts.) Then
the pretty nurse or doctor
comes in, mumbles to me;
I look up, try to smile
(this seems to please her),
and I slip in and out of sleep.
        Months later,
I'm sitting on a street corner,
leashed, with some of the nice pound
people. A lot of people pass by,
they pat my head, mumble
in that way they do, until one
couple lingers (a child or two
are with them, I can't recall).
They mumble to the pound people;
one of them (Alpha, I'll call him)
walks me; he has a firm hand,
but is gentle, in control.
Oh how I wish for a forever
family – but I don't
want to get my hopes up.
Then, the day is over,
back to the pound – sigh –
guess it wasn't meant to be.
Next night, however, there
is Alpha, and he's brought

some others. (Oh, let me be
on best behaviour so they will
take me home.) They seem
to like when I snuggle, listen,
take commands, lick the cute
young ones — they are salty sweet!
Days go by after that night,
the pound people tell me
to get ready. Maybe, just maybe,
this is a good sign. Oh, I get so
excited my butt wiggles faster and
faster. Finally, the day comes;
Alpha arrives with the others,
and I think, *This is it*. I'm going home
with my forever family — to a home;
home at last for my second chance.

Bette Lynch Husted

Fergus's Ode to Joy

Grass! It's everywhere!
Smell that? And you can eat it!
You can dig it up and toss it in the air
jump up in time to meet it
coming down and shakeit shakeit –
you can roll in it and wave your paws
at the sun and scratch
right there – oh here comes the mailman! Can I make it?
Run! I love this man because
he knows my soul. Watch

how he climbs out of his van
to touch my ears. Yesyesatreat!
My school kids know that they can
count on me. Mothers – before they admit defeat –
are cross. *That's enough. Come on home. Now!*
Then they come back to smile
through the fence. What's that? Did she say "walk"?
The woman doesn't understand: the Tao
that can be trained to heel more than a short while
is not the Tao. I listen to her talk –

"Sit!" "Down!" "Stay!"
She knows the words for soccer too. Walks are divine!
Grass and creeks and dogs and hey
a cat! That was a cat! In the evening, I recline
between the man's legs by my burning
fire (sometimes I have to bark to keep it lit),
full of good kibble and good cottage cheese
and his good smells. He says I'm learning
fast. He calls me Little Pup, his Babycakes. We fit
into one chair. We sigh. We take our ease.

John Walsh

Ergo sum

Here I am
sprawled out in the shade.

Just had some water
and a bite to eat.

All I need right now.

Those flies can be annoying.

Apart from that
life is good.

(Eyes close).

For...

Michael Heffernan

Bridgette Was A Show Girl

I have not forgotten your dog anthology, Jessie, but our little Bridgette has. She has completely gone blank on her promise to sing me one of the show tunes she used to do in the shower when she was an Upper West Side socialite in the '20s. You used to could not get her to shut up about that. But now she refuses to remember it, much less try out one of the songs. The dog has a good voice, too, really. I went out and sat with her tonight under the full moon of all things and tried at least to get her to tap into her primal dogginess and bay at it, and she would not. She simply rolled over on her back and cast those brown eyes of hers my way, for a rub. So, instead, I bayed. Dammit, she made me bay. In my own backyard. At the Moon. It's a horrible situation I tell you.

Love,

Michael

Thomas Lynch

The Blood We Paid For

Our old dog, long into his dotage, yawns –
a half-blind version of a breed that bred
among the Celts and kept their women clean
by barking off the covetous among their kind
when the husbands had gone off pillaging,
making poems and chaos in the next county.

Later, when the Celts themselves had settled in
and took to one god and wearing collars,
their dogs grew tame and even-tempered, tending
sheep and living to a good age; slept for hours
the way our own dog, sprawled on the linoleum,
listens to the breeze sing underneath

the door we never weatherstripped and hears
in some corpuscle of his ancient blood
the rage of wind matting his wet fur back,
sending a lather up from the seawrack
to float among the sea birds, hears them screech
above a band of wild men half-blind with drink,

who, having brought their plunder to the land's end,
ready their flimsy boats along the beach.
It was, of course, the blood we paid for. Spent
good money in bad times for a pedigree –
a hundred dollars, fifteen years ago
for what my wife claimed was a dog with character.

Nor will she let me, much as I'm inclined
(watching the pearlescent cataract
bloom in his good eye) when he's wholly blind,
coax him toward a stand of trees out back
and, because we've both grown overcivilised,
murder him with utmost dignity.

Ted Kooser

January 19,
Still Thawing, Breezy

Arthritic and weak, my old dog Hattie
stumbles behind me over the snow.
When I stop, she stops, tipped to one side
like a folding table with one of the legs
not snapped in place. Head bowed, one ear
turned down to the earth as if she
could hear it turning, she is losing the trail
at the end of her fourteenth year.
Now she must follow. Once she could catch
a season running and shake it by the neck
till the leaves fell off, but now they get away,
flashing their tails as they bound off
over the hills. Maybe she doesn't see them
out of those clouded, wet brown eyes,
maybe she no longer cares. I thought
for a while last summer that I might die
before my dogs, but it seems I was wrong.
She wobbles a little way ahead of me now,
barking her sharp small bark,
then stops and trembles, excited, on point
at the spot that leads out of the world.

J.D. Smith

Aubade

Dog, and I believe that I can call you that
with a high degree of accuracy,
in a purely denotative sense, though,
unsullied by cultural associations,
please listen,
since I seldom ask that much of you
(the couch is yours no less than mine,
the pillows, past and present, more so):
You would, if you possessed a consciousness
of cause and effect, self and other
and the mortality that swallows them,
be grateful to know nothing
beyond that which you know right now
because, for me,
it's seven-thirty on a partly cloudy
Tuesday, forty-five degrees,
with a sixty-percent chance of rain
and the certainty
of a commute and a day's work
in which I'll be wagged by-appended to-
devices engineered by men
who get out even less than me.
Really, they exist,
though you might have gathered otherwise
from the long and many evenings that we share –
like tonight, when we'll
resume this small symposium.
Until then, fellow traveller on the planet,
Don't scratch that spot behind your ear –
It's already bare.
A new rawhide bone is on your bed
and, as always, *cane mio*,
the kibble's in the bowl.

Larry O. Dean

Lutherans

They told me
in all self-
righteous
seriousness

dogs don't go
to heaven.
Thoughtlessly.
A child!

*   *   *

Although now
I don't believe
in their heaven,
I'd like to

believe, wherever
Lady is,
she's barking
happily,

chasing scared
Lutherans
up trees
for all eternity.

Larry O. Dean

To My Dog, With a Broken Leg

I know it's uncomfortable;
even so, I'm understating
the obvious, which is
this decade-plus, you, me,
we all took for granted the simple
inelegance of your locomotion –

bounding up or down stairs
your blind eyes knew
as surely as your paws,
or lifting a leg (usually the right rear,
the broken one) to pee, scuffing
dirt and grass afterward
in the genetic celebratory
dance of the relieved bladder. This

you always handled with panache,
no Nureyev or Fonteyn
but performing a credible variation
on their stagy themes, even
cleverer in its own way.
To stumble and fall with as much

grace – yelping bravely,
not wanting to make a fuss
or become a nuisance
in your patented unselfconscious
form, and hobbling on three
good legs to the one bad,
broken, actually hanging
loose like fuzzy dice
from a rear view mirror

– takes real zest for life,
which you've always had
and which can't be contained
in your almost-human heart
or for more than six weeks
in a nine-hundred dollar
and one cent plaster cast.

John Hildebidle

For Prince
Who Passed On Just Before Christmas

Not, mind you, that we were more than
passing acquaintances – I had a few glimpses
as he came a-courting his two lady friends.
But he seemed such an estimable beast,
at quick glance: sharp-witted, agile.
Only a dog, you'd say, missing the mark
by a hair – a dog, yes, indeed, but
only? I think not.

Sharon Young

For Pine Goose
the best dog in the history of the world
(with apologies to Jenny Joseph)

When I am an old dog, I shall wear a purple collar, with a red leash that I will chew in half when you're not looking.

I shall run down the street, ignoring you as you call. I will forget all the commands you've taught me (or at least pretend that I have, unless you have treats).

In December, if it's very cold outside, I shall imagine I'm in a big forest and pee on the Christmas tree (you'll explain to your friends that I'm confused by the piny smell, and I'll laugh to myself.)

I shall bring you a ball, but when you throw it, I will not chase it. Instead, I will lie down and go to sleep, exhausted with the effort of entertaining you.

I shall stand and stare at a blank wall for long minutes, until you get up and come to see what's there. I shall then walk away with a disdainful expression (ha, ha, made you look!).

I shall sleep in your bed, under the covers, and grumble and growl if you try to move me. You'll feel sorry for me in my old age and let me stay. I will then snore very loudly, so that I am the only one who can sleep.

I shall wander about in the middle of the night and meet monsters in the kitchen. You'll hear me crying and get up to rescue me. (Thank you.)

I shall have to leave you long before either of us is ready.

You will never forget me.

Jessie Lendennie

Zookie

The dog on the floor of the wine bar
Lifts her head at my apple pie and coffee;
Sleeps again, breathing to a Country & Western tune.

She might be dreaming of chasing sticks.
She might be dreaming of apple pie,
Or the caress of sunshine on golden fur.

I ignore the crooked mirror's reflection
And the lopsided smile of the waitress;

I want to lie on the floor in the sun
And chew sticks in my dreams.
I want not to eat apple pie on days
When thoughts turn to fat.

I want to talk with the dog about philosophy, about fur,
Ask her if she likes Country & Western
Ask her what I'm doing in this smoky place
On a sunny day.

I want to ask her why she waits for me.

Jessie Lendennie

Izzy

For Bella and Izzy, mother and daughter, our hilltop neighbours
who died from poison in June, 2010

Brave Izzy
Daughter of Bella
of the lovely eyes
Bold Izzy
who sprang the gate
ahead of the others
Brave Izzy
who loved her family her home
Bold Izzy
of the lanky legs
and silken fur
Brave Izzy
who played in the afternoon heather
Bold Izzy
granddaughter of Rosa
daughter of Bella
fond sister
Brave Izzy
who had a puppy's heart
Bella of the lovely eyes
Gone
from their mountain
from their loving world

Paul Genega

Dog

The light, my friend,
I see you standing
in a light so bright
and white it's painful.
In the distance, water
winks like a dizzy
old flirt, but here
on the soft sand
of a dune, you seem
somehow to solidify –
lean-limbed, released,
sniffing the wind of
eternity. And almost
grinning, you hold
that pose, proud,
totally assumed.
Until moved by what-
ever it is moves you,
you spring down
the slope and run,
run and run. Run,
dark speck making
for the ocean, over
the next crest and
nowhere to be found.

Desmond Gough

Zach

You were not my dog – you were her dog.
But I was there when you arrived,
A long-legged pup in her office.
We walked you home across the windswept park.
I had to carry you in case you blew away.

I let you into my bed on that first night.
That was it.
We bonded as good as any AVATAR dragon-bond,
For life.

When I'd call to her office you'd stride up
And jump and knock me backwards
That was our game
Time passed
You grew big.
I moved away.

The day I met her with you on the street
You ignored me for a while.
Then I saw your recognition
As you jumped up, front paws planted on my chest,
Knocking me back onto the pavement
I was happy to fall down to your level,
Touched by your loyal affection.

No, you were not my dog, you were her's.
Yet tears well up as I write these words
Because you loved me.

Devon McNamara

Zach Speaks

My love,
it is sunset
this is our walk after rain,
scarlet in muck, azure
in cow prints, horse tracks,
the skyey stream where I dunk
my muzzle, shake out my
blaze of splash.
            You, in your coat,
your redolent boots, call
my name, and I hear but attend
to the thrill of the smells of
the evening, sea wrack heaving
away out there, hare scut in nettles,
the byre beyond, wild pee on
this stone, chips in their papery
slick and a beer, the dark rich stink in
the ditch. Then I look back,
waiting, spangled in mist, to
raise my head to your hand.

What? You think I'm past
speech and don't love
how you lie on the floor
by me talking and stroking?
Even now, my big, ambery paws
reach your shoulders, I
open my breath in your face.

Oh my love, how your hair, wet
with sky, is my color. Don't cry.
Our lost words are shining. Turning
and turning for home, how they glisten
and sing.
                    See how I lift my head golden
and breathing beside you, the way I will
always, and you will, deep in your hands
feel my voice, hear our listening touch.

Devon McNamara

Spring Lament

Groundhog Day
the yellow clay
flies
up from
amber slugs
the maple roots
I dig
the frost line
delve
for room
to lay your limbs
mine own mastiff
sweet prince of dogs

"Loyal"
Bill Matthews
dogsbody at the vet
drives off
weeping "steadily
like an adult"

I howl
and shovel
tuck you in
thinking of him
and Sweeney's yellow dog
who leaped into the stream
and swimming after them
was left
Sputnik
called across the road
then cried for all day long

Oh earth breath
where we wail and sweat
bereft
Oh how this flailing
sounds like you
digging
your bed in summer
round and round
sweet timeless grass
Oh how
the snuff and whistle
for the beloved
rises
innocent
the wild scent
keen, keen

Eleanor Cummins

Zach
1995

Hollow bellied glistening toothed hound,
Streaks across a busy road
Golden hair points in one direction
Loping stretching gathers in
Avoids the car
Through the gate
Hurtles like a pinball
A speck
Then a gallop
Tears into the sea
Explosion of water
Canine whoops of delight.

Kate Newmann

Nobody Would Understand

Why I leaned across to a woman
– a stranger – who hadn't eaten her steak,
asked if I might have it.
I have a black labrador in the car.

How you could levitate,
a flicker of legs and light and thrill,
before leaping into water,
all seal energy as you swam,
ears slicked back earnest.

The way hotel rooms
seem so squalid without you
smuggled in through the fire escape,
chuffed and complicit.

How you could hear me dreaming,
would wake me from a nightmare,
lick my foot.

How I always thought
I could call you back
or swim out – like the time
you were caught in lobsterpot ropes –
to disentangle you.

Part of me
alive
the shape of you.

Joan Newmann

For Both of Us, Beau

The way you would
lie down heavily
and I would feather stroke
your beautiful back
with my fingers
or my toes and sing
Fintra and Falcarragh
Doonin and Silverstrand
Dickson and Barnetts
and New Forge Lane –
all that we'd done.
And I didn't know
I was calming your hot kidneys
and you were decreasing
my blood pressure.
A true symbiosis but we
never called it THAT.

William Wall

My dog Trotsky

my dog Trotsky
eats windfall grapes & apples
& lies in the sun
(when he can get it)
belly up
leg's spread
groaning

my dog Trotsky
calls to all the local dogs
in their autonomous zones
having long ago
lost interest
in their erogenous zones
encouraging
world revolution

he doesn't talk about grapes
though he will
when the time comes
they are his secret weapon
the absolute A bomb
of his life
sweet black grapes
on a sunny evening
hoovering them up
no matter what
his slogan will be
why should our masters only
love the fruit of the vine

Gréagóir Ó Dúill

Cú na gCleas

B'anseo amháin nach mbíodh sé ag brú a bhealaigh isteach,
Sa mheathdhorchadas síoraí; corrghliscearnach miotail
Ón chiothfholcaidh, ón rothar, ón speal, ón tsluasaid.
Eagla a bhí air roimh an doras a dhruideann uaidh féin.

Deich lá anois ó d'iompair mé amach
Is d'fhág é ar bheagán aithne ag an vet;
Ocht lá anois ó thug mé chun na cathrach é,
Gan de dhóchas ach faobhar dall na scine, súil le muir.

Ar crochadh de líne istigh sa scioból, mata maith an tinteáin
    fós gan ni.
Sula lasaim an lampa, feicim ceo éiginnte sa dorchadas:
Leachta bochta a choirp, iad ag soilsiú go fann,
Ina luan i ndiaidh mo Chon tar éis a bháis,
Fosfar oíche ar thoinn.

Cú na gCleas

I arrive late to a stinking dirty kitchen.
I wash the floor, clean my grey stone flags
And scour and swallow and disappear those sad stains.
I lift a towel and head out to the barn.

Only here he'd hesitate to butt in,
The permanent dark, the glistening of metal
From shower to bicycle, from scythe to shovel,
He feared them, feared too the door closing of itself.

Ten days now since I carried him out
And left him barely conscious to the vet.
Eight days now since I brought him to the city,
Sole hope the knife's searching cut – forlorn hope.

The good hearth-rug hangs unwashed on the barn line
And before I light the lamp
I see an uncertain mist in the dark:
The sad liquids of his body shine weakly,
Rotting like mushrooms,
Night phosphor on a broken wave.

(Cú na gCleas is an admiring nickname for Cúchulainn
and means the hound of many tricks.)

(Translated from the Irish by Gréagóir Ó Dúill)

Ben Howard

Greta

All day she lies
beneath the pin oak, leashed
to a post, her space defined,
her world encompassed by a nylon cord.

Looking away from us, she sees
those spruce trees in their mid-September colours,
the lilies still in bloom,
and, from time to time,
the neighbour's yellow cat, who keeps

his distance, stepping lightly.
What passes through her mind,
we wonder, watching her sphinx-like calm,
her easy vigilance.

And what, if anything, can we,
her keepers, know of that awareness,
which senses each incursion
and sniffs each unfamiliar,
uninvited odour?

And when she greets us, tail
swishing, tongue expectant,
does she not see a portion of ourselves
which we ourselves will never see,

though we outlive her lapping tongue,
her black, recumbent body?

Maurice Harmon

A Dog's Life

A chip in your neck to keep you safe, a cut
In your belly to make you barren. You have
Never hunted, known the fear that clings
To rat and weasel, fought feral cats
In the castle woods, known the odour
Of spent cartridge, or suffered abuse
At the hands of anyone. Curbs, collars, checks, and leads
A big dog in the city: dry food from a plastic bag
A bed in the kitchen, the run of the house at night
Rewards, treats, praise, in the approved approach.
We raise you like a Spock child, no wonder
You are nervous, highly strung, behave
Like top dog, that's why I crack the whip
Secure the lead every time we go for a walk.

Tiny, the bitch, fair-haired and compact
Sat in my pram without being told, protected me.
I knew fear for the first time when they dragged
A tape worm from her gut, spread it wet and glistening
Along the hedge, sign for days of something ugly.
I was drawn to it, puzzled by such filthy growth.
We had chased two weasels in that hedge, back and forth
In fierce engagement, the bitch yapping viciously.
When a hunted rat faced me, his back to a tree
I went cold, imagined sharp teeth on bare legs
Or the open mouth ripping my face, but Tiny raced in.
When pups were born she growled at me but after
She went for food I saw them, the helpless newborn.
As soon as their eyes opened she let me play with them.

Hector, her pup, was tireless and fierce.
Ratter, fox-hunter, rabbit-catcher, retriever
Of sticks thrown in pond and sea, with me
When I roamed fields and woods, with us
When we walked to the postman's gate
Magical place where stories grew from what we knew
A voice spoke from a fallen stump, where I was told
A knot would wink if I looked it straight in the eye.
Every Sunday we made the rounds of Hampton fields
Searching for rabbits, in bushes along the railway lines.
We beat bushes, cut off exit routes. Hector was quick.
We knew the best places, warrens, burrows
Tasty grass, up to the hills, then back
To the yellow chimneys, the diamond panes
Where the dog got his reward, dinner's
Scraps, while we had tea, toast, and idle chat.

I know, old girl, you fret and fume, on edge
In streets, reactive and protective, if I leave you alone
A danger to head patters, dog cooers, pushy kids.
I have to take you on a lead when my instinct is
To let you run ahead, to explore the margins
But you have no fear of crossing the road
Will lope over to sniff at plastic bags, bottles, smelly spots.
In the park you are yourself, I love the way you
Prance away, strike off through the field
Play catch as catch can with swallows skimming
Your back then zooming up and away, preparing the next attack
Where the white tip of your tail waves back and forth
Where white chest and paws shine in the sun.
Oh, my beautiful girl, you will love Ardgillan,
No restraints, no rules, nothing to hedge you in.
We do not take to curbs, masters, and institutions.
We need a big sky, love, the startled imagination.

Maurice Harmon

Conbec

from the Irish

I am sad at Conbec's death, Conbec, whose jaw was strong,
I never saw a cleverer foot after pig or deer.
I am sad at Conbec's death, Conbec of the deep voice,
I never saw a cleverer foot killing the tall stag.
I am sad at his quick death on the green high waves,
his death a calamity, his dying a great sorrow.

from *The Colloquy of the Ancients*

Conbec

Truagh lem oided conbice conbec ba lór a gloine
    ní fhaca bud chroibghlice in indiaid mhuice ná oige
Saeth lem oided conbice conbec in gotha gairge
    ní fhaca bud chroibghlice ac marbad daim gan cairde
Saeth lem oided conbice ós tonnaib árda uaine
    a hoided ba chomraime a bás fa lór a thruaige

ó *Acallam na Senórach*

Laura Lundgren Smith

Madraí na hÉireann

for Jessie

The dogs of Ireland
can whistle.
They can spin a yarn,
smoke a pipe,
tell a dirty joke,
sing "Danny Boy,"
but they won't.
They're never show-offs, sure.

Instead,
whining and pacing.
the canine queen of Clare
herds her human charges
down the Ballycotton road.
One poet in sheep's clothing,
feckless wool-free ambler,
breaks away:
lost in the bog of a writer's dream.
A furtive, furry nudge sends
her stray back into the fold.

Instead,
the canine king of Clare,
handsome as a god,
head as big as a man's,
stretches his golden body
the length of the beach.
Sticks his whole snout
beneath the cold tide,
imagines Neptune was a dog.

The dogs of Ireland
know the things we can't.
See the things we won't.
Love us,
though we will never
hear them
whistle.

Gerard Smyth

Dog Years

In the middle of the night her bark was one
that seemed to reach the point of ecstasy.
Fireworks and wind-chimes frightened her,
our little dog who lived through the changes,
devoured chocolate and Pavlova,
loved to lick the honey-jar.
Because dog years add up to so many
when she was old we thought she was young
– our terrier with grinding jaw, toothed grin,
who preferred to amble, never run,
whose silent five-word prayer was Give the dog a bone.
She slept with one eye open
to see the small, thin birds of spring
and with masterstrokes of nose and tongue
sought attention, pawing me when
I was in the middle of a Berryman Dreamsong
of *homage and soft remorse*
or one of Brodksy's sonnets to Mary, Queen of Scots.

Peter Fallon

Collie

No rutting hare's
as mad as Polo.
He'll wrestle stones,

chase birds
and not let go
a stick you throw

until he knows it's dead.
He's there eleven years
my cousin multiplies by seven

to age a dog.
Young pups come in
but he hangs round the back –

sticks and stones
the last rats that he'll catch,
the last strays that he'll round.

Peter Fallon

Own

A collie pup skims
the pebble of its bark
across the back yard.
It clatters on the slates

of the grainstore by the gate
and instigates its growling
at the echoes of its own
trespass of the dark.

Was the world ever as it seems?
Alice sees and needs no proof.
The heifers on a hidden hill
are standing on a hayshed roof.

Pam Uschuk

Walking In Snow On A Full Moon Night

for Happy

White crunch of subzero
White moon spilling the bowl
of ewe's milk Celts drank
to celebrate this ewe's moon
halfway between solstice and equinox
White wolf lopes ahead
between white tire tracks
drifted and nearly lost
In profile, his head twice the size of mine
White silence of the husband
brooding over white
piano keys frozen between chords
of loneliness for the boy
scoring his heart
White paper waiting for words
to skate from the mind's revolving rink
White smell of Crisco
of white lard bubbling around eggs
of love love love with no red roses
strapped to its burning thighs
White stars blink
White Saturn raises the moon
White windless as frost
or the philosophy of ice riming the poet's cup
The senses are where ideas die
grateful as white moths into a winter sunset
White crunch of wolf paws
outleaping the deer trail
White wolf teeth take my whole hand
and for now
do not bite down

Pam Uschuk

In Synch

for Zazu

Sun stabs the horizon of my dog's intention
as she leaps at the front door. After she's
taken a leak, she jumps six feet
although she's only a third that size. It's cold
and she's not one to suffer idiot weather.
Her mouth seldom unsmiles, black
lips neat as moist velvet
trolling for Milk Bones and hoping
that I won't go to work this Monday. Like
any god, I must disappoint her, and I wonder
if this isn't the true leash of the universe.
Not just disappointment but how seldom
our desires perfect rhythm or
are heroic couplets in sync. It's not so much
desire as duty that draws me to the car.
My dog understands duty as snarling
at shadows, blocking strangers
from entering our door. Prose
she reads as shaking a stuffed toy
like a snapped-leg rabbit until
the dismembered covers the floor.
Strange how Zazu, who must also be
part comic or abused poet, likes
it when the cat gets rough, sinking
fishhook claws into her cheeks.
Medusa of routine, she shuts down by nine,
seeks her own direction atop the quilt, shoots
me stink eye until I finally set the alarm,
sink into the sheets, where I find her warm
silk haunch cloistered all night, anchor
nailing the drift of my dreams.

Ann Fox Chandonnet

Howl For Edo

With apologetic woofs to Lassie, Timmy and Alan

I

I am sitting with Edo in his last moments –
Edo, our "Doge,"
our nine-year-old "baby dog,"
who as a pup gained five pounds a week
who has shared our adventures
who knows I am upset during these final minutes and has been
    muzzled for menacing the vet
who greeted me by taking my wrist gently in his jaws
who knew 25 words including "in"
who was teased by squirrels at Gull Rock
who loved drinking from icy Chugach creeks
who slept between us in our tent in March below Flattop
who slept most quietly as wolves came within 30 feet of the tent
who if busted in his pubic beard was mon-orchid
who roared like a lion

who would roar now but for the muzzle.
Our "Doge"
who treated our sons as litter mates
who is an Akita, a breed notorious as "serial cat killers"
who knew 25 words including "fish"
who delighted in chasing white ptarmigan in white drifts but
    never caught one
who patrolled the sun porch like a general on a hill
who had to be sat on as we pulled quills from his tongue
who wanted to pursue the watching porky as soon as the last
    quill was out
who hugged by leaning his weight against my legs
who relished salmon and beef heart and steak bones

who was in his element in snow, at zero
who was spooked by suspension bridges along Chilkoot
who was as stubborn as his owners
who perched on the toe of your boot so he could see over the
    gunnel the current denizen struggling on the line
who yearned to dive overboard to join the sea lions
who knew 25 words including "lion"
whose 108 pounds moved graceful as a gazelle
who enjoyed hanging his tongue, pink laundry, out the car
    window in the breeze
who did not like people whom he did not like
our "Doge" who danced with us in the rain outside our tent
who was forbidden our bed but left secret footprints on the
    sheets when we were at the office
who wrestled with us on the carpet like a pup
who nipped at our ears but never broke the skin
who knew 25 words including "bath"
who charmed Japanese cruise ship passengers who threw down
    candy and snapped photos
who looked reprovingly at us when attacked by loose dogs
    while he was restrained by his leash
whose ears were grey plush
whose tail was Cyrano's plume
whose legs were like pillars hewn from cedars of Lebanon
whose undercoat floated like dandelion seeds when he shed
who did not like people whom he did not like
and does not like vets – especially now
who knows I am upset although he doesn't know why
and who still stands after three fatal shots
whose name arose in crossword puzzles
who hated walking in the rain
who knew 25 words including "wipe"
who patrolled the sun porch like a Buckingham sentry
who an hour ago on his last walk, allowed off-leash to romp in
    the snow was too sick to play but hugged me for the
    opportunity anyway
who is a lion to the last, protecting me
who begins to wobble
our "Doge."

II

Moloch is the strange beast off-leash who attacks from behind.
Moloch is the growl and lunge.
Moloch is the suffering.
Not bang nor whimper
but the sliding of ragged claws on tile, the folding of knees.
Lacklove and dogless in Moloch.

III

The animal hospital illuminates itself.
Canines in their cubicles sing sweet blues.
Holy the pet!

Michèle Vassal

Cat Person

(for Dougal Mc Dougs a huge tender soul)

I didn't want you
I don't want a dog, I said
I don't want a dog
because
I am a cat person
because
a dog is a dog is a dog
a dog is smelly and needy
will dig up the hellebores
will chew shoes
will pee on the floor
and what about the cats!
and so I didn't get A dog

I got you
from serious grizzly cub
to teenaged brontosaurus
you are now the Tonton Macoute
of the Cats Junta
who brings you offerings
(or are they bribes?)
tiny velvet corpses of
mice and voles
which you hide for a while
in your cheek (so as not offend
their feline sensibilities?)
and spit out later
when they're not around

they follow you on walks

weave between your paws
share nose to nose
stories cat's mysteries
you lick them
and your tongue is
as big as their body
and you carry them
by the scruff of the neck
delicately, like a mother her kitten
through irises and poppies
crushing pelargoniums
and hellebores
and I couldn't care less
as it is obvious you and I
are both cat persons

Patrick Chapman

(for Juno)

Boxer spots a fly,
snaps into the air but fails
to stop . . .

Peter van de Kamp

Dear Mickey,

Me I can't leave you,
Though I'm all I know
You'll ever want from me.
Practically, I won't do:
With your teeth you can't chew
A bone, let alone
My skeleton. But my flesh?
You're no Ugolino:
You are sensitive,
And I shall have to live
To see your final spasm,
Thrust your body down
And wonder why, in that chasm,
I wasn't first to die.

Peter van de Kamp

Bark

Why wander where waves,
Yearning for their precursor,
Wrench the sea,
Drench the sand,
And drown?
Each, sacrificed,
Inundates,
Obliterates,
And then goes down.

Mickey, unleashed
On the beach,
Makes a dash,
Fights each crash,
Like Cuchulainn,
In abandon –
But she retreats
From each ocean frown
To where it washes down,
Wading placid water,
Then resumes her battle,
Barking at the brattle.

It's fun to watch
Our silly dog.

This isn't grace, they say:
Accept the plot;
Why bark at your lot?

But as she comes
Whenever we do call,
Shakes the foam off her,
Jumps into the car,
Her crusade over,
Why should I tell Mickey
She was barking up the wrong sea?

Peter van de Kamp

Mickey

for Mickey

I have a dog called Mick,
A gentlemanly bitch,
Who doesn't wear a stitch,
And yet looks ladylike.

It's strange: when I undress
I close the door on her.
Perhaps it is her fur,
My sapient nakedness,
Or maybe she's my mother,
And I, her panicky son,
When we're out and she seems gone.

Wendy Thornton

The Dog is Disappointed in Me

For Charlie

The dog is disappointed in me.
I dawdle over the exact same constellation
that years ago marked my way
along a sandy beach, an excuse
for some boy to stretch and point,
kisses bold as forbidden
more exciting than roman candles.
I hesitate and the dog pulls away
from the hot, silent spectacle.

Still, the burdens of years lift
sway and meld with the cloud
crossing the Big Dipper.
Return to now – from boy to man
to work and pets who need to be walked
and dark morning skies full of stars
and a dog determined to do his job,
to lead me home. He stops to watch
a meteorite streak across the sky
and I like a child laugh with delight
blow a kiss to the dog and the stars
and the soft fading night.

Adam Tavel

Curriculum

Until the thin white S of its guts
peeled like wire from a rubber sheath
my lab pup pawed that baby garter,
its stilled wriggle splitting throat
to tail. I should have swatted his hide
with the make-believe

newspaper of my hand
or ground his snout in an anthill
for the second shame he brought
a thing no bigger than a strand
of fettuccini hardened
in the colander's perforated light. Instead
I watched his small snout snatch

at flies as they dove and rose − a dervish
of herky-jerky palps lapping
pinprick drops of blood
too small for a man's sun-bleared eyes.
It was only when I saw the snakehead
garnished with chewed flecks

of switch-grass on his tongue
that I yanked my blue bandana
to wipe him clean, leaving
the swarm to their solemn
supper of flesh, secreted
in river stalks, a flesh
which gave them peace.

Adam Tavel

Ode to Noah Caterpillar Jackson, 1807-1880

Your chubby little namesake slinks
its bottle-brush fuzz an inch above your J,
softer than the buttercup halo gilding
the soil above your bones. Distant cousin
to Old Hickory, a six-gun death and still this town
of buck-knife men lost the plot for years
where your granddaughter soaked her kerchief.

So they built baseball stops, marina docks,
the jungle gym's rusty frigate wheel
above its red slide like a tunnelled tongue winding
to your new headstone, a mere twenty feet
from the rubber chips I wish they had
to pad my falls when I was young. Once
I fell so hard upon my knee that gravel
like tiny arrowheads skived beneath my skin.
With each step they scraped the cap

until that night when father's hands
pinched his tarnished Navy tweezers
and dug each scraper out. At five, my shrieks
were so shrill they drove mother
to the kitchen sink where she wept
into her shirtsleeves until she calmed herself
long enough to bring us out a pot.

Flecked with red, each stone clanked sharp
against pot-bottom steel and when the goddamn ordeal
finally ended he gave the pot to me.
My tears and snot dripped on three slimy rocks
no bigger than a pea. Iodine burn,

a jumbo Band-Aid and the final absence,
the sudden dull throb of swelling
shot through me like a vaccination
as I was held by the waist above
the creeping shadows of our yard at dusk
to fling those terrors from our deck.

That year he moved into the firehouse
barracks for good. The house at auction sold
for half its worth so I confess that my goodbye
to a room that held my infant cries
was to piss in a corner where periwinkle paint
faded in my dresser's perfect shape
as if the wall itself missed that hutch of shirts,
as if my piss could stain that house as mine

alone, the way our collie Jesse pissed
on every shrub he passed to claim
the world as his, though glassy cataracts
made him slam against an apartment's
foreign walls. When we went for walks
I missed the taut jerk of leash
at the sudden dash of squirrel so much
I took upon myself the task to name
everything that moved – there a witless jay
splashing in a pool of engine oil, there
the stoner mailman puffs a jay
on his rusted bumper. Sometimes love

is the mindless chatter of a voice
staving silence off a moment longer.
Even after Jesse nipped my arm
I made mother swear we'd save him
from the needle. The day he went she met me
at the door. Behind my aunt's willow
I sniffled through each flung shovel-full
and hours later tamped it back down tight.

Noah, one old coot says your granddaughter
cursed the preacher's sermon and like Hamlet leapt
into your grave, singing the only hymn she knew
as she dumped apron-loads of earth
on your box herself. It's only legend
but it's more real to me than Thomas
sticking fingers through the ooze
of his saviour's ghost stigmata.

Now my slim young pup lifts his leg
dribbling a mustard stream
down your name. Know I tried
to stop him. Know I tugged his leash
out of the normal superstitions. But among
Tyaskin's masts, among the musk of crab
and mosquitoes that whir like flying periods
he pees where he sees fit. He laps the sailboat names
I read aloud as we leave your trigger-itch and stroll
the dockyard to our truck: Green Gerty,
Moonlight Calypso, Bird of Prey.

Nancy J. Thompson

Poem for My Daughter's Schnauzer

If terriers were working dogs
I'd hand you the bill,
two hundred dollars for your x-rays,
urinalysis, just in case you had a bladder stone
or hormone imbalance – but no,
you piss on the floor
for the same reason Jackson Pollock painted,
to express yourself. Girl,
you'd be back to playing second fiddle
to the dog I no longer have but still love
except you don't play anything,
not ball, not chase the cat, not kill
the squirrel. You just sit outside my back door
and stare in, as if
being outside on a warm spring day
is punishment; as if longing for the fire hydrant you imagine
in the middle of the living room.

Katie O'Sullivan

Marker Of Our Lives

She was our first child's puppy,
(toddlers both, on shaky legs).
She dug crater holes
in newly seeded lawns;
chased rabbits through
babyberry bushes,
and fast cars on dirt roads.

Gentle and patient with
ear-tugging, nose pinching
serial infants.
Steadfast; a follower
to foreign homes
in exotic ports.

Aging, she lay at the feet
of her soldier boy,
off to war.
Lay at his feet
when he came back,
broken.
And, when in our arms,
time coaxed her into death,
our tears fell for her,
and for each other,
for the tattered quilt of our lives,
end of our beginnings,
beginning of our ending.

Julian Stannard

Oliver

I'm in Lorsica
and there's not a cigarette in sight.

But there's Oliver:
the most *simpatico* mongrel in Liguria.

He's small, he's whitish:
his eyes are popping out of his head.

I wish I could smoke him.

Michelle Valois

Still Life with Hound Dog

1

Red wool; hunting license pinned to a pocket puckered into the shape of a pack of cigarettes removed before the jacket is laid down.

2

Large oil painting hanging on museum wall: 18th century realism; men in red hunting jackets and crisp white pants sit atop stately horses; a pack of fox hounds leads the way.

3

Quiet dog in wire cage; one of a dozen; the others, beefy black labs and yapping mixed breeds, vie unsuccessfully for attention. The small hound in cage 3 stares as if to say *what took you so long.*

4

It takes me a long time to return from that city of bridges and islands, islands and bridges that I could never cross, where, as my mother said, I could be anything I wanted.

5

When my father wants to get Lucky back after he is done hunting and ready to go home, he leaves his jacket on the ground to give Lucky a scent to come back to. When he returns later in the day, he finds Lucky curled into a ball, asleep on the tobacco-scented wool. I, too, seek such a sign but find none.

6

Lucky is hit by a car. My older sisters watch. I am not born yet.

7

The anyone my mother said I could be is nowhere to be found. I return home, with no intention of staying. The dog in cage 3 saves my life.

8

My grandfather's dogs, each one named Tippy, wait for him, unleashed, wherever he leaves them: outside bars or city hall, package stores or his mother's apartment. Today the name Tippy makes me laugh: my grandfather emerging from a dark barroom into the light of a Hopper painting, Tippy looking tippy to the man who was dying and drinking himself dead.

9

Shelter volunteer shouts, *Daisy's going home*, hands me a form and takes my fifty dollars, explains that Daisy cannot run off leash. As I tell her I understand, I am thinking to myself, *she will*.

10

Deep snow. Little legs cannot outrun me. An obedient spaniel as mentor. A pocket of treats. Daisy comes back.

11

She runs away, but not from me. She runs because that is what she was born to do: run and sniff and roll and wander. The woods are hers, but she is mine; she always comes back.

12

She finally outruns me; I cannot follow.

13

I dream Daisy alive again after twelve years and a thousand walks in a dozen different woods, under stars and sun and moon and clouds, all swirling at once in a landscape of thickly-applied oil on torn canvas. In this dream, she is running, her short legs speed her away, but her nose and maybe even her heart bring her back for a piece of stale cheese. Leaving, returning; coming, going; running, stopping – only when I snap leash to collar.

14

This, I think, is my life's finest work: to love a thing for what it is with a heart in pieces but still thumping. So many beats as the heart asks and asks if it did all right.

Richard Murphy

Doggerel for Emily

There was a dog
Who was a mug,
He said what a soggy
Doggy
Says on a muggy
Day, with a wag
Of his wiggly juggly tag
Of a tail.
A hag
Came out of a bog
With a big bag
To catch the dog,
So he dug
His fangs in her wig,
She wriggled into a log
And that mug of a dog
Sat on it barking
"Slug, slug."

Cleggan, 14 March 1967

Mark Smith-Soto

Night Watch

Chico whines, no reason why. Just now walked,
dinner gobbled, head and ears well scratched.
And yet he whines, looking up at me as if confused
at my just sitting here, typing away, while darkness
is stalking the back yard. How can I be so blind,
he wants to know, how sad, how tragic, how I
won't listen before it is too late. His whines are
refugees from a brain where time and loss have
small dominion, but where the tyranny of now
is absolute. I get up and throw open the kitchen door,
and he disappears down the cement steps, barking
deeper and darker than I remember. I follow
to find him perfectly still in the empty yard –
the two of us in the twilight, standing guard.

Nessa O'Mahony

Circumnavigator

for Baxter, the border collie

I count the circles you've inscribed
since you came to us.
At the dog pound:
our first walks a dizzying vertigo,
figures of eight looped
on the long lead,
not certain yet
if we could go straight.
Or the border patrol that began
the first day home,
continuing ever since in a parabola
of front door through hall,
ears cocked for rush-hour.
The dizzying black and white blur,
a fairground ride as you excavate
a wall of death in the garden mud,
your signature O flattening montbretia.
Or the 360 degree joy
with squeaky toy and an open green
as you bound exuberance,
radar swerve round trees.
The widest arc reserved
for treks uphill as you disappear
into brush, emerge behind us.
We think we are bringing you;
your pink-tongued grin tells the truth of it.

Michael O'Loughlin

Elegy For A Basset Hound

Other dogs feared you, perhaps rightly –
All that weight so close to the ground
The heft of those padded shoulders
The not so comical teeth concealed
Beneath your sadman jowls and pouches.

English-bred and born, according
To the Basset experts, my neighbour plucked
You off the autostrada near Lucca
Where you were wandering confidently
Like a nineteenth century English explorer

His mind gone in Antarctic snow.

You settled into an Amsterdam bookshop
Your basket firmly placed between
The New York Review of Books
And Literature in Translation
Where you accepted the ministrations
Of single gentlemen, but fell in love
With my wife and daughter
Running away from home as often as you could
To climb like a legless man onto Judith's lap
Where you slept for hours with one eye open.

Untrainable, unbiddable, I could barely hold you
Back on the days I took you with me
To collect Saar from her school, and
You made a beeline through the crush
Of mothers and bicycles, to the class where
The children fought to touch your mighty ears
As you gambolled ponderously on giant paws
Like an ottoman pasha in his harem.

And yet I loved you for something else:
How on a brown December night
When the light had soaked into the wet ground
I saw you through the dusk of *Utrechtsestraat*
With trams and teatime traffic crashing between us
Out of earshot, almost out of sight,
You turned on the crowded pavement
And like the old god of the kabbalah
Lost in the darkness and unknowing before Creation
You raised your nose and sniffed the fouled air
And I knew that you had found me.

William Pitt Root

From One Old Dog to Another

In Memoriam: our sweet Oscar Wild

With even a casual glance into your eyes
I've seen light deep as the bones of my body
glow back out at me, your

tongue of pure pink joy hanging lathered and wide,
your heart, so powerful it leaps like a rabbit baffled by your ribs,
thumps under my hand.

      With you I regained from my youth knowledge of raw delight
          gradually supplanted, put to sleep year by grey year,
               habit by habit.

      Even our nights run parallel: Until I lay the dog of my body down
        you remain beside me, flopping curled at my feet when I sit,
             rising when I rise,

eyes upon me always, even while I mull the dull leafy white meals
I hold between us, the books you sometimes sniff,
puzzled. And when I flop

before TV, on the black beanbag you claim for you own
in all the intervals, you slink slyly behind the set itself,
to lie in my line of vision

      during the hours actors manufacture lives of moving light –
        your head resting on a stuffed toy, until I snap the TV off
            and wake

      back to our life, tossing you the belled lamb you quickly, gently
        snatch from air before it hits the floor, your eyes brighter
          than most human laughter. Once

I finally join our Pam in the bedroom, within seconds you're
beside us in the dark, at your own inalienable post
facing the door, guarding our sleep.

Now and then I've been wakened from nightmare by your nose
in my face and I've heard you, as well, whimpering in terror,
felt your legs, dream-bound, twitch.

Placing my human hand on your inhuman trembling face,
I've felt the muscles anchoring your jaws soften,
I've seen your eyes opening

go easy with that ancient glow in which I recognize myself,
and I've known things man alone
cannot hope to know.

William Pitt Root

Walking Story

for Happy and Zazu

To walk in the woods
with the dogs

so long cooped up in the house
is to be a child

hearing for the first time
those stories our ears take

straight to the heart –
each cell alert,

ears perked, body humming,
eyes dark with a forward glare

trained all at once
on everything: a search

for anything that moves
along the eyes' horizon,

anything that
doesn't move, crouching

until we've passed,
until it's safe again. Owls

in the high branches,
deer we never see,

rabbits in undergrowth,
ears laid back, breathing,

their eyes charged globes,
gleaming convex reflections

of the world
where we are walking,

tossing sticks and laughing,
joyfully oblivious

of the tale our presence enters,
of all eyes but our own.

William Pitt Root

Elegy for Apu

Apu ben Gasser, Afghan hound
And gentleman, court jester in repose
But clearly a king once he rose
To stretch or circle the room, round
And round, until his chosen plot
Of rug was freed of snakes, the grass
Of his imagination tramped down flat
As he could make it with his great black feet,

And Apu running, covering the long green ground
As if grace made his body its pure dance
Of speed and beauty, muscles flowing over bone
Concealed beneath deep fur, his elegance
Like water smoothly flexing over stone,

And Apu, who, for his mistress,
Strode across the fields of show and
Stately, at his ease,
Held firm under the judge's hand:

Apu – clown, king, champion,
Gentleman, and friend –

Apu is dead.

Patricia Robertson

Minus Forty

My dog is on fire.
She comes in from the night bearing woodsmoke, the burning
gases of stars, iced air
propelling her, heartless, to the other side of the house.

Smoulders on the sofa,
hunting the night squirrel.

Overhead the northern lights.
A vast green crayon gone out of control.

Knute Skinner

For Rimbaud (1965-1978)

1.

In the back yard
under stones

The July sun, almost warm at last,
lightens those yellow-flowering weeds
beside our garden.
There are rows of cabbages, peas,
onions and beans.
For the past two days Edna and I
have been eating spinach.
None of this would interest you at all
if you were here.

Last night when I threw at the dartboard in the kitchen,
you would have complained.

I am sitting now at the chipboard desk in my study,
stained with traces of thirteen years of ink.
I am sitting here for the first time this summer
without having plugged in heat.

Edna is writing a letter to her father.
Dunstan and Morgan are probably still asleep.

None of this would interest you at all.
You'd rather hear that cows are passing the road.
You'd have gone along with Dunstan yesterday
when he cleaned out the spring with Micky.
You'd have barked again and again at the Murrays' tractor
bringing home hay.

I set out to write a poem which would have shown
how much I miss you,
but instead all I've done is record some trivial facts
concerning my life here, which you no longer share.

2.

In the back yard
under stones,
under grasses
newly grown,

by the scraggly
sally trees
and the wall she
leapt with ease,

solitary,
Rimbaud stays
wholly to herself
these days;

nor can aught be
seen of her
toenails, teeth,
flesh, and fur

save in memories
and those
only serve to
discompose.

James Simmons

Charlie

Charlie, they bought me you for Father's Day

Now you are nearly the old woman of the sea,
neutered before you ever accomplished sex,
you only tried out vaguely on the cats,
persistently but gentlemanly.

Your bark says, 'Better to marry than to burn.'

We think of you as a loving old silly,
whining when we leave, leaping up on our return,
stone chaser and chewer, football burster.
I regret not being a bird hunter or a gillie
who would put you to clever use and teach
you skills. We throw stones for you on the beach,
and tease and stroke and cuddle you a lot.

This is a nice wild area and you wander free.

It is better to be neutered than be shot,
we said yesterday when you bit our neighbour.
It was one too many bites. We can't construe
your angers and we can't speak to you.
You always go for the postman, once our
friend, your teeth bared horribly, leaping
at his rapidly closing window. His frightened face
grown ugly. Maybe he kicked you, we speculate;
but I've kicked you to put you in your place.
You don't hate me. Is it red cars you hate?

You behave badly, and you are in our keeping.
You bark for any arrival day or night,
people or cars; but the moment they're entered

and at home you fawn and lick their hands...
with one exception, the small bad tempered
farmer, nipped in the hall, and nip is bite.
We can't talk grandly of keeping off our lands
the interlopers. We don't want to. We want
your company, but human flesh is sacrosanct.

'Get that mongrel away from my sheep,' he shouted,
'or I'll shoot him.' And he was right, Ned,
a pregnant sheep is an investment. We didn't parlay;
but you're cured of sheep-chasing this long
time. The neighbours know and love 'Charlie'.
Everyone rolls your fine name on his tongue
and smiles ... except the postman and the milkman
and the odd dandering city clan
of holiday children you sometimes terrify,
leaping over the back wall to the lane.

The noble profile poised at window sills,
our bonehead mongrel of the Baskervilles.

It was one too many you nipped with Mrs Hatrick
who drove back promptly and showered her shapely leg
with marks of teeth no friendly licking will lick
off. She said, nicely, she wasn't complaining,
she knew you weren't a bad dog. She was meaning
that country life is harsh ... no need to beg
forgiveness; but she needed a tetanus jab.

We knew someone was going to report you, you clown,
sooner or later. And then you'd be put down.

I rang the vet, who was civil and couldn't be sure,
but neutering was a high percentage cure
for excitable dogs. It cost £47.
We have no lead. I whistled you in and left.

That evening it seemed I felt your absence more
than I ever felt your presence, as a hollow
behind my legs, for up and down you follow

around the house. When I'm at stool you scratch
the door, or burst in if it's off the latch.
When I went to bed and slept I was still bereft,
your black shadow was absent from the floor.

Next day the nice girl carried you out to the car
with this plastic lampshade round your neck
to keep your teeth from where the stitches are,
and all this week around the house you knock
on door jambs and rattle like a shelf
of tin mugs when you scratch yourself.

You look up with your perfect grizzled head,
a sable silvered, a Dutch portrait with elaborate
ruff, dignified as any burgher. I wrote,
'dognified.' My daughter might well hate
a father who does such things. And Wendy said
her father had tied a dead hen round the neck
of his dog to cure his killing habit. Heck,
I can't tie a postman round you! He's not dead.

Before I hear, you hear his van, and the low groan
starts in your throat. Charlie, you aren't cured yet;
but, 'It may take weeks for every aggressive hormone
to work its way out of the system,' said the vet.

My wife was the one who knew this would set you free.
If I bite her she'll do the same for me.

Ben Simmons

Tread Softly

I heard the words, 'dog years'
and thought of my own, Charlie
a crossbreed, half lab, half collie
named after a professor, adored by
my mother, and thought of those long
drizzling days, for him; my dog,
flowing quickly like torrent water.

His days ended like his long
dead master; my father
unable to walk, but still expressing
life's simple pain and its occasional tenderness.
Where his last days to him years
each minute a fortnight of suffering
and uncontrolled bowel movements?

Did he observe, years before
my father's death like a stopped clock?
Where his last breath was a silent cry
which echoed down the hall?
If so, it gives me courage that
an animal in such pain could steer
his steadfast loyalty to my lap
offering a paw to my five
year old weeping self.
No wonder he looked so wise,
a Sensei's bread dwelling under
his canine face reminding me
in simple moans "Life continues,
a grazed knee does not cripple".

Before they carried out the casket
you howled from your cold master's feet
and expressed what the attending mourners
could not.

When I carried you, suspended
in a blanket to the white van
you looked lovingly and said
'Good night'.

Anne Shaw

Haunch

A pit bull contemplates his former homelessness

And birds, too, rise before me as I walk:
Each hangs suspended, briefly, in the air
grey whir and fear, the *coo* of them
though I could snatch them easily, and would –

When you call me good, I am good
as when you call me bad, for each thrown ball
commands me toward its joy. When we walk together,
tethered on our thread, we walk now in a tide of small gold leaves,

by the wind thrown back, in a circle cast by rain.
When you lie down to sleep I am with you
when you rise up, I awake. You go out
and you return. Your hands move

back and forth, to do, to make. Each day
you form a small hope of your life
and because I cannot tell you what I know
I dream each night of translation:

How, first, you sleep on a yellow towel
and then the street is cold beneath your haunch.
Then hunger courses through you
whether you sleep or no, and still

each moment is equivalent. Each moment breathes you
in and back, though in winter it grows dark early,
and we walk under trees of cold
where the strange light you name *snow*

is all around. And this is what I mean to say:
If there can ever, in another, be sufficient shelter,
then this is what we move toward, though it burn
against the nose and disappear.

Breda Wall Ryan

Meanwhile...

(i.m. Porter, *a.k.a.Wullemberg Count Hawk*)

Meanwhile our lives go on
much as before
but grass has grown back on the path
you wore in the lawn,
magpies menace
the songbirds in the yard
without you to chase them

next door's marmalade cat
with fire-struck eyes
stalks the ground-feeding doves
you don't come when I call
but the children still play
in the woods by the river
without you to chivvy them home

they swim in the sea
without you dog-paddling
offshore as lifeguard.
Meanwhile I chatter on
as if you were here
but you don't quirk an eyebrow
to say, Enough, already!

The door to your kennel
framed such an ache
that we took it apart
plank by plank
We've folded away
all our dog-scented things –
the brush and stainless steel bowl

your hair-laden Indian blanket
the muzzle you wore in the street
Some days I catch a black-and-tan flash
bounding over some landscape –
deep woodland or mountain, the field
near your grave. Then memory
makes you appear in a gap between dreams.

Layne Russell

chance of thunderstorms increasing overnight

under darkening clouds
in cool grass
we sit waiting

between ash and cedar
lightening explodes
in the northwest

ears cocked high
my little dog barks
cutting through sky —

lightening, Tashi, lightening
just a few drops then
thunder, Tashi, thunder

I hold her close
puppy eyes brighter
with each flash

Lex Runciman

Freckles

You want to say
it wasn't the animal but the lessons.
The first day he came from the country
he disappeared who knows where.
We walked and called, and called
and gave up. How could he know home?
Circumstance is not wish nor prayer.
Right from the first, he limped,
but seemed not to notice.
Nor did he learn: a wheel had hit him once,
and on good days he still chased them,
barking, that snout snarling so close
the lesson was persistence or foolishness.
Warm, safe, fed and happy,
he howled in the garage at night,
but not always: I thought cats,
though I lacked the proof.
And when I got off the school bus,
he'd rouse from the middle of the road
opposite our house. He would stretch,
look, cock his head waiting to be sure.
At one word, his name, he ran --
an embodiment of will, a demonstration
that, if you've known it, you can say.
After what might have been years,
one school morning my mother said
she and my father had decided:
he would go back to the country.
He could howl and chase and be happy.
He would be gone when I came home.
When she died, I emptied a drawer
and found the collar she had put there.
A beagle, Freckles had a spotted nose
and brown ears. The feel of them
defines *soft*.

Jacob Rakovan

Dog

He was good and dumb and named by a child
so his name was Duke, because children are
conservatives at heart
They like square cars and shoe-shaped shoes
And house-shaped houses and dogs named Duke
Or Fido, they grasp a certain comforting coherence to pattern

but our house was a house-shaped something else,
an unfun-funhouse with slanting floors
openings in the ceilings and walls
Strange colonies in the walls
like those miracle shacks
where water flows uphill
and tiny men become giants
and a broom stands in the corner untouched.

except it also was devoid of miracles, and most mercies.

Duke dug himself an egg shaped nest
in the brown industrial carpeting
down to the water-warped plywood.
He had a fondness for grapefruit husks
rescued from the maggoty trash

He slipped his rope and wandered the wooded lots
drawing me out of the house to call his dumb-dog name
through acres of convergent lots and hedgerows
and scrub brush. He mounted the ugly green chair
With amorous intent

He did not seem concerned with
the tricks I half heartedly tried to teach him
but like all smiling dogs he was wolf,
had to be restrained when the zoning man
came poking among the rusting cars and washing machines
the gasoline filled ringer washer
his loyalty uncomplicated

And he signed his death warrant
when the fat lady stood up on her bicycle
to peep through the grease smeared windows
And finally see just what. was. going. on. in. there.
and he chased her down
and smilingly bit out
a softball-sized chunk of her ass

Irene McKinney

For Pia

That's OK, hang in there,
make me sorry, make me weep
for your illness, follow me
from room to room making
that little low groan that is
all you have the strength for:
don't let me forget for a moment
that you're dying, that you're
limping and stumbling, barely
able to walk, but trailing me
everywhere asking for help,
because when have I ever
failed you? When you
were caught in the snarl
of barbed wire, bleeding
from many places, didn't
I pull you free and wash your
wounds? And when you
were snake-bitten, I sat up
all night with my hand
on your back so you'd know:
I am with you always.
Of course, of course, you ask that
I lift this heaviness from you,
the way your hips seem
too much to drag behind you,
the way all sounds have
strangely disappeared.
You know I will save you.
But the days drag
on as you drag
from room to room,

making that pitiful choking
sound, waiting with your
heavy head hanging down,
waiting for the saviour's touch,
waiting for your breath
to return and bring you joy.

Seamus Cashman

Welcoming a friend from the past

for Alden James Gale Price, who might have been named Tucker, but wasn't.

Welcome Alden James Gale Price
'friend from the past' whose name so nice
distracts my mind that's all a pucker
with the tongue that mutters 'Tucker'.

Tucker was a dog we had
when in Conna as a lad of tender years
and naive wit, my mam and dad acquired it.
A favourite of my sis and me, first two
in our family, we played each day
out on the street, with Tucker barking at our feet,
and God help any passer by who came too near.

But then, oh dear, there was one year
a friendly lorry driver who, often and as well we knew,
brought sweets and laughter to the day. He parked
to shop and as he did, our pet and dog sat underneath
to chew and stew the back wheel tyre and dream dog dreams.
Alas, alas, on his return, distracting all with gifts and cheers,
and jumping in to drive away, with a wave
and a 'Goodbye', that friendly trucker,
brought life's end to our dog Tucker.

We miss him still, my sis and me
though half a century has passed by
and memory is sometimes now imagination;
that happy barker with his woe-full name
is bright writ today in our family hall of fame.

To give you some idea of who
this dog was, a word or two about his looks:
– no sweet and gently cuddly guy
nor elegant nor bright;
no swift and fleet foot hunter fast
no threat beyond a hardy bark.
This dog was just a mongrel mutt
with welcoming eyes and lots of guff
and barely eighteen inches high.
Dancing with short snappy moves,
he never had the doggy blues.
His shaggy coat was white and black.
His stubby tail was cracker jack.

Our Tucker was an ugly caring friend
whose name recovers time and heart.
There's nothing I need really say
of why or what or when or where:
for every single childhood game
was tumble-loved with our dog Tucker.

George Petty

Affection

One year my birthday present
ran under a chair,
and as I reached in my hand
it growled and bit me.

When I came home from school
she shut her tail down tight
and scurried to sit on it
behind the furnace.

She worried all the time about that tail,
as if the world's bike had just run over it,
hiding it behind my mother, women united
to teach me shouts and grabs were not affection

After a while I tried being gentle;
I helped her endure her own children,
until, with eloquent reluctance,
one day she nuzzled me.

And on that first warm day in March,
headed for the park, my baseball mitt in hand,
when I whistled for her, she came, but sideways,
looking back to see if it was still there.

John Perrault

The Neighbour's Dog

Jack chased shadows.
His tail if the light was right.
Toss a stone, he sprung for the spot
Spotting the ground till it hit his nose.

Everyone cheered.
What a crazy hound they said,
Patting Jack's head, fondling his ears.
His eyes, two gray wells that never cleared.

Jack chased cars too.
To be specific, the tires
So long as they shadowed the road.
One day he got close enough to chew.

Everyone came
To the burial in Jack's
Back yard. They stood around, casting
Shadows on the stone that bears his name.

Harry Owen

Non-Dog

Dora, most solid Ridgeback,
wears her non-nylon,
non-green collar honestly, bravely,
and is, of course, decidedly
non-black

while Daisy, standard Poodle, non-bright,
wears a smart non-leather collar
around her sleek French neck
and is assuredly
non-brown.

All day,
racing together around the field, eyes bright,
reading the earth's text with their noses,
barking at strangers or just
keeping me quiet company
here in the house,
each is simply herself:
neither one is, despite everything,
non-dog.

Mary O'Malley

Anubis In Oghery

For Oisin

Our dog, Georgie is dead. She lived
with us for ten years and walked three miles a day
with me but loved you best because she was
mostly yours. Now I have to watch your face
the reddening look, as if it might break open
and think there is something about a man's pain
that cracks like chestnuts or old timber.
It is not lubricated by tears.

You buried her down among the hazels
and blackberries, made a cairn on the grave
planted two birch trees. No-one instructed you
in these rites. Yesterday you were a small boy
playing with a pup that chewed windows. Now
you walk away, a dream dog at your heel. Tall, able.

Mary O'Malley

Cleo

She was a six month Spring in a dark year.
We were waiting for fine weather
to take her swimming, nervous
she'd destroy Trá Mhór with her enthusiasm
for digging. She was everything she could be,
hovering up smells from the kitchen floor
silvery pink, klutzy one minute
a hound of heaven the next, all she. Lovely Cleo.

Chris Oke

Eastwood

Through that milky blue cloud
I am a seraph, haloed and true
any weakness or fault
concealed on the periphery.

Through that pressurised globe,
trying to leap into a world
it's been forced too long to watch,
I am that last drink

before the lights go down.
His world is black and white.
I am two-dimensional
and loved accordingly.

Only a fur covered indentation
where the other eye should be,
like a mysterious paw print
in the snow outside the fence.

He'll likely lose this one soon
and there'll be no more sleds to pull,
no more fights in the dog yard.
We'll only bark at invisible threats.

James Desmond O'Hara

Snowy in Candy Kitchen

Today I met wolf Raven

I am clearly in his world
in snowy Candy Kitchen, New Mexico

His rounds of black and thick and shine
are white lumps of furry snow

Frightened breaths are lengthening

Luminous gazes

His head now buried into my stomach

I know for sure that time is stopping

and that Raven would lie down with lambs

Tommy Frank O'Connor

Threena

As a pup we called him Coffee
Lustrous in the colour of his fur.

He would gambol with the children
Learning tricks and winning friends the more.

They scratched until his fur turned hairy.
Then he misjudged an overtaking car.

The children made a stretcher
With fence posts through the sleeves of coat and jumper.

Teardrops sprinkled their procession
Bearing the near-dead thing to our hayloft.

A parent vet was summoned
And his advice to put Coffee down out-voted.

He will live because we love him
They insisted. Never mind the bleeding

And perhaps a broken shoulder.
Just kill his pain and we will do the nursing.

Chicken broth and my two pillows,
Liver and free nibbles from the butcher.

With a rota of more children,
In three weeks Coffee was pawing and nuzzling.

One front paw was still not working,
So a new name had to be considered.

In one voice they called him *Threena*
Four working legs now down to three-and-a-half.

Soon he visited his carers
His new name and limp a signature

Tune announcing his arrival
For a snack and gambol with the children.

Sheila Nickerson

Jake and the Last Day of Summer

Perhaps it is the last day of summer
and you are sitting in the backyard
missing an old dog.
Perhaps you remember how the sun
grows an inch a year but how
a damaged heart cannot gain
back what it has lost.

The fountain still spills
water down its river bed of rocks
and warmth coaxes colour from
the flowers in their pots.
Sun comes over to join you,
but, looking up, you see
that grassy spot, Jake's favourite,
where he lay, head raised, watching.

Sheila Nickerson

With an Old Dog in the Autumn Woods

An old dog listens more carefully
than a young dog
to sounds in the autumn woods.
See – the old one, head cocked
to the falling of leaves,
while the young one romps.

Yes, Copper, you and I hear
noises we cannot name:
footsteps in the wind.
Come close and we will watch
the young one as he runs.

Pete Mullineaux

Circus Dog

Balancing at the water's edge
gripping a torn umbrella,

she has to be barking mad
to venture without even a rope, but

the ringmaster has been left at home
she rolls on her back in the sand

then throws herself into the waves
asking if they want more.

No more nonsense, tomorrow
there will be a unicycle, juggling balls!

Pete Mullineaux

Salty

She kicks her paws and spurts
along the shoreline...

bounds into the waves
to great white suds of applause,

wades through dissolving foam
shakes out her fur,

showers the world with salt –
she is worth it!

Mary Mullen

Goldie

Jack's neighbour took Goldie to the bar
a month after Jack died hoping the locals
would hoist up Goldie's heart a bit.
Maybe she could eat a left-over sausage,
jump up onto her stool next to Jack's
cold one, croon Old Man River again,
get strokes from Jack's friends
who always said: 'Good dog yourself.'

Jack used to mumble 'loyalty is for dogs.'
Goldie figured those words were a hymn
Jack had learned after his wife had left.
Goldie pranced into the bar, sniffed,
and low-tailed it out of there. She snuffled
back to Jack's porch and curled up to wait.

Noel Monahan

Clio

First an Alsatian came
To steal my dinner,
I barked, he ran off.

A few months later
A terrier came, then a cat,
I barked and they scampered away.

Now a robin robs me of my food,
I no longer bark. I sometimes
Sleep and dream the hours away.

Karla Linn Merrifield

Canticle for a Samoyed

So much fur,
four paws,
two wise eyes,
one soul,
a friend.

I ask how will my two hands
in the last moment
ever forget the thick coat,
tickling whiskers, quivering ears,
that trusting heart, even as it stops,
soon, in my two hands?

Who will feed you then?
What voice will answer your howl?
Where will you nuzzle?
When will you comfort another?
Why do you have to die?

Sweet, believing creatures,
maybe only you can teach us
in your stiffening silence
the stillness, perfect stillness
we can find in living on.

There is so much to be said
that goes unspoken except
in quiet tears years later for:

So much fur,
four paws,
two wise eyes,
one soul,
a friend.

Alexa Mergen

Yet

Since the dog went blind we're careful to put away clutter. Stepping
from shoes by the door means she'll stumble, stray magazines become
slicks, an abandoned chair a wall. Faced with each obstacle she retreats
one step and I swear you see her thinking, filing away information
in a category labelled *exceptions*. Since we brought animals inside
isn't everything an exception to their natal maps? Dogs are tireless
navigators of a human world, sofas and beds sole islands of safety.
                                                    And yet along
the river parkway, in a meadow swept clear by occasional floods, the
dog's sightlessness slips away as she flies over gullies, crashes through
scrub, olfactory compass engaged. For animals, even the soles of paws
are sensors. Watching her run I see the geometry of space and physics
of air, how with every step a response, an embrace, holding her.

Alexa Mergen

The Wilder Dog and I

The wilder dog and I walk in still starlight as dreamers reach for webby sleep. Desert animals crawl to dens, press bodies to the ground before day breaks into sun. Moon loves night, waits as long as possible before retreating like the last student at recess dribbling a red ball against time.

The dog blazes a trail through air like a comet's tail. Looking back from the low road to my house I understand why people choose hills. Winds slam our structure like a gale to a sailboat but the view over Joshua Tree and Yucca Valley places our dwindling lives in weather: wind, sun, nighttime cold rising, sometimes rain and hail. Our indigenous company is black widows slipping among stones of the sunroom wall, rattlesnakes coiling on tiles, scorpions replicating themselves in miniature. This foolishness of humanness, not adapted anywhere unless you count cars and buildings moulded to our pulpy bodies, like the Ford I drive forty miles down the grade to a new school stranded like a lighthouse for residents of low desert despair.

I found this wilder dog on a road, have somewhat tamed her though she pursues the car as I leave to greet children by 7:00, my mind spinning lesson plans that don't come off. She runs in dust until she stops abruptly where dirt and pavement meet and there she stands panting.

Máighréad Medbh

Bran

Whose bowed head and whited eyes
whose raven hunch amber fields
    moon-topped brows drooped orphan ears
    a slave act for a master

You were begging your freedom
and tides turned in our two minds
    the decision made itself
    I much less possessed than you

Your dragon-black pupils caved
sucked me into our service
    a link I thought summoning
    to love's hard obligation

We named you to conjure up
heroics we had barely read
    maybe myth could work wonders
    slice meaning into thin baps

You got no proper training
why should I make you perform
    when my life was its own game
    no boars on the teeming hills

Your father was in question
a Collie seen bounding off
    Doberman markings? hoped not
    you were gentle as meadows

Your hunts were for chocolate cakes
watching at table for scraps
 how we live rabbits are free
 and dogs must be civilised

You had no life of your own
and we in our purpled heads
 your gaze your needy shifting
 gavels for hasty tempers

No stroking ever enough
you'd scrape and paw for an hour
 at last learned the computer
 was always cosseted more

But I was the one you nudged
when fireworks bronzed in your ears
 when food was magma at night
 always my side of the bed

Nudging me head in my lap
taught me to be your hero
 not subject to dragon moods
 chaffing congenital bits

You picked the scent of my path
my panics my sudden flares
 knew my lake-bound devotion
 confused the track of service

Our sons named for demi-gods
you for a demi-god's hound
 and not a one among us
 has hunted more than a mouse

We are shadows of our myths
living in some soft notion
 but you can't see the dwindles
 think bed is bog parks are plains

Whose dragon eyes whose amber
whose raven hunch whose chaffing
        whose speed and rabid hunting
        suffered a poor translation

Learning mind was our matter
I forgave us all the sham
        the funhouse mirror of hope
        silvered by souciant skies

When I left our shared household
I held our abiding hoard
        old stories told in hundreds
        calling into the future

                        Whose

Mary Madec

Dire Consequences

Cassandra. I gave her the name, refused the metaphor.
Each day has its own supremacy of best laid plans.
Yet,

she came when she was called,
walked across the road as if.

The lorry, a second out
slid and dragged her into timelessness.
The hours after seemed as before.

She lies like Cordelia, I weep like Lear,
wonder if there was a choice of outcomes

in that moment. It took the road
two days to bleed from the thaw.
We shook woodshavings on it,

seeds to make it something else,
so she might rise like a phoenix from the snow.

I call her name into the frozen air, *Cassie! Cassie!*
I stroke her first coat. Condemned by fate,
who would believe she was never meant to go?

Something is happening inside my tense fragile skin
like ageing, warning of the future.

Cecilia McGovern

Trust

That day at the clinic,
alert again, outstaring cats,
snuffling in corners.

Under the vet's hand,
your eyes trust me
while the filling needle mocks

both our instincts
to protect and save –
you, head cocked sideways

curiously still as I wade
into a cold sea,
I, prising open your jaws

to trickle milk
through my fingers
the time you'd been poisoned

– shock of your breath
loud and fast as
your heart gives out

unconsoled by the vet's pardon
"he owes you nothing
he gave you nineteen years".

Afric McGlinchey

Cracked

He lived in the dark with rats
and rotting straw,
head endlessly cocked
from peering at the light
through the crack
under the door.

We brought him home
where he stared
at a lamp, riveted,
one eye stone blue,
the live pupil slit
to a crack.

He growled when bushes
bullied, learned to avoid
nettles like cracks
on a pavement; ambushed
wheelbarrows, lawnmowers,
left no stone unturned

knocked into gate and canine
ghosts. After six months,
he barked, an unfamiliar sound,
like crashing pool balls. We laughed.
There was more to his life now,
than light under a crack.

Bette Lynch Husted

Devotion

You did nothing, of course, to deserve this.
You gave someone money. He tumbled away from that
warm pile of brothers and sisters, climbed
into your lap
tucked his nose in the fold of your arm.

In the old Wasco story, Dog stayed with humans
when all other animals turned in disgust at our ways –

Not that yours are so terrible. Right? So you say
to the face in the mirror each morning,
or would say, but he's at the door, looking back
at you, hurry, the soccer ball's out there, the Frisbee,
the squirrels! That terrible cat!

He'd go home with the mailman, you're sure. Or your in-laws.
He sleeps by the fire, his soft ears draped into your palm.

And by God – he's fast, he is focused desire –
he catches that squirrel.
You pry open his jaw, let the squirrel survive
if it can. Blood pools deep in his mouth.
He sees you as a cloud as you carry him into the house.
Then he shivers it off, ears to tail
and looks up at you, ready.

Danuta E. Kosk-Kosicka

Luckie Shows Up Seventy Years Later

Ah, Luckie. Good dog, good doggie
You have been away for so many years
you wag your warped tail, stretch
you want me to follow

Where are we going?

Ah, towards the river
across the field unfurled
like a whitened cloth
The dew has fallen. Seems
the cows are back in their sheds for it is quiet
I can smell the milk
and the dust stirred by chains
dragged on their way from the meadows

We are coming to the bridge
of pine planks that my father
nailed together – but it is gone

Luckie, you are feathery white
like the chicken you snatched
when I was a teenage boy in the village
which is no more on the river
that now flows through us to the Milky Way

Danuta E. Kosk-Kosicka

In Salamanca: Sinbad, the Dog

He digs with his paws and squeezes
his big beige body in the hollow
of bare earth in the clasp
of banana trees; their wild green trunks
peel into dry rust, arched leaves
comb the blue cold, tearing
through horns beeping
and hammers pummeling.

In the night he runs between shadows
of roses and poinsettia bush,
tells his stories and howls in the choir
of neighbours guarding the dreaming homes.
How does he take the first strains

of a daybreak? The *basso profundo*
that rolls the night
away on the train, the calls of sirens
that suck people into
the refinery with its dragon breath
hung over the town, the chimneys
spilling hot orange flowers
of flame trees.

Now in the hollow of the day
Sinbad's chains hold him
in the clasp of banana trees.

Jacqueline Kolosov

Shelter

Through the chain link fence,
the brindle-coated Kara's eyes
yearn toward mine. Between Kara
and Mr. Brown, her escape artist brother,
is Winnie, the incontinent yellow lab
who bellows at my approach, her
baritone cry deepening as I ease through
the metal gate and enter the pen
holding Lucy, another lab, but paler,
butter-coloured, and so shy
it takes several minutes to collar her.
                  Like an old lady
baffled at her arrival in a nursing home
and the loss of everything familiar – the bed
in which she slept all her life, the sunny spot
before a living room window –
Lucy lays no claim to the name
she's been given here. And why should she
allow me to lead her away from Kara's quiet stare,
and the chorus of others, as if decibels
could sway my choice, so that all I hear is
Choose me! Choose me!

My daughter, just three, waits on the other side.
I hold the leash, she tells me, amid
the cacophony of others. *My turn, Mommy.*
                  Later,
driving home through the blanched fields
of early March, surrounded by scabbed earth
pocked with old tires and rusting farm machinery,
I will ask myself if it's better, somehow,
to know so little
of this life into which I've brought her.
How much do the dogs know?

Which doggie do you like? I ask Sophie,
the absurdity of the question equaled by my own
free-falling need to bring Lucy and
the mixed breed home – and what of Kara?
The Galilean sea of her dark eyes?

Well, Soph? I ask again.
The purple one, Mommy, she says. And then:
Can we come back tomorrow?

Philip Kingston

Local Spirit

Jake lives in a house in a cloud
Has a pretty face signalling
From a hefty barrel body
That he carries with grace
Like a deft sumo wrestler
Or Falstaff on ice.

Jake regards you with what looks like
Kindness and eagerness to please
And the gentle hope you too will
Return his urge to play
Deliriously for
No obvious reward.

Jake's sofa smells deeply of Jake;
Seventies purple, a yellow
Rug and damp Guardians curling
Amongst the drifts of hair.
Jake reclines on his front,
His side, or sits looking

At you, looking at Jake who isn't
A dog Jake's too aware of, or
Needs to be, given how much benign
Attention emerges when
You stumble across his
Expectant gaze from the

Corner of a house in a cloud.

Deirdre Kearney

Osgar

What arrived as an *Andrex* puppy
Has grown into a 40kg Exocet,
A rocket-propelled, hurtling hellion,
A surface-to-air guided missile,
A heat-seeking destroyer
Of all things non-concrete.
From his observation post
By the back garden wall
He plans his expeditions,
All-out offensives,
Ground and air, against
Garden birds in echelon formation.
This slavering slayer sallies out
To do battle with mops and buckets,
Insatiable annihilator of floor coverings
Carpet, rugs and linoleum,
Lays waste all in his path.
No downpipe safe nor garden hose,
No economy of force against
The hated coal, briquettes and turf.
Flowerpots, all growing things –
Decimated. The garden ground zero
For our hero, named Osgar,
After the bravest of the Fianna.

Conor Mark Kavanagh

Hector

One month, they said, and you
would be put down.

We bonded in an instant.

Golden paws
in the shape of crab claws.

Eyes of a woman you'd marry.

The first night I sang you to sleep;

Peace in the rise and fall of your homing breath.

Brad Johnson

The Truth About the Dog

None of it was easy
when her kidneys failed
and she stopped eating
and her pink tongue finally turned
purple. In three months all that was left
of the dog was her collar
and the lingering question
of what to tell the two-year-old
when he asks about the dog
that slept beside his crib,
that chewed through Elmo's stuffed fingers,
that followed him through
the house when he ate like a New Orleans drunk
behind a Mardi Gras float,
eyes glazed and trained for falling
beads and doubloons.

He'll know the dog's gone
and will ask "Where's Zoey"
and look for her floppy ears
behind the couch and, because everything
I know I learned, I'll tell him
what my father told me when my lab died
and what his father told him
when his wolfhound ran away.

"Where's Zoey?" he'll say.
"Ask your mother," I'll tell him.

Sabine Huynh

A Bouquet of Ephemerals

On your first day among us,
you ate my Barbie doll. I cried
when I saw the pink leg
sticking out of your mouth,
without knowing it would only be
a few years until I buried
that one-legged doll with you.

Born a Saint Bernard you felt
at home among our garden blooms.
I showed you how to smell them,
you taught me to savour their petals.
Three summers we spent
scouring the tall grass
for palatal excitement.

Mint flowers tasted minty,
red roses like strawberries,
lavender like mummy's soap,
chives like onion soup.
Dandelion buds so sweet,
their corolla so bitter,
like love-me, love-me-nots.

The spring of your fading,
every morning I offered you
my fingers dipped in honey.
Too sick for dog food, yet never tired
of the garden's bounty, you had
a daily fancy for white clover heads.
On your last day you found

a four-leaf clover among poppies.
I rewarded you with forget-me-nots,
which you chewed dutifully,
while watching the clover
wither away in my child's hand,
and sniffing the ephemeral
bitter-sweet scent of pleasure.

Noël Hanlon

Maggie

She's happy, even though
she doesn't bound with lolling
tongue. She's elegant,
her long nose is good
for sniffing gopher tunnels
and slipping quickly between
unsuspecting human thighs.

Hold a stick above her
and she's airborne,
undiscouraged by lack
of wings.

She loves her life,
tracing the edges of fields
around the house, barking
at sparrows when they settle
or catching and eating
honey-bees of all things.

She smiles, sashaying
inside her black and white,
matted fur coat,
delighted with farm life.

She's courageous, stays
outside all night – not tied up –
chasing coyotes away from the sheep,
keeping raccoons and skunks
out of the chicken coop.

In the morning she pads
back inside, kisses
the other dog's snout,
rolls over on her back –
paws up – and sleeps
until she's had enough.

Noël Hanlon

Dog

This morning – as I do each day –
I tied my dog's leash around my waist
and walked the forest trail
beside the Willamette.

Sometimes my mind travels
far away – today to Ireland
and the ones I love there –
so I was in another country when
he suddenly stopped and looked up
at me as he would a stranger.
And when I looked down
I sensed danger, saw wildness
in him; I hesitated, then offered
my hand to his scent-query.

He sniffed the back of my hand
as if for the first time,
until my voice reminded him
who I was/who we are.

He had brought me back down to the path
and to the strangeness of sharing my life
with something wild.

Gerard Hanberry

Ringo

Rescued by Mom from Death Row
he arrived bewildered into our lives.
Dad said he had the look of a Teddy Boy,
for me his shaggy black coat and tumbling fringe
meant 'The Beatles'. *Get Back* reached number one
that week so we called him Ringo Starr.

I knew straight off that his rock n' roll sneer
was a shield, his swagger a defence against the street.
He settled right in and was mine.
When the school said I had to do better
and Mom looked at me hard
Ringo just flicked his tail and licked my face.

He knew the score and probably chewed gum
out back of his kennel or even had a sly smoke
while he waited for the neighbourhood to heat up.
Bet he could tell me a lot about girls too,
not that there were any around,
not ones you could talk to anyway.

An astronaut stepped onto the Sea of Tranquillity
and someone was singing about the year 2525
but I wasn't bothered. There was serious news.
Matt Busby was stepping down at United.
I knew that Ringo shared my concern;
what would Best, Law and Charlton do now?

Dad was at home a lot that long winter while
Mom went off to a job somewhere every day.
He spent a lot of time hammering in the shed.
I could hear them talking at night. They sounded cross.
It was as if the school had written another letter.
Ringo wanted to go exploring, so we went.

Spring and Dad had work once again.
A girl said hello to me on the bus,
I thought about her all day. Back home and
Ringo's bowl lay untouched, no reply
to my calls. That night he failed to make it home.
We worried but he did have a wild streak.

Next day the search. Dad, myself, a neighbour.
Nothing. The kennel stood empty all night.
His body was found near the little wood
at the end of our lane. A farmer checking cattle
saw the black bundle – *He should have been tied
and not off trespassing on poisoned land.*

It was a fitting end given his rock-star style,
drugs in the system with a hint of foul play. Tears
when Dad laid him to rest at the foot of the garden.
Mom planted a shrub and it grew.
That was the week when Death first came to visit
and I don't think he ever went away.

Lisa Frank

Whiskey in the Morning

Six years-old, curls
barely formed, I stand
in the kitchen lined up
next to my older brother and sister.

My mother is at the counter, hands tight
on her hips, asking which one of us has taken
her nine-pound frozen chicken.

It's 8:30 in the morning.

I look at my brother, who looks at my sister, who stares
down at her feet.

'*It couldn't have just flown away!*' my mother insists.

I look out the window and up at the empty sky.

An hour later
we go outside
and find Whiskey, our
nine-year-old Sheltie, curls
hanging loose, hovering over
the frozen chicken, front paws
gripping the wings. He looks up at us
– my brother, sister and me
and then glances at my mother –
and from the look in his eyes,
his soft caramel-coloured eyes,
I can tell that he hasn't a clue
what the hell to do with a frozen chicken
either.

Gabriel Fitzmaurice

Lassie

At ninety years he fell into a drain –
That's what John Bradley tells me from his bed
(Hospital plays tricks on old men's brains);
But for his dog, he tells me, he'd be dead.
How fact and fiction make us what we are –
He fell at home at bedtime in the dark
(The drain was years ago outside a bar);
His faithful dog had more sense than to bark –
She lay down on her master all night long,
Licked his face and wrapped him from the cold,
And when the ambulance came to take out John,
Lassie stayed and couldn't be consoled.
She guards his house and lets no stranger through –
When there's nothing left, love finds such things to do.

Elaine Feeney

Sandy

for Shane

Everyone was in London
when he got really bad.
I waited at home
because I was seventeen
and in everyway a grown
up who didn't
do family holidays.
I sat on the back step
through the smell of the pine trees
and the smoke of my bold cigarette.

He walked over to me
blind, disapproving
and tired
after another hundred laps
of the house like
a goldfish in a bowl,
trying in vain to recognise
familiar things;
holes in the lawn, dirt
under the front trees,
our paddle pool
my headless doll collection.

And would eventually
flop down in a
bed we bought him in Belfast,
in a little side street pet shop
where the woman crisped her
diphthongs
to fit her rougy lined lips,

as she watched
tanks going up
the street,
sniffing
out pimply bombers
in stone washed denim.

On his coat
coarse clumps of white hair
were coming through the gone golden.
Kids who came to play with us
the odd time
thought he was a sheep.

Sandy arrived
like an adopted toddler off
a Russian plane
all blonde and ready to belong.
At the back window –
where inside
a cocoon of flowers and velvet,
we were in bed
eating an Easter egg.
We heard a tail on the
edge of the window pane
and we screamed,
all two of us.

And as mum and dad added to us,
added to everything,

he watched and ran
and barked and sat
and coughed and licked
and whined and swam
and dragged one of us
from the bog-hole water
and another
from the postman
who threw ugly stones at him,

not knowing he was body guard
to five delirious daydreamers.

He lived longer than many
the vet said,
and really it was time.

I didn't feel so grown up
but the cruelest deed is the most kind.

In the moment of dying
everything about being
a child rumbling out the back
cracked like a rash spring thaw
coming too soon.

I called them in London,
in a sleepy B&B
in some Irish area in Kilburn,
where a man from Sligo used to make tea
and complain about blacks.

My brother's reaction to the news
was that of a
kamakazi madman's mission
into hell.

In the end,
in that moment,
was where
I stayed seventeen and all grown up
and
everything about being me
with no teeth
in a nurses outfit and a
a pink coat with
freckles on my nose
riding a dog around the garden
thinking he was a
unicorn or a rodeo pony,

and not having to make plans
or meet bills
or talk nonsense
to fit in,
or be in charge of kids
in the night when they stop breathing,
from a hiding place in the brambles
eating honeysuckles,
where I was never found,
picking daisies for long chains,
and loving my siblings like
there was no other

was all over, over.

Susie DeFord

Death of a Love Junkie

For Dela

Lightning crack thunder hunger rumble stomach
quease. The banks of the Delaware River heave
water, freezing rain, sleet. Storm-shivering

angel descends covered in thick-stick brown wire.
Big triangle ears heavy with hearing, big sad mud
puddle eyes seeking safety within the trees

and arms of a couple of campers trying to keep warm.
They brought you back to Brooklyn with a bellyful
of pups. I met you on a bustling block,

you were seeking strokes for your swollen frame,
a love junkie, a poet-sniffing dog here to save us
from our heads full of words and lives

lacking reason. Then Tana came, your golden girl,
your pup that never grew up, just like the little girl
I am groaning in this grown up body, going

gray, dry, and wrinkly. You nursed us all, licking
scars to heal, ours and your own. My miscarriage
mourning-morning in purgatory park-bound,

me moping, you mischievously barking, chastising
loud garbage trucks along the way. Park reached,
lost leash leap, you chased darts of yellow,

gray, green. Carried away, you crashed backs of knees
sweeping ladies off their feet. They weren't happy.
Moved to the country, back to the storm shake,

pursuing porcupines coming home looking like a tribal
elder, a shaman, a medicine-woman-witch, quills piercing
        septum, lips, cheek. Black magic bumps grew

in your breast – no reprieve. From my own sickness
you were a pilgrimage, a Yatra, a retreat. I travelled
        to see you one last time. Lost in the lush

Catskill woods on the way and I stared out the window
and pretended to enjoy the scenery. When I arrived
        you wouldn't look at me, you just sat real close,

slower than before until your river dried up. Malignant
memory, heat out in this city, morning empty playground
        snow glow playing powder tracks clear to the dead

grass buried below. I swear you and the other dogs
of Brooklyn were sent to save me from all these lonely
        days in the autumn heat and trash confetti streets.

Susie DeFord

Wrestling a Cerberus

For Shorty, Lucky, and T-bone

For years depression's imaginary demons have doused darkness
over my eyes. Through pinpricks I peeked at their many haired

heads taunting from the foot of the bed. Biting toes and brewing
coffee before I wake, ready to tear me through the day. Unphased

by daemon ways, when their flesh and blood cousins appeared,
I was only slightly surprised by these se'irim. Shorty, Rakshasa

disguised as Yorkie, brave and true snuck up to sniff my shoe.
Not much bigger than my foot he scuttled a black brown blur

as I started to move. Tiharire T-bone, the glamourous blonde
diva hanging out on the bed waiting to be impressed or carried

around, stared, but couldn't be bothered to receive me. Asura
Lucky, loudly guarded the other two, barking and balking,

a dancing dachshund, all talk. I lean to leash and he sinks
to the ground peeing, piddling around. I leash the other two

and find I have a three-headed hydra on my hands. The hellhounds,
Cerberus, have their tricephalic argument zigzagging around

getting nowhere. I have to lead them in their hop run down
the sidewalk. Shorty and Lucky competing for the lead, T-bone

dragging behind. Lucky's tail, a feather plume, a flag-jolly roger
warning of this ship of fools. I'm in stitches, laughing, grabbing

guts at my ridiculous predicament. Even jinn have been known
to save a few. Hercules wrestled, Orpheus serenaded, Hermes,

Sybil, and Psyche soothed to sleep, add me to the mythology.
Hades hounds let me out of hell for giving them a bathroom break.

Susie DeFord

Bulls of Pamplona

for Thurgood

Lost in this world led only by leash. Your last peek
    the gray triangle of mountain peak, salt-ocean

waves brutal beat, summer seared-sun outline of busy
    Brooklyn streets. Blinked black and it was all

gone. No one explained the darkness. You just accepted
    it and moved on, slithering along rough brick

building lines, their smooth cool insides. Stumbling
    step and stump, wall bang-bump clumsy,

'til the hair scraped from your skull, holes in your gray
    grinning strands and spikes, easier ear scratch.

Before you, I was two years blind. Lost sense, music
    ears pricked, but fingertips felt for blades in back –

no sensation. Flames licked feet asleep beneath a shivering
    half-deck house of cards burning. Sniffed the char,

licked ashes but tasted nothing. Only the beautiful screech
    of guitar feedback and tinnitus ring and thump

of locust drums beat until your excited shrill scold and bark
    for being left alone sniffing around for that damn

cat who's always just one step and nine lives ahead woke me.
    Reckless abandon until then, launched the Chupinaxo,

we ran full boar, bulls of Pamplona bucking bodies buckle
    into the encierro. Broken broncos beat a *Fuck it*

into fences. The crash came too soon. We sat, legs splayed,
    stunned. For the first time, I felt your soft ears

and rubbed the collision from your head as you nuzzled
    your impact into my palm. Lying there, we smelled

the cut grass and the sun. We crawled from the crevice
    where we'd crammed ourselves to sleep safely.

Forced to feet, we learned to walk slow feeling our feet
    notice steps and green growing though cracked

and soiled cement. As we paced the parkway sirens sang
    and signaled us to hear outside our heads'

cacophony. Short sight lengthening, we taste spring
    and all the growth that the cold rain brings.

Jack Brae Curtingstall

The Luckiest Dog in the World

I have a dog   with spots   like a dice;
she's my charm,   she's my luck,   she's my fortune;
she's a roll,   she's a jump,   she's a gamble.
The Six are her teats,   the Five   are her paws
                    and the tip   of her tail;
the Four   is her side to the left;   the Three
                    is her side to the right;
there's a Two   on her back   and One   on her skull.
When she rolls   on her back   she brings me good luck,
when her head is down   it's just awful.
When she runs round the park   it might rain
                    it might snow   it might thunder;
day might be night,   night might be day
the sea might be up,   the sky might be   under.
Her bark is the laugh   of a woman enthralled,
her snap leaves a frost   in the air;
her whine   makes you give   up your heart,
you give up your heart   at her whimper.
Children draw bones on her fur   with crayons   of cheese,
draw bones   on her fur   with butter.
She sleeps on a bed   made from burglars' coats,
she chews on the rib   of a whale.
She licks up the stars   with her scarlet   tongue
and wipes   off the moon   with her tail.
I have a dog   with spots   like a dice;
she's my charm,   she's my luck,   she's my fortune.

Nahshon Cook

Nick

At two years old,
Nick was a ceaselessly
scream-barking
little wild child
with almost no home trainin'
and strong feelings
about everything.

Which – I think –
made Marti afraid
that he'd end up
an unsuccessfully adopted orphan
in some animal shelter,
standing helpless
in a wire cage
waiting to be mosquitoed out
of all of his blood
to provide transfusions
for more well-heeled dogs
with owners who loved
and wanted them,

like she had asked us
to want and love him
before she died
early one cold
and snowy morning
in a room shown to us
by the nurse who
suggested over the phone
an hour earlier
that we bring Nick

up to the hospital
so that Marti could see him
one last time:

she couldn't speak
but she did smile and
reached for him
and we put him in her arms
and that was that.

Thomas Cochran

Domestic

The husky is unfathomable
nosing her biscuit along the carpet.

Satisfied at long last
she circles into a position

from which to guard it from us
who gave it to her a little ago.

Now we are enemies is all,
threats to her very existence.

When she growls I tell her,
'Keep that up you'll find yourself

looking through wire at the pound,'
a lie she is too busy to attend,

being in a deadly circumstance.
Her eyes never leave the treat –

two ounces of who knows what,
in truth, but plainly to her something

still warm, still reeking, her mouth
still dripping from the kill.

Sarah Clancy

Farm Dog's Comeback

For Pebbles RIP 2010

It's dark so early this evening it could be November,
the lamp's throwing shadows around my old house,
my long-term old mongrel stretched out on the rug,
is a picture of tiredness, not a paw or ear twitching,
just slow steady breathing, there's a book on my lap
I'm not really reading, my guest in the spare room already
sleeping – jaded from tramping tourist trails down in Clare.

In the morning we left her at the interpretive centre
(as if you could explain the cliffs and the sky),
dog and I in agreement, we didn't need it, instead
we strolled down a sloped field to the sea,
mud in the gateway, something we both remembered,
giving its way to tufts of sparse boggy grass
and a fine herd of bullocks there grazing in clusters,
I timed my pace to the old light and slow dog.

I absently walked along the ledge by the sea,
half-thinking of waves and the softness of limestone,
watching hang gliding seagulls surveying the cliffs,
until the cold and the sea spray finally intruded
but my whistle was lost to the wind in my face,
and far up the hillside I could see cattle flowing,
in unanimous motion, like those waves on the sea,
in their wake was my old dog, low slung,
steadily working the bullocks uphill.

With old-school learned patience she stayed well back,
keeping them all in unthinking retreat,
remembering her old work as easy as breathing,
as she moved the small herd to the edge of the pen,

but then when she paused, looked around for instruction,
I was foot dragging, picking my way in unsuitable shoes,
and she barked out frustration as the cattle dispersed.

In a ten year old gesture I called her back over,
hoping to stop her from beginning again,
she came at a run, slowed as she neared me,
feeling the strain of young work on old bones,
still purpose-filled though, awaiting lost signals,
she circled me all the way to the car, nothing
could persuade her that we were just strolling,
seems I'd forgotten how fishermen seldom swim in the sea,
and that neither farmers, nor farm dogs, ever go walking.

So, sitting on Sunday with the book I'm not reading
the guest and dog sleeping, with the full darkness fallen
and work thoughts invading, bringing a structure
and a sense all their own, I find myself glad I
have to get up in the morning, consoled that I have
somewhere to go and I hope when I'm older
I will still feel so useful, and that no-one
will park me in a car by the sea.

Kelly Cherry

Another Ode to Joy

Duncan, cairn terrier, b. 1979 - d. 1996

my love, my heart
small miracle
and work of art

my (adopted) son, my (platonic) spouse
my man of the house

hope on four feet
(until age played its mean tricks:
no more chasing balls and sticks)
faithful friend
        O charite!

left for me are a red plaid collar,
the soft bed for old bones,
the bowls, treats, remembered special places

("won't come even when i holler")

you are ashes scattered
beside the trees
and hydrants
you made your own.
        No more mad dashes
after squirrels or cats, or
girls wearing long, red sashes!

my Valentine boy who follows and pants
my Halloween hoot (born October 30)
my midsummer dream
(my coffee with cream)

my celebration of every good thing,
best blessing –

O my joy, my adorable, doggone boy –

Louise C. Callaghan

Death of a Dog

i.m Rob

He stands for hours on end you said;
those pool-black eyes focussed on one
table leg, or wonders in the persian rug,
as though minding some secret. Or
maybe sensing that void in the hour
we children used to call angels passing.
You only, who hear the uneven heartbeat.

He turned aside from your minced liver,
the warmed-up milk, I suggested –
instead he went outside to the *Weisenau*
and answering a deeper law, drank snow-
water from a puddle in your back yard.
Isn't this how we should die too,
stop eating – stare down the future?

Sandra Bunting

Paree

You were a black poodle
without the pom poms,
a scruffy ball of fur
with the unlikely name of
Mademoiselle de Paris.

You were constantly by my side:
in the carnival house of horrors,
in the university residence,
sleeping with me in a snow bank
when I didn't want to go home.

Sandra Bunting

Foggy Dew

You loved everyone but old men—
you'd pin them against the wall.
You herded swans three times bigger
than yourself into the sea,
and you herded us, tried to keep us together,
wouldn't let us stray behind,
checked to see if anyone was missing
until we found we were missing you.

Brian Brett

Old Dog

She's dying, my dog
a grey-muzzled, black muscled
big bullet of a dog.
She broke her back
chasing a racoon up a tree
and survived the arthritis
for the last five years.
Now she leans against my thigh –
trembling, full of pain,
all hungry to live.

Pat Boran

Fetch

Again and again she comes back to me
to place it by my feet, today's
old piece of flotsam or bonfire debris
dug out from the heap and blessed
with a kind of magic.

Dog-given, the least of things
may be treasure for a day.

And how she spends these days,
this love-struck mutt,
stretched out along a neighbour's wall,
comically shadowing the postman,
or, despite the wind and ice-flecked rain
that keeps every other dog indoors,
bounding out across this desolate park
as if it were a summer's meadow, alive
to the possibility of play.

Hours, I imagine, she has spent already
running like this between her home
and mine, her world and ours,

to bring me a stick,
to chase that stick, to seize that stick
and then come back with that stick so tight
between her jaws it sometimes seems
she will never release it, that she has changed
the rules and very purpose of the game,

and had I the strength
I might lift her clear
or she might lift me clear
of this rain-locked planet.

Marck L. Beggs

Kilty Sue

Instincts jammed by lack of sheep
in this region, she attends to babies, ducklings –
anything small and in need of care.
A border collie whose eyes, opposite
shades of brown, offer the look
of a slightly retarded devil-dog. And,
if you must know, she bites people:
my brother, presumably, because he was mean
to me at a younger age; the UPS man
because he carried a package too quickly towards
my pregnant sister; my mother-in-law, I suppose,
to keep in shape. And various relatives
and strangers – Kilty Sue reminds them
of the precise location of the Achilles' tendon.
Mind you, she never actually rips it out,
but merely offers a sharp touch. Like a pin-prick,
only deeper, her bites spring out
from a sudden vortex of silence. When Kilty Sue howls –
in a voice high and piercing as a drunken soprano,
and you wish your ears would just drop off and die –
you are safe. She is protecting you.

Celeste Augé

Turn Left

Murphy's ghost wags his tail
whenever I round the bend.
I follow him through reedy fields,
slip out to the main road,
tracking gentle nose and sense.

He mimes a bark at the cars and I wave,
taunting them with our freedom–
to be able to cut across the bog,
feel dew and brush and squelch,
dance a forgotten prayer.

When our shadows get too long to chase,
we yield to the umbilical pull of home.
Back safe on the low road
a sign reads *Turn left at the black lab*,
for anyone who can see ghosts.

Joan I. Siegel

Nick's Dog

All the while,
the dog, part shepherd–part lab, watched
at the bed, rushing from one side
to another when Nick turned, tracking
him to the toilet and back, licking wildly
his hands and face and that time
the ambulance rushed Nick to the hospital
for a week, the dog howled his wolf's
howl on the front stoop all day, guarding
his bed all night until Nick came
home and finally when Nick went off
to the funeral home for the viewing, they let
the dog come along, but he broke loose,
jumped in beside his man and after
they quieted him, he lay nearby,
good dog, keeping watch
like Argos.

Joan I. Siegel

The Blind & Deaf Dog Named Jack

She reads wet leaves
undergrowth for signs
of dragging where he lost
himself. A drift of fur snagged
on vines.

All day rain had swelled
the creek, spilled
its banks, sculpted
mushrooms pale as wax, washed
the trail away.
          All night
coyote howling
from the ridge, his body
electric, wired
for her scent, the leash.

Joan I. Siegel

Dog Outside a Grocery on Broadway

It was how he waited
how he waited where somebody told him to wait
how he paced outside the grocery store
how he tugged on the leash tied to the signpost
how he looked at the man coming out of the store
how he looked at the glass door swinging shut
how he looked at the man tearing cellophane off a pack of cigarettes
how he looked at the cellophane falling on the sidewalk
how he looked at the girl stuffing a red purse in her pocket
how he looked at the old lady opening an umbrella at the crosswalk
how he looked at the boy who looked at him
through the window of a bus
how he looked at the bus turning the corner out of view
how he sat down on the sidewalk and got up again
how he pushed his nose against the glass door
how he scratched behind his ear
how he waited

Joan I. Siegel

Dog

Sleepless
that last night
obeying
the body's will
to unmake itself.

Feverish
she crept outside
to keep watch.

The December moon
blank.

Her belly bloated, pressing
into the snow. The body's
waste, draining.

Eyes begging.

Anne Kennedy

The Dog Kubla Dreams My Life

I acquired you, old companion,
on impulse from the Palo Alto pound
to satisfy an adolescent
urge for someone all my own.

You crouched shivering on the back
seat of my black '48 Chevy, shedding
fair hair, your obsidian toe-
nails slipping on slick upholstery.

Transported into the redwoods
you tore off down the old highway,
a gold whipcord,
lured back with a bit of steak.

In the cabin bathroom, your corner
stake-out made ferny wastes our outdoor
toilet, as you snarled comic guarding
your own ceramic reservoir.

Tamed with coos and coaxings
into a loyalty hard-won,
I called you *Kubla*
after that nervy invader.

In an attic in Berkeley, you shredded
the socks of my first lover, pawed
ravelled strands beside the rumpled bed,
then patrolled the narrow stairs.

Pacing the pine floor-boards, those wolfish
toes tip-tapped a sentry song. Nobody's guide
dog, you wore no harness, roamed at will.
You could be gone for days prowling

lanes and harbour wastelands or snoozing
contented in some student's kitchen.
They called *Kubla* on Telegraph Avenue,
you glinted sidelong.

When I moved to L.A. I entrusted you to a friend
until I settled in where dogs were welcome.
He said you got lost, wandered off, followed
some family back up to the redwoods.

He claimed I had made you too friendly.
Year later I heard you were killed
the week I left,
running towards a woman
calling *Kubla* from the kerb.

About...

Patricia Monaghan

The Dog As Oracle

A cajoling dog signifies the future.
Macrobius

Inside the building, bloodhounds
give chase down endless corridors.

In the dark forest, a white terrier
snuffles along the shadowy path.

On the roadside, a border collie,
too old to work, limps slowly by.

In gray winter dawn, the great
black mastiff silently approaches.

Death is near if you meet one of these.
Another predicts wild sudden hunger.

A third, remembered joy. The fourth?
Ah, that I cannot say, nor can I tell

which threatens which, nor why.
Which promises which, nor when.

But I can tell you this: every dog
you meet is an oracle, a guide,

a guardian, a muse, a holy thing,
every dog stands half in this world,

half in that, signaling to us:
here, look! the answer! here!

the answer! look! look here!
can't you smell it? oh, yes here!

The only truth I know is this: no dog
is ever far from god, not far at all.

William Matthews

Above the Aquarius Mine, Ward, Colorado

My dog clatters up a talus pile. Is there a key-stone, that when he steps on it will organise a slide? The thin air hasn't got to him yet. He pranks down toward us, stiff in his forelegs but his head's not back, it's jutted toward us and his tail goes in circle like a pump-handle, he's dancing as if there'll always be enough water, enough air.

We trudge up a swale, happy, 9500 feet. Locusts clack past. One makes its first stroke just as it passes my ear: it sounds like a bowstring let go.

As we near the ridge the view drops away. We go out onto a promontory and stare over the trough. Just as I turn to go back down, a locust, going the other way, loops over my shoulder, over the edge. My dog's so tired he slinks back down. He looks as if he's claimed this place in the name of something he's ashamed of, now that he's done it, but he's only tired and keeping close to the ground, wherever it goes.

Alicia Ostriker

The Drink Tryptich

Well what can I say
said the old woman
a glass or three of wine was normal at dinner
but one also enjoyed martinis
gin and tonic to celebrate spring
in summer rum straight up or margarita
champagne for
especially festive occasions

You see said the tulip
we who drink nothing but pure rainwater
remain awake and alert perhaps we shiver
and cannot but notice
the way you stumble getting home
after one of your evenings
while we remain upright on the spine
of our stems our petals locked

My long pink tongue said the dog
is one of my best characteristics
they put the bowl out
and I drink from it
slurp slurp lap lap
slurp slurp lap lap
making a great deal of noise
to show my appreciation

Alicia Ostriker

Deer Walk Upon Our Mountains

When they see me said the old woman
they stop where they are
and gaze into my eyes for as long
as I am willing to stand there
in the wind
at the edge of the forest

You are speaking of my mortal enemy
said the dark red tulip
they have eaten many of my family
they do not spare children
they are pests
beauty excuses nothing

Oh cried the dog
the very thought of them
thrills me to the bone
the chase as much as the capture
the scent weaving ahead of me like a flag
saliva spinning from my teeth

Thomas Kabdebo

Cheesy

I was three years old, fair and lively
my dad brought home a dog
a bitch, as it were, for my birthday.
She was fair and lively, and
could only speak English
because her former owner
was the British consul in Budapest.
He was recalled to London
and instead of quarantine
gave the dog to my dad.
Was she happy with us? Bouncingly!
She was becoming my playmate
and – learning Magyar words fast –
became my dad's hunting beagle.
She collected pheasants, hares
wild ducks, found lost toys,
keys; got married and
had six pups. Eventually
she reached the grand old age
of ten. Around us the war
reached its climax. The Soviets
entered our home, she barked,
they shot her dead.
Her bark is locked in my memory.

John Montague

Walking The Dog

Recovering from an illness
I walk a neighbour's dog
Each day in the Champs de Mars:
A sleek Cocker spaniel
With long golden ears –
Thirty quid's worth of silky hair.

With a visage as grey as Richelieu
Contemplating the state of France
He examines his universe
Of smells and excrement:
Every puddle provokes
A sensual trance.

Across two lawns
He sights a friend
Possible for love
And gallops to attend:
The excitement is intense –
Inspection at either end.

Watched by three gendarmes
He tackles the roots of a tree:
For the sake of a putrid bone
Commits lèse-majesté.
I suppose I should restrain
But, vive la liberté.

He circulates a bench
To distribute his signature
Adapting to double purpose
This rank poetry of the poor:
Generations to come
Will know his noble spoor.

Pulled from pillar to post
By this most pampered beast
I certainly ought to protest –
Enough's as good as a feast –
But follow in baffled awe
Shameless manhood, golden fleece.

Andrea Cohen

Seven Dogs

The life of a man
is measured by seven dogs.

The first dog says: and now
we shall eat and lap

water and walk in the woods.
We will sleep often in sunny spots.

There will be much
chasing of squirrels, but we

will not speak of death.
Then the man speaks

of death to himself, but
not to the second dog, who

must learn to heel
and come, and this goes

on. Seven dogs. And then one
evening the seven dogs

come to him with seven
sets of slippers. It is a trick

they never mastered in life.
Is it time? he asks. And

he follows his pack, good
dog that he is, into the woods.

Andrea Cohen

Eureka

Eureka! she squeals at the town pound,
meeting the beleaguered beagle, leading him
home on a taut, frayed rope. The hound is short
on smarts, long on devotion, following
our heroine, Boswell-like, from room to room.
His own past is part mystery, part trauma, having
arrived at the shelter with a note that read,
Don't Blame Me. Aside from following,
he likes planning to follow, guessing
which way she'll cross the kitchen, practicing
his shadow walk or shadow dash.
He doesn't bark, doesn't howl, suggesting
any prior voice got booted from him.
He likes dry kibble, the odd tuna melt.
Mirrors make him turn and run,
as if he's seen what can happen
to a mutt like him, and when she leaves
the house he hungers hard,
gnawing at the bedroom door, the pie chest,
even the Frigidaire, causing lead poisoning.
At Angell Memorial she says, *I blame myself,*
though the pooch survives to chew
through another and another door, insisting
that what he's missing lies behind some stubborn portal.

When he chews through the screen door,
chasing her unrivaled fragrance, he sets
off a vicious evening of circling–the woman
trawling dark streets in her rasping Impala, screaming
Eureka, Eureka, causing insomniacs to wonder
what wild discovery's in their midst before realising
it's that woman who frequents the shelter,

who inevitably wakes neighbours
yelling *Flood, Fire, The Second Coming.*
They've heard it all before: *Free Money, Point
of No Return, The Sweet Hereafter*, enough
to know no creature could live up to her calling,
that she and the dog, exhausted, will end up
next morning at the pound, where
they'll pretend they're strangers. She'll christen him
anew: *Liebchen* or *Die Trying*–the way people
give a different name to every hurricane
that blows their way, though really
it's the same air, same troubled sky, same
last minute scurrying to board up windows, secure
the lawn chairs, same mule-headed insistence
to dig in, rebuild, to reinvent themselves.

Andrea Cohen

A Coonhound on Lieutenant's Island

Yes, I'd bury it too,
even though the fish

is dead and washed not
of its own accord into the eddies

stung with eel grass stubble,
even though the flesh

is rotting, though the backwash
of brackish sea is shifting,

coming back at us, and
the bridge that brought us here

is disappearing, as it does,
twice daily in high waters.

Yes, I'd bury the corpse.
I'd use whatever tools

my body had, I'd work
my human brain hard and wish

for instinct pure as yours,
imagine I'd be coming

back, that whatever the sea or earth
might proffer would sustain us.

Adam Wyeth

Food is For Me

(for Mike)

When Einstein came back as a dog
it felt improper to make a mathematical
genius sleep outside in a kennel.

But since his occupancy in the body
of my four-legged friend, he tends
to think of little else except his stomach.

Each day I'd lay out in bone-shaped biscuits
his ground-breaking formula: $E=MC^2$
which he'd devour in one fell swoop.

Till one day, he pondered upon the pattern,
cocking his head to the side, before
slowly reshaping his equation –

eating a few bits of bones while sniffing
and shifting parts with his nose. I grew excited
at the prospect of *my* little Einstein stumbling

upon a new formula, cracking some great sum
which would unlock the secrets to the universe.
I pictured us splashed over the morning papers,

the top story of every news board:
EINSTEIN BARKS BACK. But as I began
to decipher his new formula

I realised he was up to his old tricks.
You didn't have to be a physicist
to read: $F=4ME$.

Stephen Dobyns

How To Like It

These are the first days of fall. The wind
at evening smells of roads still to be travelled,
while the sound of leaves blowing across the lawns
is like an unsettled feeling in the blood,
the desire to get in a car and just keep driving.
A man and a dog descend their front steps.
The dog says, Let's go downtown and get crazy drunk.
Let's tip over all the trash cans we can find.
This is how dogs deal with the prospect of change.
But in his sense of the season, the man is struck
by the oppressiveness of his past, how his memories
which were shifting and fluid have grown more solid
until it seems he can see remembered faces
caught up among the dark places in the trees.
The dog says, Let's pick up some girls and just
rip off their clothes. Let's dig holes everywhere.
Above his house, the man notices wisps of cloud
crossing the face of the moon. Like in a movie,
he says to himself, a movie about a person
leaving on a journey. He looks down the street
to the hills outside of town and finds the cut
where the road heads north. He thinks of driving
on that road and the dusty smell of the car
heater, which hasn't been used since last winter.
The dog says, Let's go down to the diner and sniff
people's legs. Let's stuff ourselves on burgers.
In the man's mind, the road is empty and dark.
Pine trees press down to the edge of the shoulder,
where the eyes of animals, fixed in his headlights,
shine like small cautions against the night.
Sometimes a passing truck makes his whole car shake.
The dog says, Let's go to sleep. Let's lie down

by the fire and put our tails over our noses.
But the man wants to drive all night, crossing
one state line after another, and never stop
until the sun creeps into his rearview mirror.
Then he'll pull over and rest awhile before
starting again, and at dusk he'll crest a hill
and there, filling a valley, will be the lights
of a city entirely new to him.
But the dog says, Let's just go back inside.
Let's not do anything tonight. So they
walk back up the sidewalk to the front steps.
How is it possible to want so many things
and still want nothing. The man wants to sleep
and wants to hit his head again and again
against a wall. Why is it all so difficult?
But the dog says, Let's go make a sandwich.
Let's make the tallest sandwich anyone's ever seen.
And that's what they do and that's where the man's
wife finds him, staring into the refrigerator
as if into the place where the answers are kept—
the ones telling why you get up in the morning
and how it is possible to sleep at night,
answers to what comes next and how to like it.

Maxine Kumin

Widow and Dog

After he died she started letting the dog
sleep on his side of the bed they had shared
for fifty-one years. A large discreet dog, he stayed
on his side but the tags on his collar jingled as he sighed
and especially when he scratched so she took his collar off
and then his smooth tawny bulk close to her but not
touching eased her through the next night and the next.

One morning, a chipmunk and his wife somehow slipped in
through the screen door when neither of them was looking.
She got up screaming from her coffee and whacked at them
with a broom. Dog pounced and pounced but they were faster
than he was and dove under the refrigerator. After a while
he stopped crashing into chairs and skidding around corners
in fruitless pursuit and then they came and went untroubled
even drinking out of his water dish, their tails at right angles.

That summer it just seemed simpler to leave the window
by the bird feeder open for ease of refilling. Some creatures
slipped casually out and in. The titmice were especially graceful.
She loved to watch them elevate and retract their crests
whenever they perched on the lips of the kitchen counters.
The goldfinches chittered and sang like drunken canaries
and once in a thunderstorm a barred owl blundered
into that fake crystal chandelier she had always detested.

Autumn fell on them in a joyous rush. The first
needles of hard frost, the newly sharp wind, the final
sweep and swirl of leaves, a swash of all-day rain
were not unwelcome. Hickory nuts ricocheted
off the barn's metal roof like a rain of beebee-gun pellets.
They both took afternoon naps. They both grew portly.
While Dog in his dumb allegiance dozed on the hearth,

sometimes he ran so fiercely in his dreams that he bared his teeth.
Reclusive comfortable Widow scribbled in her journal.
It did not matter how much she woolgathered, how late
into the night she read, it did not matter if she
completed this poem, or another.

Maxine Kumin

The Apparition

True to his word, our vet
comes in late afternoon
and kneels in a slant of sun.
A pat, a needle stick
stills the failing heart.

We lower the ancient form
to the hemlock-shrouded grave
and before the hole is brimmed
set a layer of chicken wire
to guard against predators

so that the earth we broke
reforms, a mild mound.
The rock we place on top
common glacial granite
is mica-flecked and flat.

That night the old dog works
his way back up and out
gasping, salted with dirt
and barks his familiar bark
at the scribble-scratched back door.

I pull on shirt and pants
a Pavlovian response
and stumble half awake
downstairs to turn the knob
where something, some mortal stub

I swear I recognise:
some flap of ear or fur
swims out of nothingness
and brushes past me
into its rightful house.

Maxine Kumin

Seven Caveats in May

When the dog whines at 5 a.m., do not
make your first mistake and let him out.
When he starts to bark in a furious tom-tom rhythm
and you can just discern a shadowy feinting

taking place under the distant hemlocks
do not seize the small sledge from the worktable and fly
out there in your nightgown and unlaced high
tops preparing to whack this, the ninth of its kind

in the last ten weeks, over the head
before it can quill your canine.
But it's not a porcupine: it's a big, black, angry
bear. Now your dog has put him up a tree

and plans to keep him there, a perfect
piece of work by any hound. Do not
run back and grab the manure fork
thinking you can keep the prongs

between you and the elevated bear long
enough to dart in and corral your critter.
Isn't it true bears come down slower
than they go up? Half an hour later do not

give up, go in the house and call the cops.
The dispatcher regrets having to report
there's no patrol car at this time, the state
police are covering. No doubt the nearest

trooper, wearing his Smoky Bear Stetson
is forty miles up the highway.
When your closest neighbour, big burly Smitty
works his way into his jeans and roars up

your dirt road in his four-wheel diesel truck
strides over the slash pile and hauls your hound back
(by now, you've thrown something on
over your not-quite-diaphanous nightgown)

do not forget to thank him with a sixpack.
Do not fail to take your feeders in on April One
despite the arriving birds' insistent clamour
and do not put them out again

until the first of December.

Jean Kavanagh

The Dogs on the Rez Speak Lakota

Indian Reservation dogs
Are teenagers run wild,
Hanging around gas stations
And grocery stores;
Dozing in shadows
Or gathered on corners,
Staying out after dark,
No one calling them home.

Sore-pawed
Tourist-hustlers,
Patch-furred
Trash-rustlers,
Whip-tailed and hungry,
Long-legged and lean;
Teeth sharpened on pine cones,
Surviving
The ticks, fleas,
And porcupine quills.

They roam invisible spaces
Between American highways,
In their eyes, the secret landmarks
Of legend's terrain;
Four-footed emblems
Of ancestral nomads,
In liminal places
Ignoring defeat,
They remain.

C.K. Williams

The Dog

TAR 1983

Except for the dog, that she wouldn't have him put away, wouldn't let
    him die, I'd have liked her.
She was handsome, busty, chunky, early middle-aged, very black, with a
    stiff, exotic dignity
that flurried up in me a mix of warmth and sexual apprehension neither
    of which, to tell the truth,
I tried very hard to nail down: she was that much older and in those days
    there was still the race thing.
This was just at the time of civil rights: the neighbourhood I was living
    in was mixed.
In the narrow streets, the tiny three-floored houses they called father-
    son-holy-ghosts
which had been servants' quarters first, workers' tenements, then slums,
    still were, but enclaves of us,
beatniks and young artists, squatted there and commerce between everyone
    was fairly easy.
Her dog, a grinning mongrel, rib and knob, gristle and grizzle, wasn't
    terribly offensive.
The trouble was that he was ill, or the trouble more exactly was that I
    had to know about it.
She used to walk him on a lot I overlooked, he must have had a tumour
    or a blockage of some sort
because every time he moved his bowels, he shrieked, a chilling, almost
    human scream of anguish.
It nearly always caught me unawares, but even when I'd see them first,
    it wasn't better.
The limp leash coiled in her hand, the woman would be profiled to the
    dog, staring into the distance,
apparently oblivious, those breasts of hers like stone, while he, not a step
    away, labouring,

trying to eject the feeble, mucus-coated blood-flecked chains that
    finally spurted from him,
would set himself on tiptoe and hump into a question mark, one
    quivering back leg grotesquely lifted.
Every other moment he'd turn his head, as though he wanted her,
    to no avail, to look at him,
then his eyes would dim and he'd drive his wounded anus in the dirt,
    keening uncontrollably,
lurching forward in a hideous, electric dance as though someone were
    at him with a club.
When at last he'd finish, she'd wipe him with a tissue like a child; he'd
    lick her hand.
It was horrifying; I was always going to call the police; once I actually
    went out to chastise her –
didn't she know how selfish she was, how the animal was suffering?
    – she scared me off, though.
She was older than I'd thought, for one thing, her flesh was loosening,
    pouches of fat beneath the eyes,
and poorer, too, shabby, tarnished: I imagined smelling something faintly
    acrid as I passed.
Had I ever really mooned for such a creature? I slunk around the block,
    chagrined, abashed.
I don't recall them too long after that. Maybe the dog died, maybe
    I was just less sensitive.
Maybe one year when the cold came and I closed my windows, I forgot
    them...then I moved.
Everything was complicated now, so many tensions, so much bothersome
    self-consciousness.
Anyway, those back streets, especially in bad weather when the ginkgos
    lost their leaves, were bleak.
It's restored there now, ivy, pointed brick, garden walls with broken
    bottles mortared on them,
but you'd get sick and tired then: the rubbish in the gutter, the general
    sense of dereliction.
Also, I'd found a girl to be in love with: all we wanted was to live
    together, so we did.

Glenn Shea

The Moon

A bit at a time, and a bit more,
I leave my dream, I'm back in my body, awake.
The dark shapes sort themselves, my room
at home, 2.20 morning by the clock.
I'm weighted, sopped, breathing heavy in the panic
of deep night. What brought me –
but then I know, the shade's pulled back
in the chill room, and the silver spherical
bright full moon illumines the yard, unseemly light.
The pear tree, utterly still and counting:
how many years alone, how many more?
The German Shepherd two houses down
barking in fury, not at a burglar but at the moon:
why should the dark be shown so clearly?
why should he be made to feel like this?

Gary Percesepe

I Keep Hearing How Life is Not a Bowl of Cherries

So I ask the dog of the family if he wants to take a
Ride and we find a summer fruit stand that still sells
Bings in an out of the way place I know and there we sit
Happy as clams, me pitting and he finishing and when I
Pause to seal the bag, a half eaten cherry in my reddened
Fingers I hear him pant and ask you gonna eat that?

Gary Percesepe

Stuff of the Marriage

Couches and chairs and lawn mowers and canisters
Bubble bath and ducks the kids floated like wishes
Down streams now forgotten

Tennis shoes (sneakers!) and broken laptops with
Sputtering screens and dot matrix printers
Business cards and raffle tickets and one guitar

Belts and ties, suspenders and cummerbunds
Spackle for nail-printed walls and Hockney paintings
Coleus and cactus and pictures taken at the beach

Legal pad legal tender legal thrillers
Christmas cards from off shore ports
Ashtrays filled with half smoked cigars

Tennis racquet presses, barrettes & pony wraps
Shaving kit and tinsel from the tree re-laid in
Cardboard boxes. The marriage bed, unturned

Some sighs we let escape, the jangling black
Telephone that makes our nerves jump and the
Dog of the family, waiting now at the door to be let out.

Goya's Dog

1.

Particle dog.
Dot on the horizon.
Paddling for all she's worth
Into the oncoming wave,
Into material, into density.
Out of velocity.
Into position.

2.

The black dog on the creek bank tracks a smudge of deer dashing
through deep woods. The squirrels are so enthralled in their spring
frisking they're oblivious to the dog, muscles tensed, nose quivering,
all her intricately-tuned-ballistic-system senses now locked in on
those luscious twitching tails. She dives into the ravine after them,
paws digging into the yellow clay heavy from recent rains, kicking up
the scent of lichen, log pile, and leaf rot, and in a single brushstroke
scattering the squirrels up trees and out of reach. The air is golden
because the light is golden and up is lighter than down.

3.

Go into your yellow, we are told, and so we do,
Easeled to a view of sunflower fields fronting the
      nuclear cooling towers.
The painter squints at my efforts and says,
This black splotch here looks like the head of a dog.

Heat looms like a car too fast around a bend.
We work like dogs panting in the sun, brushes in hand.
Like the universe expanding from the first hot bubble.
We want to know, we said.

4.

Because on their first and blind date in 1957, my mother is wedged up against my father who is driving the whole gang on this joy ride. She's trying to study for her final biology exam. The notes in her lap are diagrams of the male reproductive system.

5.

A law of nature has been broken
In a laboratory on Long Island
In a quark-gluon plasma soup
For a millionth of a billionth of a billionth of a second.
When gold nuclei travelling at 99.999% of the speed of light
     smashed together,
Up quarks moved with magnetic field lines; down quarks
     travelled against.
A break in parity, symmetry.
Maybe this can tell us why we're matter more than antimatter.
Why we matter.

6.

Because fifty years later, my mother sits with my father in the urologist's office, looking at the same diagrams of the male reproductive system while the doctor explains prognosis, treatment, progressions. And after the bladder is removed, chemo, radiation. And then maybe.

7.

Maybe the dog is an up quark.
Maybe the dog is a down quark.
Maybe the dog is in the soup.

8.

One day years ago, walking with the dog. Not my dog, my father's dog.
A dog named Man. A golden yellow dog bounding in and out of golden
rod along the country road.

9.

Then, a car coming too fast around the lonesome bend. After the collision,
my father closing the window of the dog's eye; shoveling a hole in the
field. That break in symmetry. The heaving of his shoulders. Still.

10.

Because the world is made of atoms,
Because symmetry underlies the laws of the universe,
Because the universe is expanding,
We count on the universe being neither right- nor left-handed,
On being even-handed, balanced, fair.
But the weak force of nuclear radioactivity
Isn't balanced. We've known this since the fifties.
Who knows where we'd be if we didn't
Matter more than antimatter.

11.

Around the bend, the black dog finds a possum carcass – putrid lump of
bone and gristle and tissue – and gives herself to it utterly, bending her
front left leg and lowering her shoulder, the way we'd ease into a hot

bath. Then she's fully down and on her back, twisting her torso to
and fro to rub it in, to embed the stink deep in her hair and skin.
She's painted herself for us, grotto and gutter, pigment and fume.

12.

Wiping the brush on a linseed-oiled rag:
The stain, a murky brownish yellow.
Don't see a bladder-cancered father's urine.
Don't feel the certain seasick uncertainty
In prognosis, treatment, progressions.
In the way Goya painted the dog.
In the way the pigment of an end looms.
Go into your yellow, the painter says, and so we do.
Nuclear cooling towers overflowing their basin of
    sunflower fields.

13.

Whatever the season, the dog sees autumn and winter, mostly. Violet,
indigo, blue. Yellow, yellow, yellow. Some red. She sees better at night
than we because her eyes have more rods, and a reflective surface
behind the retina that ricochets light back through. Her *tapetum
lucidum*: beautiful tapestry. That's why dogs' eyes shine yellow in the
shadows beyond the fire beyond the cave in the darkness our eyes
clutch at, pleading for scraps of vision, of understanding, of mercy.

14.

Because it isn't fair,
This pigment, or this yellow.
Because, as we were saying:
We want to know who and what
And where and when and how.

All the way to the beginning.

Why at the heart of every large galaxy

There's a massive black hole.

Dog scratching at the back door.

15.

Strange matter, a dog, warm and panting. Slurry of black fur snuffing dung and death and dirt. The way she bounds through the fields, chasing what we've thrown. Explorer, emissary, inventor, strong force withstanding extreme heat and colossal density. Plunging into the yolk, the very birth pangs of the cosmos. Because we've asked her to.

Rita Ann Higgins

Rat-Like Dogs and Tattooed Men

for Cathy La Farge

In Creepy Crawley
in West Sussex
big men with tattoos
walk rat-like dogs
into pubs.

When the rat-likes
go for the ankle bone
you are told
'Wouldn't touch you.'
Another says,
'He'd lick you to death.'

These big men,
one with his elbow
on his knee,
bellow down the ear
of your friend,

'He's a pisser,
pisses everywhere,
but I'll knock it
out of him,

a few round the head
and he'll sit up.'

You try not to look
at his tattoos
but you can't help it,
they're everywhere,
even on his lips.

'That one's a snake,'
he says,
'an anaconda
could eat elephant eggs
and spit out the shells,
could wrap himself
round the belly of an ass
and strangle it.'

Later, and glad to be home
the whole scene
dances in my head.

I question nothing
but the elephant eggs.

Rita Ann Higgins

Dog is Dog is Dog

'Xadore, come here,
Xadore, don't urinate there,
not there, not anywhere here.'

If that heap of failure
with the varicose face thinks
that us canines have
the same urinary tract
as those two leggers
she's got another thing coming,

                              on her ankle.

'Xadore, you stupid boy,
come here at once or you will fry.'

Xadore exits to greener lamp-poles.

Renée Ashley

I Am Still Here

I

O, the dark the dark of it. What we were
And the constant moon shifting. The body's
Shiver and spit – and not one star speaking
Night's language. Ask the dogs how to do it:
Keep barking, they'll say. Let the heart burn.

II

They'll say: keep the nighttime leaning.
They'll say: lock the gate. Close the book.
They'll say: possum, woodchuck, vole.
Listen: abstract, concrete, whole.
Really: abstract, concrete. Whole and

III

I am still here – with a wing like the be of it.
The wiggle and fart of it. What we are:
Tinkle & twist. O, just tinkle & the tin-
Skinned rattle of the hammered heart and all
Those howling dogs under the howling moon.

Renée Ashley

The Dogs

I

Discover love at the bottoms of their pockets.
They'd reach for a beer but such love and its sudden
brightness seems simpler. This week they are into
denial. Into repression. Into it-won't-happen-to-me.
What they know is, the butcherman's on strike,
the garbagemen are not. Rattle and drum. No
meat on a plate. Here come the wheels, the cans.
The word is *We know that.*
The word is *lacking,* is *absent.*

II

A sense of what's taken away. Or never been.
Those abstractions account for it: all the nothing
and everything that changes. And the solid moon
dangling from its socket. The sun still pacing the lighted sky
and all the shadows tilted away, away. Oh, these distractions,
the dogs say. Listen, the stars are all in place. The sky
is full of reason and the dog door's open.
Tonight is the only horizon.
All our bets are on.

III

But here's the reason one worries: this appetite
for the difficult. This strange taste and the night
which slides over them like oil, over their heads
like dark oil – they are so likely captured. And out there
so many starlit pastures billowing. Here and there
whole worlds light up like promise, like flint, like

sudden traction. There's something up there.
The dogs are keen to it. They'll
tell you what's to see.

IV

Leaf and candle. Pocket and beam and the heart
of some dark banging against that slice of sky.
Even their slow and stupid shake off their dust and shudder
beneath such incantation, such traipsing on those
little feet. Now here they go: the odds are shifting.
The fortune teller's bound to earn her poor gray
dime. Nothing's standing still; the air around them
is riddled with risings and fallings; the ground
is littered with hope and stones – and somehow,
anyhow, the dogs find friends
among their frequent blessings

V

and their shadows wind amidst the shadows,
one dark through another called *this* night.
The dogs look sidelong at a shade called *sorrow*
and what defines the heart strikes there:
some hard edge of minimal light, the brackish soil
that breeds love, its opened body steep on both sides.
Bones there. And *oh* and *again.*
The dogs' eyes roll backward – their dancecards
have gone to hell, their licenses have lost their wings,
and no one living offers solace. They flash a tooth.
Wag. Oh, they look forward.

Patrick Cotter

The Singing Bichon

My dog sings arias but only to me.
Mahler's *Kindertotenlieder* he knows
imperfectly. The *In Paradisum*
of Faurè's requiem he renders
with a strong nasal strain.
He can't quite reach all the notes
of Purcells's *The Plaint*,
but hey, he's just a dog.

He began to sing
when I began to ignore him.
Neither of us can stand the other's company.
When he shakes his Bichon curls,
doggy whiffs tinged with bitter fermentations
assault the upper reaches of my nostrils.
His piss perfumes the corner of my living room
with a pungency made worse by the addition
(without obliteration) of the mop-bucket's
ammonia-based floor fluid.
I can't stand him because he smells.
He can't stand me because I'm impervious
to his plaintive, glistening eyes.

Regularly we each need to elude
the secret inner lives of our separate solitudes.
I, by listening to my music,
he by stepping outdoors to sniff
the arses of other dogs
or to beg attention of passing children.
After I ignored his whines to be let outside
he learnt to sing. That first night
I could not avoid paying attention
to his original interpretation
of Raphael Courteville's *Creep, creep, softly creep*
I released him. He arse-sniffed.

The following night I ignored his Courteville
and he sang something by Dureflè.
I once tried to arrange a soirèe
where I planned to accompany him on cello,
my living-room too bijou for the pianoforte,
but with the house full of guests
he had no solitude to escape
and no need to sing.
He doesn't know I know
he sings Rufus Wainwright
when he thinks I'm not around.
Smelly bastard.

Siobhán of Carna

Bean na Leabhar

Bean na cúig ngadhar
Bean an gheansaí álainn
Bean na mbróg shocair shócúl
Boiscín beag de charr
Is plód boscaí ann

Tháinig sí is d'fhan
Le bheith ag scríobh, ag scríobh, ag scríobh
Gur nocht
An bradán feasa

Greanmhar, láidir,
Bean mhór
I measc mná móra.
Is sa cairrín-bhosca
Fanann cúig gadhar
Le mór-mhí-fhoighead

Bean na cúig ngadhar

The Woman of the Books

The woman of the five dogs
The woman of the beautiful jumper
The woman of the comfortable shoe
A small boxy car
With a load of boxes in it

She came and stayed
Writing, writing, writing
Until she revealed
The Salmon of Knowledge

Humourous, strong,
A big woman
Among big women.
And in the boxy car
Five dogs wait
With great impatience

The woman of the five dogs

(Translated from the Irish by Siobhán of Carna)

Mary O'Donnell

Wilderness Legacy

I leave two books, as promised.
The Buddhist one on suffering, and
The Rubayyat of Omar Khayyam,
for the sake of a verse about
a loaf of bread, a jug of wine
and 'thou beside me in the wilderness'.

For myself a dream of the Isle of Isla,
imagined from long ago, cottage
near the sea, black dog to guard me
when I wasn't communing with Gallic poets.
You, occasional visitor to my wilderness,
would bring an extra seam of light,
that indefinable male gleam, itself a speech-
form conversing with the body.

Mostly it's wilderness I seek. Buddha
can't ungrow the harvest of suffering.
when you read the Rubayyat you'll know
the huge joke on all of us, will sense
a ruthless finger, its protracted prodding.

To the shore now. The black dog
waits. He loves the way I smell
and how I speak to him.

Mary O'Donnell

Galician Watch-dog

Manoli says the farmers are not sentimental.
The chained fawn dog guards the house, watches
what moves within the mists, his ears like pinnacles.
If the sun flares on a wet stone, he barks.
If the farmer's granddaughter exclaims at new lambs,
his ears swallow her voice, he barks thrice, then stops.
She speaks to her grandfather in the mother tongue.
Manoli says that once they go to school,
they lose the words. The fawn dog watches cyclists,
children, sheep, caped men bound for Finisterre,
frustrated by those with permission to walk.
Around him, the world gulps some words, vomits others.
He knows his place. He knows he has no say.

Steven Ray Smith

Those two

He walked in behind her one Sunday,
cashmere pedigree and a waggish laugh.
I try to shush her growling and shoo away
her over-sniffing but half hound and half
Doberman in her struggles both to hunt
and guard, chase then chase away – like me
yap yapping with indecision while in want
of the Jersey girls stroking my buddy's
curls in our New York bar. Yap, yap, yap.

The puppy watches the squirrels in the yard
beside her, eyes them, wags at them, laps
his water, goes nose to nose. She tries so hard,
barks at once to scare and then recall.
For him there's no decision – none at all.

Amy Dryansky

Happy as I Believe Myself to Be

Three days I was all yes, seeing only luscious,
early summer light. For three days
grateful, pompous even, I idled
in my blowsy garden rampant
with vetch, forget-me-not, trumpet vine
springing forth from the head of a split pin oak
in crazy, vegetative fireworks. My car
sat in the driveway so long a spider
rigged a zip-line from roof rack to lilac;
not a web, just a filament
catching the breeze. *Why there?*
I asked, watching the dog puzzle out
the perfect spot to bury his bone – *here,*
no here, not here, no, yes, here –
and return dirty-nosed, triumphant,
like it was a game both of us won.

Amy Dryansky

Dog on Hind Legs

Every night the dog down the road
asks the same question in an afflicted howling
I don't understand. But I picture her
tarpapered house with its upside-down U,
her metal stake sunk into a patch of cement,
and the rusted chain's rattle — which I do
understand — as she paces its length
in the packed dirt circle she's worn in the ground.
When she barks I listen —
because she's found something to protect
in this neighbourhood. I see only silhouettes
of what no longer exists: every dependable stick,
every dream with marrow gone

Amy Dryansky

The Space on the Floor Where the Dog Lay

feels warm to my bare feet,
and I think I see a dark outline
his body's left, and picture crossing
through shadows, following him
from one vacated dream to the next.
He stretches and yawns
with all his teeth showing, obviously
something I admire.
Who watches me while I chase rabbits?
Who points and smiles?
Then whispers against my neck:
Turn over, stop shaking,
the small beast is already caught.

Sebastian Matthews

A Tale from Ovid

The moment Echo saw Narcissus
She was in love. She followed him
Like a starving wolf
            "Echo and Narcissus"

I had come back out
end of a late afternoon walk
at the entrance of river trail,
sun already casting itself

up over my head, tops
of bare trees softly alit.
It was getting chilly. Urs
lagging behind, leash

dragging in tall roadside grass.
Looking back, ready to reel her in
if car rose up onto bridge,
I found two dogs

had joined her, appearing
out of nowhere. Up sniffing;
tails neither wagging
nor stiff with aggression.

Urs, too, nonplussed,
Chocolate Lab *love-me* mode
percolating low. Both dogs
short-haired, both mutts;

one scruffy, black-and-white fur,
other half-Airedale, half
something vaguely hound.
They were strays: their odour

rife with freedom of river.
Then Black-and-White got jumpy
and loped onto the road. A car
coming so I stepped up

and raised a warning hand;
Hound crossed road when
car got over bridge.
And together Urs and I

watched the strays run
through the garden, picking up
speed as they veered
toward each other, converging deep

in rows of plastic-covered seedlings.
They didn't look back. Their stepped-up
pace called out something, though,
for Urs started to whine softly. If

she had been off the leash,
would she have crossed the road
to join her new pals in the shadows,
following them behind barns

and back under cover along trees
lining the darkening river?
And I, straight out of a tale
from Ovid, suddenly transforming

into dog, or wolf, what would I do
but pursue my companions
through the fields, on up into hills,
clothes falling off me, last flickers

of thrown light.

Sebastian Matthews

Night Pee

As though some part
had been waiting under the surface
all these years, waiting

for that felt-tip nose to touch
my cheek, to pull me out of sleep
and on my feet, heading for the door;

as though all those years
had vanished and I was back
with Underdog in our half-empty house,

brother Bill gone away to college;
back in the dark
with the dog's moist snout

at my ear and that low,
urgent whine in the back
of his big dog throat;

and up, following the shuffle beat
of our decrepit German Shepherd's
two-step down the hall;

and outside, where I sat
for some unclocked time, half-awake,
dreaming on the stoop

while Underdog rooted around in the dark
to pee and – for he was a crafty dog
as well as loyal – to sniff out imaginary

truffles and scout out varmints,
waiting until he came back, finally,
long after my urgent whispers, to join

me on that half-dark purgatory of a stair.
As though some part awoke tonight
who had lain dormant all this time,

present but undetected; and so
when she came to me this our first
night as dog and man with wet nose

to cheek, I was ready, alert
to the dog's myriad needs.
Up before I could tell I wasn't

sleeping, then outside,
waiting on the stoop in the abundant night
while she snuffed about

and peed, and came back on the stair
to look out on the shifting canvas of night.
There was this looming dark form,

I swear, we both thought
might be another dog ready
to lead us out on a long night scout –

but it was just shadow
and so I came in
to lie down next to you.

Pat Boran

A Man is Only as Good ...

A man is only as good
as what he says to a dog
when he has to get up out of bed
in the middle of a wintry night
because some damned dog has been barking;

and he goes and opens the door
in his vest and boxer shorts
and there on the pock-marked wasteground
called a playing field out front
he finds the mutt with one paw

raised in expectation
and an expression that says Thank God
for a minute there I thought
there was no one awake but me
in this goddamned town.

Susan Millar DuMars

They Put Down Ronan's Neighbour's Dog

For Ronan Scannell

He'd bitten someone's leg.
Not 'put down', *killed,*
that's how Ronan says it,
killed him. Great fucking dog.
Ronan, can you sit down?
Ronan, please don't curse!

Ronan says he wants to be
a big dog. White.
And what would this dog say?
He'd bark, he'd HOWL.
Chase cats, BOW-WOW-WOW.
He'd dig up your garden.
Ronan, can you sit down?
Bow-fucking-wow.

Joseph Woods

Kerry Blue

The year I walked
you kept the dog
and took him
up the mountains.

Unleashed, he put
so much daylight
between you,

then disappeared
into the woods
forever.

Beautiful blue kerry blue,
wayward wild mutt
and black sheep

who could never be broken
and more beloved
because of that.

Whistling would never
bring him back —
once a black

bundle herding
all the deer
in Phoenix park.

I like to think of him
up there, settled
on some farm
still bold as brass.

Scot Siegel

Fire Poker

The dog that lives in a house
is the broken dog

The man who dwells in the wood
howls at the dog-eared moon

The house that holds the dog's bowl
is a house of iron & stone

No man is ever home
in a dog house—

But a woman, a real woman,
stays home

With a broken dog,
a man who howls at the moon

When she stokes the fire, that cold
fire grows

And the children know, as children
always know,

who's master

Scot Siegel

Thermodynamics

It's dark. The dogs are late for an
appointment. They perform a circular
ritual involving the ghosts of previous
occupants of our house: Cats; Bees behind
the clapboards; Bats in the shutters;—The
dogs won't stop until I'm persuaded, until I
rise like a newly-thawed moth & lift-off...
Raindrops are not cold on my scalp. They
just lack heat.

Kevin Simmonds

Seeing Eye

Chosen
because you didn't run
from the ball or ringing bell
You go to school a believer in treats
for complete stops and avoiding fire
Habit
becomes pleasure
And there will never
be anything more delicious for you
than obedience

Emily Wall

This is not a poem about dogs

for Jessie

This is also not a poem about cats,
with their terrible grace,
and the way they make any woman ungainly.

This is not a poem about
babies and their hungry mouths, mewling
through the night.

This is not a poem about
books, the fresh glue smell and uncracked
spine of an unread novel.

If this were a poem about these things,
it would be a poem full of wishes,
and heartaches.

It would be a poem about the way

a dog looks, running along the hard-packed
sand of an Alaskan beach, April, long sun setting,
herding a flock of sandpipers and gulls –

symbolising the old things
we all want –
joy, grace, spirit.

If this poem were about that dog,
it would be a poem of such longing,
and such regret.

And who has the time, anyway,
for such indulgences?

Anne Le Marquand Hartigan

Dark Goddess

It is Maytime and my black bitch
Is on heat. Her many suitors
Old, pure bred, or shaggy
Throng the doorstep

Making their music with the blackbird.
Warbling whines and much leg cocking.
Meeting her sometimes nose tip to nose tip
Through the glass door. She growls,

Spliced between desire and territory,
O Prisoner of Love.
I, the wicked stepmother
Keep constant guard.

Hard hearted to her wistful eyes
Her whimpers and placating tail
Whisk her to the car, with well aimed boot
Towards the love lorn there.

It will soon pass poor girl,
And they so constant now will flit
Towards mature attractions,
Dustbins, O fickle Love;

Black Goddess, so soon to be dethroned,
Your heady incense
Moonlike, is on the wane,
And when out walking

Down the street again
You and your faithless lovers meet,
A hackle raised, a sniff,
Formalities complete, jog on.

Home, lie sunning in the grass;
Heigh ho, for it is spring,
The silly season;
How love can pass.

Christopher Woods

The Bank Robber's Partner

Patient, so patient, for hours now
in the old green van
while the master is gone,
wearing a cat mask of all things,
disappeared into the building
where, later, something went
terribly wrong. The police arrived.
Much shooting, then silence.

Patient, so patient, for hours now
never knowing the heist
was to get money for the hound's
operation to take the cancer away.
The sun is high in the sky,
the heat inside the car rising.
Patient, so patient, for hours now
waiting for the master
who will not return,
longing for the ride
on the open road,
head out the window,
the wind in his hair.

Christopher Woods

Old Dog Watching the Sunset

The fiery red globe
Slips behind the trees
Beyond the pond
Already dark, a deep blue
That precedes the gloom,
Dims the distant green hills.

Wizened but still alert,
His paws flat on the grass,
He watches the last light
Feels the rhythm of hours.
Silence cloaks him
Like a Zen master.

Laurelyn Whitt

Animal Memory

A dog
black, lop-eared and wary

fills the shelter with her waiting.

Someone enters one day,
or does not,

looks deep into shadows,
or away.

Her bruised body trembles,
a hesitant tail thumps

eyes haunt impossible futures.

When the door shuts
it is much too late:

longing spills from the cage

pours through cracked windows
down the streets, among us.

Without expectations.

David Wheatley

A Dying Animal

lifted

its empty waterbowl
heavier in my hand

than the full

as if

a shadow
alone casts
no shadow

departing to no
goodbye it
can receive
or return

it goes
without saying

David Wheatley

Three-Legged Dog

Pitching crazily earthwards with each bow
and scrape, then yanking back in crippled pride:
dogged; no getting off, no helping now
the see-saw for one his whole dog's life he'll ride.

John Walsh

Tranquillity

Why has that dog stopped barking
in the middle of the night,
just when I was getting used to
the sound of him?

It's not right.
There should be a law against it.

I think he's blind. Never barks
until I get a few steps past him,
after he picks up my scent.

Right now he's freaking me out.
All I can hear is the wind and it reminds me
of this book I'm reading about the moon,
where there is no such thing as wind,
so in reality the flag could not have been blowing
when Neil and Buzz staked it in the lunar dust;
which seems to prove, to some people anyway,
that they never went there in the first place.
Thank you very much.

Wherever that dog has gone,
he's robbing me of sleep. And
that moon doesn't look
like a face to me anymore.

I wonder what Neil sees when he looks up,
being the first man and all. But they say
he's the type wouldn't tell you
in a million light-years.
Well, that's okay, I think.

I only wish that dog would bark.

Gordon Walmsley

Seaward

for Jessie Lendennie

Who could imagine
her love for those dogs
would fall as light among shadows
on walks by a wall of birds so white
you could feel the salt foam rising
the dogs moving out
to coax the peninsula
releasing invisible threads
so the soft dome might lift
covering both her and them
with one triumphant sphere
a sphere to move among the others
nearing
that place
where the land
choking with memories
gives itself
over

Micheal O'Siadhail

Lame Dog

He's lame but won't go away,
This dog will have his raving day,
A madcap chance to dream again
One perfect moment he'll attain.

Look! This dog is doing his best
And yet both plot and telling contest,
So all this give and take's a slight
Bit off the mark, as though despite

Himself his nature seeks recall
But over moments his shadows fall
And caught in themes of all and each,
Beyond its own our eye can't reach.

Sharper the eye, the more disturbance
Between ourselves and radiance,
Heisenberg and this poor cur,
One eye here and the other there!

For ages we try to find such laws
As nature long before us knows,
We can only trust our hunch may fit –
If dogs are lame, then so be it!

Padraig O'Morain

Dog Latin

Canis lupus familiaris. That's dog
in Latin, he'd brag. Too bloody familiar,
she always threw back, resenting his mongrels
who mocked her in their dog thoughts, she suspected,
trailing her as she stomped around finding fault.
They see you as head bitch my darling, he sneered.
Well, someone appreciates me, she'd mutter,
softening for a moment. Then at it again:
When we married I married your bloody dogs.
The barking stopped for weeks after a black fog
stole her spirit, puzzled them into silence.
I have never got anything I wanted
in my life, she cried then. He sniggered. They sighed.
After a month she lifted up her head, smiled:
Well, it should be *canis lupus vulgaris.*
Tails began to wag. Tongues lolled. Dog breath wafted.

Drucilla Wall

Bullet Dog

My dog is not a hero.
He hasn't tunnelled 100 yards through dirt and snow
in 40 below to drag me firmly but gently by my hands
from certain death to the road. He might someday
bark and scramble over the bed in spite of smoke
just in time to wake us people to get out of there.
So far, he has never treed a bear or run off
a mountain lion, or hauled a child out
of a river, or dialled the police all by himself.

His skull is so thick his neck gets tired. He sheds
enough to clog the vacuum cleaner. He's good
at eating, but not digesting. His farts bubble up
the paint on the wall at the exact height of his ass.
He hasn't yet braved a four-lane highway to drag
an injured fellow dog to safety; never used his nose
to locate someone in the rubble; or dashed
under the hooves of a charging bull to distract it
from a man knocked to the ground.

He's not as big as he ought to be. One eye
looks sideways all the time. His hips aren't right.
We never knew he could jump at all until that one time
he flew at that man kicking down our door on a dark night
in ordinary April. The muzzle flash and the pop froze us,
as the bullet grooved his skull right down the middle,
ricocheting into the kitchen, and, evidently,

the sight of my dog's big head shaking off the blood
and surging forward, with the rolling sideways eye,
and the streaming slobber from the gap-toothed
snarling maw, determined beyond all sense

on a not-big-enough body with its clattering paws,
was just enough to make that gunman fall
back out the door and run. My dog has a scar
on his head like the map of a river.

Wendy Thornton

Building a Fire

For Bradley

The neighbours disapprove. They're too near
to ignore the flaming drift of wet wood,
the staggering boldness of the forbidden.
The house needs painting, there's plastic on the roof.
This is exactly what they would expect
from a woman who can't keep her ferns alive.

The dogs don't care. They lie beside
the drifting blaze, content to dream
of summer and preceding days in the sun
under pompous clouds riding rowdy winds
before the chain link fenced them in,
back when they superceded the alarm
and pre-empted the electric blanket.

And the woman doesn't care. She's in a trance,
transported back to a pyramid of wood
beside a spring, when the last thing she did
before turning in was to bank the coals,
and the bones of youth could stand
the ground and fire kept the beasts
from coming around
except dogs.

Matthew Sweeney

Dog on a Chain

This red setter was another red setter
who ran with his red tongue out
down the road, over fields and sand
into the sea; who came out shaking water
and loped by himself the long way home,
then lay on pebbles in the sun.
But after the car from over the border
mashed his hip, he lay on a rug
then limped for years, till a lump
grew on him, and the vet brought a gun.

In this second life he is lithe again
and doesn't howl at the chapel bell.
He howls at his long chain instead
that keeps him from the car-filled road,
and from the sheep and cattle
and their farmers who threaten guns.
But the next time he slips the chain
he'll run with his red tongue out
down the road, over fields and sand
into the freezing, gull-cluttered sea.

Matthew Sweeney

The Dog

He was walking an imaginary dog.
He'd stop and yank an invisible lead,
turning to growl at the creature
that he hadn't got all day, that no dog
needed to pee every five yards,
that any minute now rain would fall
from a sky as blue as his one eye.

He brought the dog into the pub.
He tied it to the leg of a chair,
got a pint of stout and sat there
as I followed him in, pretending
to look for someone, then sitting down
with a beer of my own, to stare at him
talking to the dog and to himself.

He drained his glass and got another.
He leaned down and stroked the dog,
muttering to it things I couldn't hear,
straightening up to smile to himself,
then I had to go, out into the November
sunlight, looking behind me, listening
for the faintest whimper or bark.

Matthew Sweeney

Bones

The horse fell in the harbour,
was splashing in the water
with the cart strapped to his back.
And a cyclist with sunglasses
and a woman with a pram
kept on going – but not the man
with the mongrel in a sack.
He dropped all and dived straight in.

The horse kept neighing
while the man was saving him
and the dog was chewing free.
Maybe the horse knew
that the man was on his way
to drown the dog. Maybe the dog
had barked this to the horse.
Oh, there were bones in the cart.

Matthew Sweeney

His Dog

Where is this dog he sees and I can't?
Why is he pointing to the window,
then beckoning me to rise from bed
and herd his sheep back to the hills?
All around me sick men sleep through
his hissed commands, his tearing cries
that the night-nurse runs to calm –

a calm that night-lights can't prolong,
or daylight either, though his daughters
when they come with wills that lack
his signature, don't get a sound
or a move from him, don't get the farm,
although they plead and squabble.
Where is his dog now, where is it?

Scott T. Starbuck

Warrior Says People on 17th Street in Portland, Oregon, Are Dreaming of Dogs

I'm at a potluck block party
listening to a black-haired 30-ish single mom
discussing her dream of rottweilers
chewing red striped pieces of cloth

when another single mom says she too
has been dreaming of dogs,
only these are tiny irate poodles
barking indecipherably into microphones.

The lad who works in the bookstore
says for him it has been St. Bernards
appearing in blizzards, but as he touches them
they flash into skeletons.

No one mentions the war.

Julian Stannard

Dog Talk

Why be adrift
when you could be a dog?

Why be a heaving breast
when you could be a dog?

Why take on a mortgage
when you could be a dog?

Why take a trip to Nam
when you could be a dog?

Why be an Oxford Blue
when you could be a dog?

Why be a blue stocking
when you could be a dog?

Why drool over a mozzarella
when you could be a dog?

Why stake your reputation
when you could be a dog?

Why do a Ph.D
when you could be a dog?

Why pen a sonnet
when you could be a dog?

Why broker peace in the Middle East
when you could be a dog?

Why be a lunatic
when you could be a dog?

Why be twenty-third in line to the throne
and why be Home Secretary

and why be a triple jumper
when you could be a dog?

Why be a crock of shite
when you could be a dog?

Why go to the trouble of preparing a bong
when you could be a dog?

Why be the morning mist
when you could be a dog?

Why have two legs
when you could have four or even three?

Why be a dog in the manger
when you could be the dog?

Joel R. Solonche

My Dog

So many people with dogs in the park today,
it makes me wonder what kind of dog
I would have if I had a dog. I never had a dog.
When I was five, I was chased by a dog.
I think it was a bull terrier. It looked like the dog
on the old *Our Gang* comedies, but without
the black ring around its eye. It chased me
into the alley behind the apartment building.
I climbed up onto one of the iron bars
that connected the iron railing to the wall.
The dog kept barking as I kept my balance
as best I could, but I was five, and I lost it
and fell off and split my nose open.
Maybe this is why I never had a dog.
There's one I like, a big black one.
The one that looks like a bear.
The one with the big brown doleful eyes.
The one that looks like the only reason
he gets off the couch is to go out to take a crap.
The one whose master is pulling hard on the leash
to get to cross the street into the park.

J.D. Smith

Policy

Because Nubians are still enslaved
I walk my dogs twice a day.
Because a child conceived tonight
will inherit addiction
I leave my dogs offerings
of fresh water, with ice cubes.
Because envelopes and marketplaces explode
I hug my dogs and even carry them
where no shrapnel flies.
Because a manatee is sliced
by motorboat blades
and the last wild tiger
has been born,
I keep my dogs' tags and shots
up to date.

Now that any fact can be known
in an instant,
the smallest love is news.
Things touch at a near or far remove:
jays pass raspberry seeds
over fresh fields,
armadillos, burrowed into freight,
widen their range.
Word of my program
will ride the jet stream,
and land like a petal,
or it will bounce, devoutly,
off a satellite.

Dog in the Road

The dog lies in the middle of the road
indifferent as an occasional car
manoeuvres around it.
Only once, when a driver honks,
does it lift its head from its paws
before settling again on the gravel.
Is this what they have in mind
when they call it a dog's life?

Whatever those words mean,
it's the life I'm living, I suppose,
stuck as I am by this window,
looking out this window at a dog,
at a dog I don't know,
and asking which one of us
will be the first one of us
to get out of the way.

Dave Lordan

Street Dog Song

In the long exodus of dogs
Whatever went down yesterday
is very much a minor episode

Who the bullbars turned to mud
Who the scissors snipped
Who got screwed on whose front lawn

Who's in heat and flaunts
their raw and carefree meat
to everyone

Who stood against the hunt and fought
Who bared their teeth for sake of form, then ran
Who got caught and culled
Who won

All apocrypha to singing dogs
All very much of no concern

Nor is the moon the altar of their song
Every lamp-post in the world conducts
to that majestic urinal

Make like any night-seeing animal:
Disconnect your ear from history and listen
Listen to the canine song

What they bellow from the hollow
In next door's creeping undergrowth is nothing sorrowful
It's absolute conviction, it's howlellujah

Tomorrowwww
Tomorrowwww
Tomorrowwww

Is all they've ever sang, will sing
They have no other lore.
They've nothing more to tell or show

They're the dogs in the street
And I believe in them
They know

C.J. Sage

How to Keep a Setter

Understand that attraction
to the birds is only natural.

He might be trained to sway
from posturing and pointing,

but don't demand prostration
of the face. A high-held mask of pride
helps him become your champion.

Don't just pat his head – stroke
the golden apple of his throat.

On balmy evening walks, don't hurry.
Let him nose the honeyed air, the grass.
Maybe take a tumble in it with him.

When he comes to your sweet call,
remember you aren't the only creature
singing. Applaud the concentration.

For some it's a question of chemistry.
For others, a matter of best-friendship.

And oh, what people do for such
companions. Learn to love the dirt
or if you love it learn to show it.

Learn to love the killer instinct,
and the dumbness that's the basis
of loyalty. He wears your leash

and prances happily at your side.
You lead sometimes, sometimes he.

Eileen Sheehan

Memo from the Residents' Committee ref Dog Ownership

Dear Resident, it has been brought to our attention
that the number of dogs in our Estate is increasing.

Dogs must be prevented from running loose mid-morning when
the postman is calling
Dogs must be prevented from running loose in the daytime when
traffic is flowing
Dogs must be prevented from running

                  (eye-witness accounts of
car-chasing have been recorded)

Dogs must be prevented from barking late at night when people
are sleeping
Dogs must be prevented from barking early in the mornings before
people have woken
Dogs must be prevented from barking

                  (reports of unsociable
barking have been noted in the minutes of our meetings)

Dogs must be prevented from digging in flowerbeds where
people are planting
Dogs must be prevented from digging in the park where our
senior citizens are strolling
Dogs must be prevented from digging

                  (the health and safety
aspect of holes has been investigated)

Dogs must be prevented from fouling the footpaths where
people are walking
Dogs must be prevented from fouling the green area where
children are playing

Dogs must be prevented from fouling

(evidence of such fouling
has been lodged with our Chairman)

Although none on our committee are dog owners,
per se, we do welcome dogs in our estate
but would gently remind you, dear resident,
of your **legal obligation** to practice responsible pet ownership.

(the use of bold typeset,
above, was unanimously agreed on when drafting)

Eileen Sheehan

midnight

and the dog   also   is restless
nosing through rooms   sniffing out
evidence of you

throws herself down   resigned
to your absence   big sorrowful
eyes   the odd whimper

John W. Sexton

The Bark of a Dog

The blackboard was smudged with the ghosts
of wiped out words, stale lessons days old.
Sister Mercedes wrote out a new word: Laika.
She said it was Russian and meant *never stops*
barking. She said it was the name of a dog
that the Russians had sent into space.
She said that the dog had gone round and around
the world for five whole months until the spaceship
had burnt into nothing. She said that Laika
had come back to Earth as a shooting star.
She said it in such a way that we couldn't be sad.
She made Laika sound like a wound in Jesus,
a tear in the flesh that could never hurt.

I believed every word and thought that the sky
was a dog, that Laika was there as particles
of cloud; that she would come down with the rain
and then evaporate back up again.

Superboy had a dog too, a bit like Laika.
Superboy's dog was called Krypto and could fly
into space; he chased comets as if they were cats.
Krypto was indestructible and so Superboy
would wash him in the lava of volcanoes,
would scrub his fur clean with a brush of barbed wire;
and all the time Krypto would just bark,
like *yip yip yip*. His life was nothing but fun,
even in the cold of space; he was like a wound in Jesus,
a tear in the flesh that could never hurt.

Our next-door neighbour in number sixty-
seven, Fairfax Road, had a dog called Digger;
a dog as black and coarse as soil. Dad would say,
"that dog came out of the ground".
Digger could bark shapes that entered sleep
and which often entered mine; shapes like boxes
that I could sit inside; shapes that would take me
into space, right up close near the eyes of the moon;
or down, very deep down, into the ornamental pond
in the local park, whose eight inches of depth
were a trick much deeper when you travelled
in the bark of a dog. A bark like a wound in Jesus,
a tear in the flesh that could never hurt.

John W. Sexton

The Dogs of Ourblood Road

Buried in the gardens of their owners
no one owns them now. Their bodies are made
from the tears that were shed for their lost lives.
At dusk you might catch sight of them, solid
no more than rain. They guard the city, night
after night. While you sleep they may even stand
vigil at the foot of your bed, alive for a moment yet
in your sleeping breath. If you wake they'll be gone
but you'll know they were there. Their names
are sometimes forgotten, or sometimes repeated
in the names of other dogs. Those dogs know them well,
sniff them out on the evening walk, turn back
with a pull of the lead to bring you to them. You
may rarely see them but will feel them sometimes
nuzzling into your heart. Their bark will sound
like your own gasp. In that moment they are you.

Breda Wall Ryan

Raftery's dog

I feel Spring stirring in Raftery
he eases his bench
back from the hearth's fierce heat
feels his way
along the settle-edge and table
to the door

day is night behind his eyes
but his bones sense
a stretch at day's end
his skin warms as the wind's colour
veers from blue to violet
furze flames saffron on the Bens

he hoists his bundle and fiddle
damps the fire
I shake my coat free of winter's ash
bow to St Brigid's sun
we walk the winters' poem-hoard
across the nubbled Mayo bog

I nudge him along the mid-line of the path
under his hand
my hackles rise to warn of ruts
bogholes, strangers
I tread the tussocks flat where we stop
to share cold rabbit in the heather

At word of our return
neighbours crowd
the rambling house
to hear new verses I, Seol
know by heart. They write his rhymes
toast Raftery in whiskey and buttermilk

but his heart sinks often into its own dark
I sing a canine dirge
bring his light back, spark the words
to win us the *file*'s stool at the hearth
I tongue his blank eyeballs till they shine
then sleep curled to the master's feet

Gibbons Ruark

Wallace Stevens Welcomes
John Crowe Ransom to Hartford

Wallace Stevens ushered John Crowe Ransom
And his dog back on the New Haven Line.
It was time for tea, and he feared the dog
Might piss on the palm at the end of his mind.

Gabriel Rosenstock

Koan

Mar go ngabhais thar bráid
Is mé go haclaí ag glanadh fiaile
Reoigh an spáid
I dtochailt na cruacheiste
Bhfuil dúchas an Bhúda ag gadhar?

Sea is cinnte go n-áiteodh saoithíní orm
Cuimhneamh ar an tSalvadóir seachas scráid
Ar ghorta seachas gortghlanadh intinne
Ar dhiúracáin núicléacha seachas mo phaistese dúrabháin.
Ach nuair a ghabhais thar bráid
A ghadhair
Faoi thromshiúl daitheacha
Bhí freagra an tomhais agam láithreach

Koan

Because you passed by
When I, supple, cleared the weeds,
My spade froze
Digging the insoluble question:
Does a dog have Buddha's birthright?

It's certain that pedants will persuade me
To contemplate El Salvador rather than turves
To contemplate famine rather than weeding my mind
To contemplate nuclear missiles rather than my patch of loam.
But when you passed by
My dog
With painful plod
I had the riddle's answer straight away

(Translated from the Irish by Michael Hartnett)

James Silas Rogers

Dogs in Passing Cars

You have to admire those dogs
riding by toward who knows where:
glass down a few inches, they thrust
black noses into the air
with the bravado of wildcatter oilmen,

or subway daredevils plunging
heads out open windows
to let the breeze peel back their lips
and pop their eyes like a bad face-lift.
Yet they know the first rule: *Stay*.

Ears jostle, like bell-clappers
in the hands of a child, or a clump
of flapping socks pinned to a clothesline.
Always, the dogs reach and stay, reach and stay –
inquisitive, eager, contained.

James Silas Rogers

Dog and Squirrel

The dog looks up, and up, and up, but no matter:
the gulf into which it peers is unbridgeable.
An islander without a boat. Meanwhile, above,
the squirrel has, for now, stopped scrabbling .
Compact and solid and balanced, the S of its tail
wraps along its back like a tooled machine part
in a socket.
        The black-and-white dog will soon tire
and walk away, sniffing. The squirrel, instinctually back
in its own improvised plane of tree to tree,
will find and follow instantly forgotten tracks,
moving over branches, rooftops, fences, utility poles:

testing the rims of a steadier world.

James Silas Rogers

Past Guessing

Thirty years on, she still
pulls out an occasional rabbit,

lets it slip that she can hear
a music others never do

or will reach into a place
not just hidden but unlearnable.

I am thinking of a day
when I came home at five p.m.

and my wife told me
she had lain on the floor

all afternoon beside our dog
who could barely lift his head,

and who shook for some reason
past our guessing.

Sunlight filled the kitchen. She'd run
her hands along his ribs, saying

you've been a good dog
and can give yourself back to God,

until, like ripples losing themselves
in a pond, the tremors stopped

and he slept at ease
there on the white linoleum.

It seems right to me now
that her first word was "light."

Billy Reynolds

The Beagle Factory

You've squeezed the problem to death. But the door still whines shut, and the huge fan in the wall chases down the programmatic smell of shit. You think, get on with it, but your hands turn to fists and you swear under your breath, but the fan roars back. So many snouts sneaking up to the silver bars. Then you're wheeling them out into late sun and back into the artificial light of another room with its metal desk, stopwatch and thick manual you know by heart. Summer's about to wander off, and you want these creatures to know the grass heavy with morning dew or the rain coming down hard. Your renderings have no place to go, like these dogs beseeching you. You surrender to the work of petting, on your knees your fingers seeking matted scruff. The barn swallows beyond the concertina swoop in the half-light, at work, too, inches above the grass. It is summer but it is dusk; it is anything but pity lost in this place, and it hurts while outside the dark grows, a natural thing moving with such imperceptible slowness.

C. R. Resetarits

Dog Gone

My dog has gone after dreams again.
He stops a moment to contemplate
a scrubbing at the garden hedge
then through he darts – one of his many
alchemist skills. My dog is gone next
piney gust, next whorl of leaves.
We both traverse worlds too easily
called out as we are in shifts or spills.
His cosmos rife with shooting smells,
with riffs of *musica universalis*
or the lopping beat of spaniel ears.
A kin to my own palimpsestic ways.
Cold dark kennings, ionised hearts,
from dodging bits of broken stars.
Our rilles-braid heathland holds acres of chance,
our cloudless sky pales blue so blue that shamed
rust hills take violet veil, and this light too bright
for eyes and mind – lemon pith white –
fruit clean and spare as nova grace.
And there is my dog gone far afield,
a black feather blown cross a gold-green land.
He's worn and ready for fate to move.
Only once past wasted does he think of me,
only once the wind has gathered and turned –
drowning smells and harms and words.
I'll meet him halfway, whistle him home.
We'll both sleep deeply still battling stars.

Bertha Rogers

Dog and Girl

Dawn prods trees
grated against sky,
gaudy green limbs stretched
above sharp green grasses.

The girl, barefoot on dirt,
toe-clambers hill
to the low chicken coop,
where she sprays grain
from clasped then spread fingers,
a child's hand-dance
for gathering, dispersing
skittish chicks.
Her dog, his fur night-black,
cockle-burred,
laughs and follows.

Then, down
to the sun-blared,
ramshackle-eyed house.
The door handle has vanished;
the spindle-frame claps,
its toothed screen
scratching at fingers.
That happy dog's
right behind his girl.

Those two,
hands and paws lifting,
working, running in that place
where it always seems
to be summer,
and sun's morning.

Bertha Rogers

Wild, Again

When the forest was field, after
orchard (after field, after forest),
when these spruces had not been thought
by grasses encumbered only
by wild red strawberries,
the dogs ran in there, every day –
they corralled and cowed speckled Ayrshires,
whooped and barked for their farmer-lords.
They herded those cows to stalls –
until the milk was gone, the barns fell down.

Then there was a rainy planting –
fingerlings slippered into bladed
soil; rocked, clayed soil – followed
by slow growth, passage to sky's eye,
patient, steady renovation
from green staves, red fruit, earth's increase –
to stippled, needled, knotty ground.

And, at last, only this slant-lit
site where primal dog-paws pound russet
spurs shed by leaning, lithe under-boughs.
Ah! Wind soughing, susurrating –
and just there, the doe's immigrant
eyes – home, again, in her found wild.

Barbara Regenspan

Introduction to Teaching Nietszche

Think about your adorable dog
with head cocked
and weightless spirit
he's without a history
in the context of History

That backpack full of books
that load you down
the record of centuries
even if calculus,
is still recorded culture

You traded that cocked head,
that rapid-fire tail
for the pleasure and pain
of listening to me
right now

And in the moments
when it doesn't feel worth
having depth, a thing Nietszche
prized, despite his love for
dancing Greeks,

Roll down a hill,
wrestle with a friend,
dance to your
next class, but remember
you

can act like
a dog
whenever you wish
but your dog
is dogginess
all the time.

Jacob Rakovan

In the northern country

Robins starve in the thin snow,
their bloody chests a false fire
in glass branches.

There is a river that is falling,
over stone and ice.
It has fallen
since the stones ground flour
that now decorate unused parks
and an empty museum with a gift shop.
Each day, I sit in half-burned down factory
where 36 men burned alive
beetled on the edge of the cliff

From the empty office
across the hall you can hear
the same river that carried a trained bear over the falls,
killed Sam Patch the daredevil, in 1829

The engines that ran the streetcars
rust in a disused bar's basement
and the river, indifferent
to living and dead

drops through the broken wheelhouse
riming the bones of abandoned scaffolding with ice.
This is a brutal country,
beneath suburban streets
old hotels and whorehouses
keep their secrets
masquerade as chain restaurants.
at night, with my hound
trying to hang himself with his leash
howling at the swollen udders of the moon,

we chase deer across the frozen lawns.

Moira Rhoarke

The Pound

Brown, liquid hope-filled eyes;
Tails swish on metal cage bars
Gore encrusted boots.

Cold concrete floor feels
Like ice on raw open sores;
Bone-jagged skin.

Accusing looks, bitch
Watches her newborn litter
Swaddled in a steel bucket.

Filth streams through yellow glass;
Stinging light over rough-raw paws,
Puddles in a death-bleached drain.

Moira Rhoarke

Waning

The dying day spills droplets of crimson;
Shadows pool on grassy hillocks.
Colours run, greying in the fading light
Washing through the dusk in rivulets
Of navy blue and purple.

Wrenching belly-cries of freedom
Rising from the fringes of the light
Lupine shadows dance before the crimson orb
Their calls tugging the waning consciousness;
Wild and violate the notes entwine.

Through cataract-clouded eyes
She struggles to put form to shimmering shapes
Feebly she lifts her grizzled head
The old tail thumps on the cold ground.
Diaphanous shadows evaporate with the day.
Wait.

Alexis Quinlan

I wish I believed in the soul

I wish I believed in the soul
so that I could sing sweetly about it
like a real poet. I would
focus on yours, of course,

since I know yours, or I know
that soul-ish thing in you
and I love it, too,
though it is blind greedy omnivorous

as a dog. As my dog
Arthur Rimbaud, who will
eat anything from cigarette butts,
apt for the French poet in him,

to pine cones to styrofoam
peanuts, apt for nothing and
surely invented by someone else who
doesn't believe in the soul. Above all

Art longs to feast on every snot-slicked
ketchup-crusted napkin rumpled and
dropped to be stomped on the streets
of New York. He leaps to their gray

with a fleeting furtive glance
and a spritely bounce away
for he's long since worked out
which things we do not share.

Susan Pilewski

Sleeping With Your Dog

She aligns her diminutive frame
first chin, then chest, then dorsal spine

at last, her belly slopes along the crescent of my ass.
Somehow she knows I'm a fitful bedfellow,

who will occasionally rise to ply her with salty chorizo
on the off chance she would spill your arrival time,

whereabouts, intentions, agenda, transgressions
a dossier compiled through bribes of processed meat.

In the kitchen she blinks at me through beatific eyes
one of two at home smart enough to never sleep alone.

There are no atheists in foxholes
only bones of true believers.

Richard Peabody

Walking to Dublin

I live with three women
of varying ages.
My doc says,
"You're surprised that there's drama?"
I am.
My best friend dubs my place
"The House of Estrogen."
I buy a boy dog
to even the score.
My daughters are always
campaigning for a puppy.
So this is perfect.
Now when all hell breaks loose
over who's using who's brush.
When *Princess Not Me* splatters
nail polish on the wood floor.
When *Miss I Didn't Do It*
spills her smoothie into the laptop.
I can go walk the dog.
For hours and hours.
Just walk and walk
and walk some more
and keep right on walking.

Harry Owen

The Language of Hooligans

There they are as usual, hanging around,
rushing about, beating one another up,
their mad eyes and loose-tongued lunatic grins
scrabbling the ground for something, anything,
to do. Not stupid (far from it), just what they are –
bored fur-faced ruffians.

They growl an empty patois of delinquency,
a coarse, manic vocabulary of yelps
and snarls flecked with canine expletives
belching through the fence as challenge, all threat,
bark and bluster, sneering, spitting, running away –
graceless young layabouts.

Not starving either (they're healthy enough)
and plenty of space to wander; everything
you'd imagine they'd need, including their own
rough company. But these are our neighbourhood chavs,
street corner vandals, dogshit graffiti artists
squawking their gross monoglot nonsense,
the only language they know.

James Desmond O'Hara

Needing Puppies

In my bed on an aesthetic snow night
I hold a compunction
and throw about a towel
get up and hit the switch on the Macintosh

I need to catch them
to record about my short haired puppies
pushing noses hard in searching ways
in order to extract tugs on full hydrated ears*
and underchin pullings and chewy slavers
undeveloped understandings
puppies after all
of snarls and lickings sentiment
on any teasing available fingers

There

When I get you home from this nightscape
I will pull on your healed cropped tails
and make you cross
and demand from you an impossible
forgiveness and

go to sleep

* These half-tail puppies have juicy ears.

Ron Houchin

Haunted by Dead Dogs

(for Art & Sadie)

Their heads down, walking stiff shouldered
toward a door they can't remember is closet,
even their spirits need out to pee.

Like the best aspects of us, they're left
to nap on an island of folded blankets
down the hall.

If I were wealthy, I'd keep a Quonset hut
of memories for all the dogs
I've ever known.

Dobie, Trixie, Matty, Sadie, Teddy –
all their long e-sounds crying
at the end of the names we gave them,

like our wailing at the end of their lives.
I would gather them in from their plots
beside aluminum outbuildings in backyards,

from under special trees in the oak woods
outside of town. It would be a convention
of memory, a conference of elegies

like this one, perhaps, better left
unwritten – all their sweet old eyes
and gray muzzles lifted in half-round air,

at once yowling nostalgias for us
whom they miss more than
their own lives.

Ron Houchin

Heaven Without Animals

"The soft eyes open."
— James Dickey

Those beneath salvation, flitting
flower to blossom or humming among
sugar saucers on the back porch
and darting away, those howling

at the blue cone of night sky,
and all that live as if life were its own
end won't be there. Imagine no
mockingbird to help mourn

the broken branch, no squirrel counting
off autumn in acorns, no snow
leopard to remind us, in winter, how
to live; most of all, the brown dog

of any kind, warm devotion –
like I always wanted
from my parents and my kids –
in his eyes. I won't go then.

I'll kill my neighbour who beats
his wife, preaches to his boys,
hurls snowballs at his cat, and hangs
mourning doves up in his garage.

Ron Houchin

Rituals

He paces in an ever-shrinking circle,
leans against his tree waiting for
time to unwind the chain,
then naps in the warm middle of the day.

From the tightness of tree
and loud links, he runs at the world
that surrounds him, that always gets away.
At dusk, a dish of dry food falls within reach.

The windows of the trailer light up
and open. Laughter and threats pour out.
Nearby, the ghosts of cars prowl the traffic river,
looking for him in dense night.

Sprawled on his bald spot of earth,
under a loping moon, he dreams
of the hostile stranger, the uniformed
talker, the loud walker. It's

as difficult for him to be grateful
for isolation as it is for those inside
the metal box, giggling in the flicker
of TV light, to appreciate anything.

Les Murray

Trees register the dog

and the dog receives the forest
as it trots toward the trees

then the sleeping tiger
reaches the dog en masse
before the dog reaches the tiger:

this from the Bengal forests
in the upper Kerosene age,

curry finger-lines in shock fur.

Les Murray

Two Dogs

Enchantment creek underbank pollen, are the stiff
  scents he makes,
hot grass rolling and rabbit-dig but only saliva
  chickweed.
Road pizza clay bird, hers answer him, rot-spiced good.
  Blady grass,
she adds, ant log in hot sunshine. Snake two sunups
  back. Orifice?
Orifice, he wriggles. Night fox? Night fox, with left
  pad wound.
Cement bag, hints his shoulder. Catmeat, boasts his
  tail, twice enjoyed.
Folded sapless inside me, she clenches. He retracts
  initial blood.
Frosty darks coming, he nuzzles. High wind rock
  human-free howl,
her different law. Soon. Away, away, eucalypts
  speeding –
Bark! I water for it. Her eyes go binocular, as in pawed
hop frog snack play. Come ploughed, she jumps,
  ground. Bark tractor,
white bitterhead grub and pull scarecrow. Me! assents
  his urine.

Theo Dorgan

I Will Be Gone...

I will be gone when these green trees are bare
and a last taxi climbing up the hill
breaks the night silence and its echoing chill.

I will be gone and that black lonesome dog
will still be casting back and forth
with her small head going this way and that way
under the cold moon.

It will be winter everywhere then,
a hard frost on everything in our world
that is no longer my world or your world
or any place that poor dog can ever again call home.

Pete Mullineaux

My Captain

Wasn't the only one to go down with the ship.
I was there, faithful to the last
as he clung to the wheel in torment,
cursing the world's woes and folly.
We sang his favourite song –
the one that goes 'bow wow wow' –
wrapped ourselves around the mast.
There were tears enough to sink the boat
even without the storm.
'Rats' we cried – but they were long gone.

Pete Mullineaux

The Stray Dog Café

Where everyone sings for their supper
has to beg or roll over
for attention.

The main menu is always bones
starters are a chair leg
a napkin

or the waiter's trousers –
dessert a selection of tins
from a trolley.

The cabaret will feature
shaggy dog stories
and shaggier poets

patrons may 'Howl'
all they like at dancers
in postman uniforms

(some of them Russian)
or the moon
if they prefer

scratch and sniff
at whoever
takes their fancy.

The Stray Dog café
a woof and a whistle away
from the pound

where no one is on a lead
but the hair in that soup
is most likely yours.

Susan Moorhead

I need the dog tonight

It's a night of worries fretting me like old bones
malformed by years of disease, the dull aching
pain flaring up when it threatens to rain. I wander
through the house, everyone asleep, checking
door knobs and window locks, but it's the thing

in me that can't get out after years of trying
to leave it behind. I walk the rooms turning off lights
I have just turned on, not restless but looking
for direction, just the old whirrings of a mind stirred
up with no ease in it, no place to curl up and rest.

I need the dog tonight. I find her, the furry snoring coil
at the foot of my daughter's bed, a bit of fluff and canine
neurosis that my sleeping child feels can guard her
from harm. The dog looks up, quizzical, waiting for my call,
but I see the peace of my daughter's outstretched arm, the slack

of her mouth, her long dark hair careless on the white
pillowcase, and I bid the dog goodnight. I will hold fast
to this in the long hours waiting for me, this hard wisdom
of what I have learned to give and what I have learned not to take.

Susan Moorhead

July Twilight

Heat stillness,
the thickness of cupped air

as night begins its slow press.
Sky, pearl to slate like an opened

abalone shell turned over in a gathering
hand. Brief sparks of fireflies search

the darkening quiet, flicker nocturnal code:
here – the last findings of day. The old

white dog totters to the spread of pachysandra
beneath the tilted pine. Stands, swaying

slightly, looking as if she remembers
something beyond the first shadows.

Susan Moorhead

Concerns of the Old Dog

Who will protect her? The old dog frets,
attempting to rise from her soft bed
on the floor, legs quavering,
the ache of old hips.

Her owner is walking out of the room
so she must go as well, following
from living room to kitchen, each step
of her stalk legs a reinvention of pain.

Her owner measures the coffee scoops,
scribbles a note on the pad by the phone,
turns to fetch a cup and trips over
the old dog who is angrily waved away.

In the hall, the old dog watches her owner,
feels the tightening wheeze in her lungs
and frets. How will I keep her safe?
Who will keep watch? Who will protect her?

Alan Jude Moore

Magione Umbria

raindrops on the dog-dish
like Japanese bells

some absence signalled
by these foreign tones

footprints on the slope
marked
and lightly washed away

melancholy canines
rest beneath persimmon

then take back to tracing
truffles

or some other recorded item

Agi Mishol

I. The Ascension

As I ascended to heaven
and hesitantly opened the gate,
no magi shone within
just a huge white furry Great Pyrenees
couched on a resplendent cushion,
surrounded by animals,
down to the smallest:

the poodle from the Humane Society
and the mongrel from the road to Rehovot
and the one abandoned in the Yavneh station
and not only:

generations of cats whose spirits were refreshed
by the Friskies kit I keep in my car,
puppies from the coastal plain,
one frozen heron I fan-dried in winter,

mice I returned to the field from the house,
spiders I saved from the cleaning lady's broom,
a porcupine whose fleas I removed
with a tweezer
all of them
all of them were there

the Great Pyrenee's softness
and the grace his eyes bestowed
filled the temple and the animals

not one word remained in the world
all of them
passed away
passed away

and only my love quoted his love,
my head resting forever on his fur.

(Translated from the Hebrew by Lisa Katz)

John Menaghan

Two Black Dogs

Two black dogs
on a snow flaked
field wandering
about among bare
brown trees ignoring
each other ignoring
me making slow
snuffling progress
along invisible trails
that curve and
loop and bend
and end nowhere

John Menaghan

On a Lavatory Wall
(a found poem)

Why are dogs
superior to people?
Three things.

One:
Dogs always know
where they are.

Two:
Dogs always know
what they want.

Three:
Dogs always know
what to do.

Kevin McLellan

About more

a leashed dog stops the
business of smelling to be
a part of the wind

Iggy McGovern

Canine Haiku

Life's big mystery:
There are days you are the dog
Days you are the tree

Garda station log:
The body found by a man
Out walking the dog

Would it be stranger
If The Magi had found a
Dog in the manger?

Those Wise Men might say
(Like Elvis) that any hound-
Dog will have its day

Yo, yo doirty rats!
Yo tink yo're really sumtin?
Yo, yo doirty cats!

Hi, Old Marmaduke
Wants to be (man's best) friends with
You on Muzzlebook

In Wagga Wagga
The tail, undoubtedly, will
Something the dogga

Afric McGlinchey

Rescue dog

He stands near,
to steady her shakes,
crumbling language,

creeping dark; nudges
his nose into her knee
on the sun-swept bench,

fetches a carnival of memories
for déjà-vu innocence
at eighty five. He's her first

love, and last. *No pets
allowed*, but they let her
care for her push-along dog.

Tom Mathews

False Start

I and Pangur Bán my dog.

Caroline Lynch

A Moment of Woof

Woof chased a bumble bee –
Woof chased a bumble bee –
Woof chased a bumble bee –

Woof-woof-woof! a bumble bee.

Come back, Woof! the bumble bee –
Come back, Woof! the bumble bee –
Come back, Woof! the bumble bee –

will sting you if you catch it...

But Woof chased the bumble bee –
Yes Woof chased the bumble bee –
For Woof chases bumble bees –

forever chasing bumble bees.

Caroline Lynch

Photographs with Poodles

First

The poodle pups are not spooky.
She clutches them to her,
their round, soft heads
echoing the bloom of the rose
pinned to her breast.
One puppy yawns, two wriggle,
and the fourth –
upright on its hind-legs –
leans against her and gazes
out of frame, its eyes
solemn and dark as a child's.

Second

The hedge across the road is bare.
Rufus, Nicolette and Lucy
(Lucy wears a little vest)
gather round her at the gate.
Her left hand rests
on Rufus's head; from her right,
three leashes dip
like maypole-ribbons to the dogs' necks.
Rufus has jumped up
to put small paws on her heavy coat.
They are too excited to be returning –
they stare up at her,
beg her to open the gate and go.

Third

Her hand is to her face,
fixing her glasses.
Or perhaps she has been struck
by a thought
that gives her sudden pain.
She is on her knees.
Sunlight shows up
the strain in her mouth.
Behind her,
the garden border is unkempt.
A leaning trellis supports nothing.
On the crumpled rug,
five poodles are not
lined up neatly before her.
They stand and sit
at sixes and sevens.

Colour

As children, going to visit the old lady,
we saw only
her magnified eyes,
her shapeless habit of dogs,
a handful of tempting kittens.

In the dark

She crawled into the recess under the stairs.
It took a day to find her,
the garden, fields and river searched first
while the poodles gathered round her in a pack,
their thirty pom-pom heads and hers
indistinguishable.

For those hours, picture a tin of light around her edges,
the frame broken, the image melting away,
until only sensation remained –

the feeling of poodles, clustered to her.
Afterwards, she was taken away
and the dogs put down

as punishment for something:
madness, truth, straying beyond the white border
of what can be contained by a photograph.
But I know her now
moving towards love,
finding it in the unseen, loneliest places.

Yahia Lababidi

Dog Ideal,

without the need to stifle the cry of consciousness
through drink or drug or violent distraction,
disinclined to wreak havoc on self or other

free of the sustained illusion of written words
and images, with their enduring damage
or turning to the senseless spell of art for oblivion

their memories are not material
but perish at birth, still-born

always the present, unoppressed
by the burden of past or future
the unspoken and unspeakable

without the complication of human sophistication
or impossible longings beyond dog and dog world
they dream of food, shelter, air
and wake to find them there

without false divisions
among mind/body/soul
so without perversions

honest in their need to give and receive
a love neither tormented nor tormenting
nursing their wounds without meditation,
which is the creation of more suffering

a spirituality of the earth
a piety and humility that accepts
the man and God-given crumb
expects nothing

unconcerned with the pursuit of truth
and other lies
they live in Truth

never lost in the labyrinth of self
they are without self-image,
thus without self-deception

blissfully unaware of Schopenhauer's Pendulum
which from pain to boredom swings
their tails sway contentedly
always at home, in their bodies

nonchalantly, watching the world pass by
with benign curiosity and sideways glace
slipping in and out of untroubled sleep

they do not know the gloom
of deliberately darkened rooms
suspicions, fears and worries
real confounded with unfounded

or artificially purchased dreams
long after an inexhaustible mind
has exhausted its hapless frame

without question, they accept the deposits of Fate
without the added interest of personal doubts
questioning their place in the universe

unconcerned with peace, justice
and other human nonsense

impervious to the charm of philosophy or psychology
the conceit of thought, the paralysis of analysis
all idle speculation, and monstrous civilisation

neither prisoners of Time
nor victims of temperament

without necessary occupations
or unnecessary preoccupations
with sanity

out of reach
out of reach
out of reach

work like dog
live like a dog
die like a dog.

Jacqueline Kolosov

Guidance

No dog seeks a master who pins
on wings and flies almost high enough
to kiss the sun, only to fall back
to earth, trailing the hapless dog
in his wake. Not even the most
desperate of the dog's kind seeks
one whose heart rattles when he walks,
whose own shadow flees at his approach.
And no dog seeks one who has forgotten
the cool mystery of gardens.
The dog, who understands almost
better than anyone that hope
is the hardest, most necessary
bone we carry, seeks one who listens
to the crickets skittering into night's
deep ear. One who opens
his mouth to the rain. One who knows
that tenderness alone can break
open the smell of the earth.

Noel King

Even the Dogs Drink Beer Here

In The Blue Lagoon café of
Stockholm's *Gamla Stan* / Old City
she pushes her dog
and pulls a shopping trolley
– in the city for the day
from God knows where.
The plush building is all blue light,
posers and composed and rock-musiced.
She ties the dog to the leg of a table,
her eyes darting everywhere,
eye contact with everyone,
duck-walks to the counter, and orders a beer.
Cautious, she takes it to the table,
pours some into cupped hands
for the dog to lap; laughing
diners watch behind hands
muse upon her origins, and me;
I spill coffee right down into my crotch.

Noel King

Three Collies

Nickie was black and white
and grew bigger than me. I know this
only from photos we used have.
He got killed I was told, by Dad
reversing the car on him in the dark.

Billy was black and white, a bitch
actually. Can't figure why we called her that,
Mam and Dad laughed. Billy would meet me
on the road from school, got burned alive
by fellas down the avenue, Halloween night.

Barney is black and white. He has behavioural attitudes.
My baby sister named him. She is fourteen now,
alone at home with Mam; couldn't care less about
the dog. Dad lives in England.

The vet will have to put Barney down, Mam says,
I can't take him, I'm in Boarding School now
and pets aren't allowed. I am sad. When I finish,
and have my own place, I will have another Collie
I'll take my time choosing its name, a proper name.

Fred Johnston

Le Chien Malade

Il a tombé malade, mon chien
il n'a pas un voix —

le monde chante
ses douleurs violentes

dans un monde pareil
mon ami souffre en privé —

il dort et il songe
des choses le plus simples

il ne connait pas
les rêves minables

et barbares, des gens
qui n'ont pas des âmes

sous la croix gammée
il prend la nourriture

qui les soldats lui offrent;
même sous le crucifix il mange:

le ramoneur et le politicien
lui donnent des os à manger

et, sous un fascisme parfait
il trouve des abats

parmi les briques
de maisons abandonnées —

il protège son âme
contre leurs péchés brutals

les péchés humains
qui hurlent dans les rues:

mon pauvre,
je veux qu'un chien

juge ce monde: enterres-le,
dans sa propre merde lépreuse.

A Sick Dog

My dog fell ill
But he has no way of talking about it

The world sings
Of its violent agonies

In a parallel world
He suffers in private –

He sleeps, dreams
of very simple things

He is unaware
of the shabby and

The brutal side of life
of men without souls

Under a Swastika
He eats away

At what soldiers give him
as he would under the sign of the crucifix

The street-sweeper
and the politician offer him a bone

And, under the solid fascism
of bankers, he finds offal

Among the stone-work
of abandoned houses –

He guards his soul
against appalling sins

Human sins
that howl in the streets

My old buddy, I want
a dog

to judge the world: bury it
under its own leprous dung.

(Translated from the French by Fred Johnston)

Holly J. Hughes

The Wounded Dog Theory: My Dog Responds

"Powder of sympathy" could heal at a distance – apply it to an article of the wounded person and it will heal the wound. But it causes pain as it does this, so they came up with the idea of sending a wounded dog aboard the ship. A trusted individual would dip the dog's bandage in the powder precisely at noon and the dog would then yelp, letting the captain know that "the sun is upon the meridian in London."

Dava Sobel, *Longitude*

The grid's one thing, but really, the wacky ways we've made our way.
History stacked with stories but consider what's left out.

Those wounded dogs, for instance. Did they come with wounds
or were they wounded? Did dogs apply for this position?

Imagine the job description. *Wanted: dogs that bark only when in pain.*
What about dogs that bark at tax collectors, bright arc of ball?

Was punishment meted if a stray let slip a yelp?
Did the ship sail in circles until the dog next cried out?

I imagine ships sailing, captains hanging on every bark:
Noon in London? Time for a walk? He must consult the chart.

I turn to my dog, read this account.
He whines in sympathy, clearly wants out.

Adam Houle

After Watching a K-9 Assault Demonstration at Lackland AFB, 1967

Back north, we'd praise soft teeth
in a dog, and a sleek body
paddling a steaming marsh at dawn,
a golden eye nested between
the gentle jaws that could but didn't
splinter bone into the meat.

Our best dog kept the bird unbruised,
that's what my father taught.
He held up in the blind's half-light
each drake or hen Sissy brought in
and twisted the wing to gauge how hard
she clutched the bird. She got good

quick, sparse praise alone urging
her release. He'd say, *That's how it's done.*
I believed him. Believed I always would.

Adam Houle

Nomenclature

If I bred shepherds they'd take their names
from your favourite things. Desert Rose and Sandstone,
the only two welcome in my home. The only two
I'd collar. The rest kenneled and pacing
the same worn patch of silty loam until I'd walk
the dogs into woods, loose them on ground squirrel.

Your postcards come. You've found yourself or something
close, I suppose. I tape them over nail holes, where paint
we laid together has peeled, and sheetrock freckles
like eggshell. From the kitchen sink, I see the runs
I'd make from cyclone fence and cars parked
on the road's shoulder to witness my fine dogs.

I can almost see you, back with no notice, pulling
the grass I let sprout between flagstones and tufts
bunched at the mailbox's base. The dogs whine.
They press their fences, pop the gates, and rush
your hands, eager for the music in your voice,
eager to prove that all you love is already named.

Adam Houle

Begging Home a Stray

I'm told this county coughs
its dogs up roadside, whole litters
left in a burst of exhaust, road
dust, as if loss could be lessened
by the simple acts of recurrence.
At the park, though, it's just one
brindle pit, a four-finger gap
between his eyes, shrunk withers
like razor blades in the high
headlights of trucks, a red
sun just cresting the low clouds.
So I call to him, say *treats, ride.*
Say, *you're a good boy, let's go
home now.* My heart's odometer
rolls over to zeros, and still
he'll have none of it, shies
thin hips away as I ease closer.
Oh, shovel-head, oh bull terrier
of our interminable nights, try
to believe there's home yet to come
home to, a vast and verdant yard.
Think of the tennis balls, the rope
toys, the instinct that drives you
to love the tug-of-war. And prairies,
dog, where you run for running's sake,
grasses trembling with all you have
left unnamed. I'll call out your new name
as you scent the far-ranging winds
for rumour of all that has been
lost. Look at me, damnit, all the roads
we follow can lead us homeward.

Diana Thurbon

The Dog in the Crate

*The story of Chok Dee (formerly Haan), rescued by the Soi Dog
Foundation, and his rehoming to America*

The brown dog fills his hospital cage,
Twists around, turns his head, and grins at me.
I gently push a liver treat through the bars.
He gulps, and grateful grins again. I see!
I find another – we could do this all day.
I notice bandages wound round his legs,
"What's wrong with him?" I softly say.

Reggie replies, "He has cuts, a broken back."
"Can they?" "No! The vets can't fix his spine:
hit by a car – now he drags along the concrete track.
The nerves in his back will never align."
So, he'll never walk. I'm in a Buddhist place
I know he will be cared for – allowed to live.
I pass a second treat; see the smiling face

again; gobbling gulping grinning.
As I sprawl beside his cage, rub silk ears,
I see tomorrows sadly – my Spirit spinning.
I visit him again. I'm filled with fears,
But the dog is in his present moment,
His eyes sparkle though his tail is still
He licks my hand; joyful spirit, but I lament.

Sometimes souls forge strong connections;
There is no turning – no walking away,
Putting bits of life in forgotten sections.
And I have seen a place on another day,
a sanctuary – where lame pets run free.
I'll find a place like that – I know I will.
I whisper, "You will run, you will see."

Worth the strife and struggle – every bit.
So many donate. It's soon now that he will fly
Legs sprawled in front he will somehow sit
in his airline crate. Sleepy eyes – a sigh.
He cannot know, that his wheels await –
That soon he will play, have fun and run.
But he will, and I know it's great.

Diana Thurbon

Siam - A Thai Stray

The sun goes down, dark, sudden, tropical, over all
the barren, sea-wet rocks exposed by tide.
The tourists and her shelter deck chairs gone – night will fall.
She curls up small and sandy; all alone she will abide.

I lament that a different life she will never know.
Her puppy-hood is solitude and scraps,
she scavenges her patch up and down, to and fro.
Always tired, this chocolate brown dog naps.

Sunday morning I watch – people
walk past her – laughing, eating, uncaring.
Then they go to their prayers in the temple; steeple
their hands in prayer. Pointless ritual, all un-sharing.

I give my new friend some bacon, rub an ear.
I *hate* the people who don't see starvation at their feet.
A passer says to me "Careful they bite." I wipe a tear,
"She is starving!" "Nah they do OK on the beach or the street."

She is just ONE dog, I know. All over Asia they forage and fret
cats and dogs with scabs and sores. No one sees. No one cares.
Just another homeless pup. At home her cousin sleeps on my bed,
I can't understand. I rub her ears, rub my eyes and my heart tears.

Siam was rescued by the Soi Dog Foundation

Amy Holman

Or, Something

I don't know myself, at all, I am certain
of nothing. Why do I say exactly what I mean
and add, or something? My favourite English professor
my senior year tried to tell me during the evaluation of my thesis
that all my poems about my women friends were love poems,
that he knew me better than I did. As if a woman couldn't want to be
like her friends and like them as they were and like to write
portraits of women, without that sexual bit.
I was betrayed and muffled because I wasn't myself yet, and plus
my advocate in the room was rumoured lesbian and living
straight, adjunct faculty, to boot, muzzled by the power play. Also,
too, I often failed to capture the attention of men I liked, a cubist
at the impressionist party. The professor did grant me
honours after dishonouring me. That's power,
or something. He was dating the French professor
who lectured on feminism and had a high-pitched, little girl voice.
She was my best friend's advisor and once asked her
when she proudly displayed my winning poem,
"Oh, is she really serious about writing?" Yet, we'd never met.
I was skimming the surface of writing, skimming the surface of being,
or something. Now, I'm certain being uncertain is good
for the brain, mystery refining the clues to how we change.
I had a dog, recently, who walked me into every scene
that made me uneasy because he was certain the world was open –
outside the corner bar where the sexy platinum guy shot pool,
the bookstore that could stock my chapbook, the mafia
block's patio crowd. He took my shyness from me and when
arthritic in old age, reclined on sidewalks, drawing
visitors to us, teaching me. Never be restricted, never be depicted,
be love. This poem reveals my bestiality.

Amy Holman

Drawing Near

after paintings by Philippe Vasseur

You were home asleep
so you arrived only as a sketch
on my afternoon.
I walked away as you sat
looking at the sea.
I really want to be with you,
and I walked away.

*

I dreamt my lean dog
died while I was far away
because someone
shocked me
by thinking I was cruel.
My lean retriever is a dusty one lane
road, he disappears in being
alike. Weeks
after my misleading
dream, he's been very
reassuring, appearing in outline
on every street I lonely walk.
When I wounded
my right foot, he started
favouring his lefts,
appearing in being alike.

*

The rails my brother
always liked end broken
by the sea. After inviting me
over he and his wife

keep talking to each other,
and I could be a photograph.
I took the train. Only now do I see
the rails curving around a bend
ended, we passengers riding
into our versions of life.

*

A man brushes
against another man down
at the port of call; he is unfinished
and that is the freight
the brother carries by being
complete. It figures that
this is how I've learned to love,
lingering too long for a way
to be retrieved when I'm not gone.

*

No explanation is offered for
keeping broken track yet here I am
keeping track of broken ties –
tense, furious. I have been trained
to disappear to reappear,
a present perfect for anyone
looking. I'm nearly there.
What I rail against is broken by the seen.

Kevin Higgins

Regime Change

No more sitting on white window sills
minding our own whiskers.
The age of cat is over. Now comes
the community of dogs.

Sniffing each other's backsides
is the new global greeting. No more
sitting on white window sills. The daily news
a sound only we can hear. We do

all our business in the public park
and don't care who sees us. No more
sitting on white window sills. In the name
of loyalty we go happily after

our master's kill, return
with peacocks between our teeth. Our walks
always someone else's idea. No more
minding our own whiskers
whitely on a window sill
we thought belonged to us,
now the community of dogs
has come.

Patrick Hicks

Nose Cone

When Pan Am 103 exploded over Lockerbie, Scotland,
a rainstorm of bolts, seats, and bodies cometed through the sky,
spewing out a debris field that punched the earth.
Men combed the ground, finding loved ones here
and there, gathering them up for funerals.
Cadaver dogs were brought out and they shepherded
the last pieces of human tissue into steel coffins.
    A dusting of peace settled onto the town.

But the jet fuel was an invisible fog in the grass,
and it filled up these dogs with cancer. They died,
one after the other, in quick succession,
which made the whole town grieve
in a way they hadn't yet done for the passengers.
A great outpouring was attached to these dogs
who bent their snouts to the ground,
hoping to fill themselves up with our scent,
hoping to please us even though the nose cone
lay smashed in the distance.

Richard W. Halperin

I didn't think I could be this kind of happy, my dear, ever again

A nervous woman and a solid block of blue
sea. The sea twittered, the woman waited,
the sun promised nothing. 'I thought I was just born,'
she said, 'yet I watch in a wheelchair. What happened in-between?'
A dog ran along the shore. 'Emery,' the woman said. 'My dog.'
'Never yours, let's be clear about that,' said the dog.
'I was what love is,' then cut out over the solid blue
to behind the sun. 'Why no one else?' she said to no one else.
'Surely I loved my husband, my child, my par-ee-ants more.'

The sea twittered, the woman waited.

'Why my dog?' 'Arf,' Emery corrected. 'Why Emery?' she said.
'I was four when I got him.' 'Arf,' Emery corrected.
'When we were,' she said.
'Do we only have here the one we loved the bestiest, just the one?
Or the one that loved us the very bestiest?
You'd have thought Susan would have been someone here now.'

'Arf,' something said.

'Well,' she said, 'I've plenty of time to think about it.'

Richard W. Halperin

Our Cassie

The signs were up all over Glendalough for a year.
'Has anyone seen our Cassie?'

There followed
A brief description of the world's most lovable dog,
With faded colour snapshot to prove to anyone with eyes to see.

I read it. The valley shook (and not for the first time).
Years before, months after my wife, yes, had died –
ashes scattered, hugs received, wonderful letters reread,
phonecalls 'You OK?' levelling off –
I'd been walking thinking of nothing in particular; a boon, that;
When I got exactly the same impulse as Cassie's owners.
The only sensible thing to do, really.

Desmond Gough

The Lama's Dog

Talking about reincarnation,
one can come back as a dog.
That could be your primary karma.
But then again
there is secondary karma which could make you
The Lama's dog.
So you would have a comfortable armchair
to meditate,
a warm bed to sleep,
the company of humans,
a dish of water waiting for you
on every floor,
the best of dog food,
the company of women,
someone to open the door for you
and expansive lawns on which to pass water.

A better life than many.
Why you'd be on the pig's back.

Whose dog
do you want to be reborn as?

Desmond Gough

Words of Wisdom from My Master

Look at the word GOD.
If you spell it backwards
It says DOG.
There is no escaping this fact.

Peter Joseph Gloviczki

queen-size bed
the dog lets me
sleep there too

Philip Fried

Theogony

First was the spinning Wheel of Fortune,
travelling through the fair-going throng,
dogging the heels of the lucky one.
I felt it roll to my palm, and nuzzle,
then a barker dressed like a checkerboard
told everyone to circle round me.

There on a flimsy, folding table,
he stitched blue eyes to a pelt of cotton,
which he stuffed with straw and cups of sawdust.
He stroked and sewed this rag until
it leapt in my arms, yapped, and wriggled,
dangling a red lappet of tongue.

This toy became my revered companion,
guard, and guide to the language of wolves.
Smoothing it to my cheek, I listened
into the cavernous dark of its innards
where the unremitting, random howls
mixed with an acrid chemical musk.

NOTE: The stuffed dog is theriomorphic, a deity in the form of a beast.

Janice Fitzpatrick Simmons

Cocoon

I love to walk on the strand with my old,
good dog and my son on a warm day in September.
The pain of my husband's death is still present and
walks with us on the cooling sand. We walk far
and throw stones for our dog who is blind and deaf,
and over protective. I thank God for what I have
and there is a sort of peace that comes with grief
after the cocoon falls away and you stand naked,
shaking before the future. Nothing will ever be the same.
You don't want it to be. Let change come. Let the changes
come, let them all be good ones.

John Fitzgerald

Seven

I used to try and trick my dog.
I'd sneak up the driveway, on the other side of the brick wall.
There was no way he could see me, and I was quiet, catlike.
I could hear him sniffing, but he wouldn't bark.
At first, I thought I won the game. Later, I figured it out.
He not only knew someone was there, he knew it was me.
Hell, he knew what colour socks I was wearing.
He could smell bones through flesh.
He could smell straight up your ass and into your soul.

J.P. Dancing Bear

Dog

for Jack Large

first off: Dog knows you are watching: as you should be: even when you are trying to hide your observance of Dog: because Dog is the centre of everything: is the universe: the world: the fountain in the desert of your life: an unending isle of wet-tongued delights: he is the one true Dog: all others are false dogs: not worthy of your attention: Dog is watching: you and over you: when you confide in him: he cocks his head at you: Dog says *enough about you: scratch behind my ears*: it is always very humbling to be in the presence of Dog

J.P. Dancing Bear

Man with Dog

for Jonathan Kevin Rice

Most of the time the man is a shadow in the dog's life: even now
trundling the sidewalks the man is minor tension on the leash: dog
has to make the most of these times: there is the business of dogliness:
a world (no matter how concrete) to smell: stop for other like-minds:
it's all wags and chuffs this close to the ground: the man follows at
the dog's leisure: scent of discards: all things making ways to the sewers:
dog listens to the music coming up from the grate like some Ophic
dog rising up from love

J.P. Dancing Bear

Dog in the World

for Jessie Lendennie

you say *there is something about a dog: that reflects the rest of the world*: in its perked up ears: wagging tail: ready for the next moment's joy: certain it will come: and the dog reflects the eagerness of the dog: off every appendage: as though its coat is one of mirrors: a million moments of happiness all within one moment: as the tail reflects the image of the ears: reflecting the body and the tail again: until the whole of the dog is: shimmying with excitement: and you cannot help but smile: which is reflected back at you: from so many different parts: and angles: of the dog

Dallas Crow

Regret

Despite the date on the divorce decree,
I think the marriage ended when we gave
the dog away (the lab who sometimes shared
our bed, our seven year old son's best friend)

because of your supposed allergies,
which apparently aren't triggered by your
new beau's dog (who barks at me — the stranger
at my old house — when I pick up my sons).

In retrospect, perhaps it was a test:
what kind of guy gives away his son's dog
for a lying woman he never really knew?

Dallas Crow

Separated

The kicked dog forgives the foot,
so I whimper, wag, hope – return.
I want to roll on my back,
and offer you my throat, but

my man-brain keeps intruding:
Not the throat! Anything but that.
The world is my doghouse now,
but you're my only home.

Nahshon Cook

April

1.

I woke up with the thought that my brother
must have already fed them

because the sound of her nibbling on kibbles
drug me outta sleep like a rope being pulled to shore,

before I opened my eyes, sat up, put my house shoes on
over my socks, and walked up the stairs into the kitchen

where she lay on the Diamond Limestone Chalk linoleum floor
with her blue trimmed, yellow glaze ceramic bowl

in between her white feather laced front legs:
elbows flat, chest heartwarming the ground, belly arched a bit,

knees up and hocks down on the outside of either
of her wide sista-hips, as if on command.

2.

When told her good morning, she, all at once,
opened fully her half-shut eyelids, feverishly
wiggled her little docked nub of a tail from side-to-side,
and perked her politely folded back ears heavenward,
before gobbling down the rest of her breakfast
in a scramble to her feet so that she could give me a hug.

And she did! I told her how much I loved her. She snorted
and dug her claws into my back, right at the belt-line.
I leaned forward to give her a peck on the forehead.
She slung her paws over my shoulders and licked my chin
in a quick slobbery swipe of the tongue.

I sat on the ground. – And before rolling over
in my lap so that I could scratch her belly,
she freakishly drew back her inky black lips
and bore her teeth in an happy, ugly doggie smile.

Susan Cohen

Yowl

True to his wolfish heart, that dog next door
bares his teeth, yips from his rooftop,

poised to jump me as if I'm a burglar
at my own gate. He's got it all:

territory and certainty; surefootedness,
not to mention lungs, to be a pack of one.

He also howls when I play jazz, his notes
outlasting John Coltrane's.

Sometimes I laugh and say, that dog can swing.

Sometimes I yell: Dumb dog, how many years
before you know where I belong?

But he just barks when I pull up, barks
as I'm unlocking my front door, until I fumble

like the stranger he knows I am. He's so sure
that I've come home to the wrong life.

I wonder if his ear can catch my true life swinging
somewhere else, improvising without me.

However long I live, it won't be long enough.
I'll still be longing, that same dumb human longing.

Next door, a different dog will bark.

Jennifer Clark

Lives Overlapped

She does not want to break the chain
of knowing him so

to touch the past
each dog is obtained
while the current one lives.

May each, she prays, pass down
the memory of the first one:
a curled up, resting-in-his-lap memory,
upon ever thinning legs, covered in Hayband pants
the man had ordered from Reader's Digest.

Enveloped in the cherry smell of his pipe and
lulled by the television's steady hum,
the dog observes lazily with one eye
as the man's lips form an O and
release puffs of cloudy, white rings;
the girl attempts to marry this moment,
reaches high above her head and slips
a tiny finger into already vanishing rings.

She does not want to break this chain
of knowing him.

Sandra Bunting

Old Cats

After an absence I return
to discover the passing away
of several old cats of my acquaintance,
missing parts of the landscape now
at the homes of different friends.

I thought they'd never disappear
but go they did, and the names
Sultana and Georgie won't be called
and I'll not be asked to mind them
when their owners go away again.

Even old dogs are getting older,
parts not working as they used to,
and I sense a quivering in the air
as if my ghostly terrier is around,
digging up flowers at the university,
chasing blowing leaves, and old cats.

Megan Buckley

Seventh son of a seventh son

In a September night in a concrete kennel,
in the presence of a dozen baying greyhounds,
we watch him work. You lean against the wall,
I perch on a dirty upturned bucket.
For once, you are silent.

We watch him hold each dog between his legs,
see him divine where the problem lies
in each lithe body – spine, paw, knee, joint;
he feels the error with his fingers,
then, with his butcher's grip, he twists
the pain into each animal and out again.
You and I learn the art of reticence, so unnatural to us both;
we learn to hold our breaths together.

We learn that he effs and blinds while he works,
grunts punctuated with "fuck"'s;
we learn that healing is guttural,
all dirt and sacrifice,
and that dogs scream in human voices when they suffer.

Later, you tell me he is proud, but I tell you he is humble;
it took years to realign the clean bones
of his own life to accommodate the healer's curse.
Now, at forty, the physician cannot heal himself;
the animal aches have pushed him far into old age.
And you and I, amid the smell of hurt and fur,
learn our own craft of the hands;
to let the suffering come.

Eva Bourke

In Duiche Iar

The fields were no larger than the green envelopes
our dead-and-gone Greek teachers used
to post reprimands to our parents.

We climbed stone-walls, got lost in a maze,
round every corner we feared the minotaur
might come crashing through brambles

but, as luck would have it, we met face to face
only the serene local bull,
a youngster with six female dependants.

In Duiche Iar light dripped from rocks, the tarmac
glittered in thousands of punctures,
the mountains were studded with pinpoints of silver.

Thigh-deep in marsh reeds we watched the Atlantic
turn over once more on its back.
I don't know why the crows reminded me of seminarians,

maybe because they were huddled together, celibate,
starving and black in the one tree
not blown inside out by the storm

which crashed raging against a bolted gate
somewhere beyond the hills,
bundled us through the graveyard

where the dead in their coffin ships
were slowly sinking towards bedrock.
We were amazed at an old sand stealer

who with his donkey was busy rearranging
the planet, a job more futile, we thought
than that of Kind Sisyphus.

On Duiche Iar strand the sea rolled up
a scroll with its signature in fresh blue ink
left urchin shells dotting the shore

white a fairy skulls and as bald,
we could see the stitch holes of elfin embroidery
where their needle work was unpicked.

In Duiche Iar we discovered dogs own six senses or more
and all the boreens. One appeared to us
out of thin air, tailed us wherever we went

to shield us from harm, barked at anything
that moved, the neighbour's Labrador,
a tractor rattling past. We knew well

we couldn't take a step without her
and submitted counting our blessings
this windfall of kindness on such rocky ground.

Let our companions on our travels always be like her
with her wind-blown coat
in true local colour, black and white,

her tilted left ear and her unlikely eyes,
one a deep liquid brown
the other blue and changeable as her native sea.

He dark eye saw a future raught with danger,
her blue eye looked into a world
where metamorphoses were commonplace as rocks

gods walked on hind-legs, stars fell into tin pails
and the ends of the earth
rested on the shoulders of mongrels.

Drew Blanchard

Winter Dogs

Tonight, in a sudden wind, the sky vanished
into an ashen wall: winter's first snow, heads covered
in wet-white; and in peoples eyes, not a glinting exactly,
but an acceptance of autumns passing, and the first flakes

undeniable magic. And at the Mayakovskaya stop,
a babushka drowning in the weight of her woolly dress
and gray head-wrap, hunched against the metro steps;
the cavernous descent as impressive as the yellow-blue

mosaics depicting Soviet fighter-planes and socialist warriors
with ornamental machine guns. Stalin said the metro stations
were the palaces of the people. And on these palace steps,
the babushka, staring up at the colourless sky, repeated,

to the constant swish of legs – square-shoed businessmen
smoking cigarettes and teenagers shoving through the mobs –
Pomagee karmeet sabaki (Please help me feed these dogs.)
She had five hounds tied to the handrail. Each one skilled

in the art of sadness, each a master of the frown, cringe and whimper.
Above her, a steady drip of melted sidewalk snow, the steaming
warmth from women behind kiosks selling bruised fruit,
blini and pelmeni. The dogs knew the routine well:

go for eye contact, begin whining two feet before the passing legs.
Then from below, beyond the shadows of the escalators,
a chorus of voices splashed into the snow-flaked air of the city.
Four young men emerged into the shadowed light,

sprawling in all directions, their arms locked at the elbows
like a chain link fence blowing in the wind. As they approached
the babushka, one of the dogs, agitated from the clamour,
began to panic and knocked over her bucket of change,

sailing it down the steps. The woman whacked the dog with a paper.
One of the young men flung his bottle of beer at the woman,
screamed, "Idiot!" The bottle shattered on the wall above her head.
Two of the dogs broke free and ran into the gray night.

Richard Berengarten

from The Manager

He's a lurcher not a whippet, said Steve, shifting his bulk from his
   bar stool to pat the creature's head. Nice colouring, eh. It's that
   white patch over the eye gives him that wistful look.

He can sniff out a pheasant at 300 yards. Go for it like Casanova.
   A little on the big side but he sleeps under the duvet. Don't you old
   feller. Two more Harvests and another Dubonnet please, Ray.

Watcher mean Casanova, sniffed Vicky petitely between us, nudging
   him in the ribs. At least he doesn't snore. Which is more than
   can be said for some people. Your pullover smells like a museum,

She said, and turned on me, conspiratorial. You ever seen him with
   out it. He won't let me wash it. Never takes it off. Sleeps in it
   too, you know. Says it's got Special Sentimental Value. Cobblers.

And what with him and Hound Dog here hogging the bed between
   them, it's a bleeding miracle I get any sleep at all. And in the
   morning, she said, snuggling her neck into his giant elbow

And addressing the bar at large, His breath's like a filthy ashtray.
   What I have to put up with, she sighed, I don't know why I bother.
   You're not exactly Nice, you know. Not what I'd call Respectable.

I don't know about that, I said. He looks all right to me. No nasty
   infectious diseases. And he doesn't squint or stammer. What more
   do you want. He can't help being small. What about a game of darts.

Rather watch the pro's, said Steve. 'S an international on. He
   ferried our drinks to the public bar and sat at an empty table. The
   dog wagged its tail and snoozed on its ribcage and haunches.

The TV blared in the corner. Darts is made of tungsten, confided the commentator. And you need tungsten nerves for this game. This lad's a son of Peterborough. If he wins this final or not

They're giving him a civic reception when he gets home tomorrow. If he was my son I tell you I'd give him Peterborough. I hear they show Shakespeare on BBC 2. But you can't beats darts for drama.

His table manners aren't bad, said Vicki. And, true, he hasn't got rabies. He's just a great big healthy animal. Aren't you eh, Midget. What about foot and mouth, said Steve. Disgusting man, she said.

Marck L. Beggs

Still Life With Farmer With Hangover

Last night, I dreamed that I woke up inside
the burn-barrel. A smouldering hangover
itched deep in my brain.
No, I woke up as our youngest dog
learning the hard lesson of a tractor
bumped over his neck.

Actually, I can't remember. My neck
is sore, pain clear to my brain.
Outside the window, morning is a pink dog
licking my face with its dry tongue. From inside,
I stare out towards the iced-gleam of my tractor.
The garden is dead, there are leaves to turn over

into mulch, dirt-food. Autumn is over,
as winter sets in with its thick-necked, hair-of-dog
warmth. Boiler makers pulse through my brain,
twitching lightly at my limbs, spine, and neck.
I don't feel young anymore, feel beside
myself: fumbling with my overalls, stumbling out to the tractor.

Red, Canadian, built in '48, a damn good tractor.
Thirty-nine years old, and I drive this Ferguson over
two-hundred acres of land, king of everything this side
of some living, breathing swamp swarming with moccasins, wild dogs,
and mosquitoes—I imagine a black helmet of them fitting my head
    and neck,
opening veins and arteries, blood-letting my brain.

But this is winter, after all, even more numb than my brain.
The insects are asleep, as are the snakes, although the dogs
live on, glare-eyed and hungry. Their thin necks

stiffen in the frost like a branch leaning over,
about to break. From my tractor,
I pity them: their wild and bony sides.

Cranking the engine, I feel the knot in my own side
creak like a rusty screw. When the engine kicks over,
at last, I look back, once more, past the tractor,
to the dogs lifting howls from deep in their throats.
My fingertips push against my temples, touch brain,
thinking, this truly is a dog's life. When I see one dog,

tall as my tractor, on the north side of the swamp,
staring over at me: a Great Dane, limping and jerking its neck
in distress, watching me shut the eye's brain.

Marck L. Beggs

This Lesson

I ought to move. The half-schnauzer
lockjawed to my knee still foams
while I lumber about like Ahab
on his whale-bone. So I've been sitting,
a lot lately, thinking about
sex and time-zones and how
if we could fuse them we might never fall.
How we might never die,
or if we did, how it would take forever at least.
But the only thing I discern of physics
is that apple knocking on Newton's door.
Every great fall is a delicacy. Sin, gravity,
we suck them dry over breakfast.
We garnish them with logic and personal
amnesties against the odds of our own undoings.
We write *areopagiticae* to allow for our imminent
fuckfacedness. My dog doesn't get it. He wants to know
why his leash is so long and how many
hours he will have to strain against it.
I explain how it keeps him from
discovering the natural selection of
the front grill of a truck. He drools on my leg.
I could take him for a walk along the sidewalk
of Burnt Weenies, of Aimless Children on Skateboards,
of Turtle Wax in the Sun, but then
I think we fare well lounging on this porch,
staring up wide-eyed into a fall of sparrow-shit,
pondering how far away it comes.

Paul Barclay

Communication Skills

it's partly their long useful fingers
that make raccoons, like humans
appear to be intelligent
like it or not, it's telling us something
when they open doors or garbage cans with such ease
dolphins don't have this advantage
and thus don't manipulate much
or make or use tools but
by swimming in tricky patterns
and emitting a certain aura
they get their rather sophisticated point of view across.
birds do it by shitting on those they preach to
at appointed times
and once a dog, having found a new kink in our old sock game
ran fast around me 10 times, barking
it wasn't just excitement
that he was communicating.
indeed, he was demonstrating an insight
into the very nature of things

Michael Augustin

In a Pavement Café

The fat lady who walks by with a little dog, stands still all of a sudden, pulls a gun out of her handbag and shoots twice into the air. Then, she takes the frightened animal on her arm and scuttles away. "She did that on purpose!" says the waiter. "Otherwise the dachshund would never have allowed her to have him on her arm." "But she was really having him on, ha, ha!" I say jokingly. "You're right," says the waiter, "and lucky! Because sometimes she forgets to shoot into the air, and simply fires straight ahead. Last week, for example, she accidentally shot a young man who sat there exactly where you are sitting now." "Oh," I say, "then these are not wine stains on the tablecloth?" "Hell no!" says the waiter as he walks away, "that's blood!" At that moment, I see the fat lady just turning around the corner again. Next to her trots the dachshund. "The bill," I call out, "but please hurry!"

Michael Augustin

Dog

This supposedly selfless little dog, who for weeks, yes, even for months, holds out by the grave of his master and doesn't even feel like touching his bowl of food: a shrewd beast, cold-bloodedly seeking nothing but his own advantage, a hypocritical mutt who simply knows exactly where the best bones are hidden.

Scott Edward Anderson

Redbud & Pitbull

The mining bees are emerging.
Males zipping around
tiny holes in the ground
where females are burrowing
beneath the redbud.
The males have a curious display;
more manic than romantic,
expecting a mate to think crazy
is sexy or superior.

I guess we all
fall prey to a little crazy
love now and again,
do something foolish,
cross a line or two.
But the bees flying too close
to the ground are just frantic,
can't imagine they'd make
suitable mates.

They course and dive and zip
(yes, that's the best word for it, *zip*),
while females wait below the redbud.
My pitbull Calvin watches
the mining bees swirling
above and into the ground
beneath the redbud. He thinks,
Who or what are these (things)
buzzing and drilling in the dirt?

Truth is, the mining bees
– neither food nor friend –
pay him little interest.

Now Calvin grows bored,
slopes over to the sidewalk
flopping down in the sun.
The redbud's waxy leaves
glisten in the same sun,
green edging into red.

Calvin is mottled, piebald,
brindle and white with a big brown
eye patch that makes people smile.
He's a lover, not a fighter.
He cares little why the redbud's shock
of fuscia flowers, like scales or
a rash running up the limbs hasn't shown.
He has no word for flowers
and little time for bees.

Jane Blanchard

A Dog Howls

A dog howls when it hurts.
As a passing siren strikes its ears,
It lifts its head and sounds its pain.
It doesn't wonder what its owners will do;
It doesn't worry what its neighbours will think;
It doesn't even know the reason for the noise
Interrupting its usual repose –
Whether a house has burned
Or a heart has stopped,
Whether there's a wreck down the road
Or a thief on the run.
It only knows what it feels,
And it doesn't hold back –
A dog howls when it hurts.

Aimée Sands

Dawdle and Scent

Mawkish beast, gaiety at a gallop,
rogue, tongue-dweller, regular soccer-mutt,
what stench did you rut in today, mongrel
of the compost, muzzle caked with smut, coax me
at the door, reckless badger of the brook, snouty one,
remorseful one, high-fours atop a squirrel,
musty, pokey girl: come calling, calling me,
come calling where I whimper. Come, Molly, come.

Ilsa Thielan

My Brother

Moon is rising
amber
in the dog's eyes
mirror
of an ancient spirit

they hunted you
killed you
projecting their fears
and darkness
onto you
brother wolf

moon is rising
amber
in the wolf's eyes
mirror
of gentleness
mirror
of wisdom
and light

Simmons B. Buntin

Coyote

I cannot follow the river of her myth.
Perhaps Papago, or Hopi.

In legend, she was born of the sharpest
cactus – the cholla – and spread her thin

roots into the desert soil.
She broke the underground river

and blossomed into life. As punishment,
the Great One gave her thickened fur,

and naked pups. Confined
to the desert,

she was weaker than the wolf,
could not hide like the fox,

took heavy heat from the white sun.
She ate the horned toad spitting blood

into her eyes, the Gila monster leaking
venom through her veins, and the prickly pear shooting spears

through her tongue.
And she became strong.

I said, I cannot follow the river
of her myth; but I can

follow her sweet desert song
like a stream through the fiery hills.

Anatoly Kudryadivsky

3 Haiku

beach at sunrise
two red setters chasing
the shadow of a cloud

barking at a pug puppy,
his reflection
in the water bowl

first snow
a westie's eyes deeper
in her shaggy hair

Jacqueline Kolosov

Refrain

is another morning's walk, the two dogs
tugging towards the park before I've steeped
tea, or paused to comb sleep from my hair.
It is the midsummer breeze in the old dog's
rough coat, the young dog's
raspberry tongue along my ankles,
the pungency of just-cut grass
between my sandaled toes. Refrain
is the harnessing shape of *hush now*,
slow down, and *go get it!* The search
for throwing-sticks, the chaos
of leashes tethering tired legs.

After rain, circles weave around
puddles, inca doves flurry away, and paws
splash through pools. But refrain
is also the morning I will wake, not
to the duet of just-contained barking
rushed out of the quick-bang screen door,
but to the body of the old dog
buried beneath the climbing rose.
To the young dog's surrender
of her sunflower of joy.
On that day, refrain will become a woman
salting her hands and feet
in the hopes of recovering the kisses
she once dared to push away.

In Old French, *refrain* is the restraint
I must surrender to this gift
of another morning's walk, the pair
who love without asking why

yearning towards the live oaks and willows,
and above the trees, a migrant hawk
bearing its way
into the heart of a red-shouldered wind.

Jeanne Wagner

Conversation and Its Discontents

When people start talking *dog*, I tell them how each morning my own dog grovels with delight; the Sun King, at his leveé, never had it so good. But also, I tell them about nights when he's barking mad, the raccoons ignoring him as they grapple their way up the tree. How his feet scumble and skid, his nails etching graffiti into my hardwood floor. How the coons taunt him, playing god through the skylights, fixing him with their implacable stares, their ghostly posturing, watching as he flings himself against the sliding glass door. They have a sixth sense for invisible walls, the raccoons! But these people who talk to me about their dogs only look sorrowful and confused. After all, they've been talking of love. They wonder why I've unburdened myself this way; should they offer their tips on dog-training, their acrylic floor polish, their prayers? Some reach out in sympathy, one arm extended tentatively, as if they're about to pet a stranger's dog, to brush their hand along its unfamiliar coat. Their faces leaning near, their breath clouding up the glass.

Theodore Deppe

Orla

One moment she is a leggy girl of ten, walking the strand alone, invincible,
the next she's peering over the rails of a hospital bed, waking

as her husband sits up in his chair, wrapped in a fraying blanket.
She greets him with the smile of one about to go under the knife,

and he says, *Do you remember talking about a sheltie dog last night?*
She shakes her head, and he says, *You started talking about this little silky*

dog, you said it was sort of a sheltie dog, and dressed in the finest furs, regally
dressed. I asked if you were dreaming, and you said, Yes, maybe I am.

This morning, she can't remember, tries to be sure
he's not making fun of her, but he's delighted by her words,

a silky dog, sort of a sheltie…No, she says, *I don't remember,*
but just now I was on a beach, I was a girl again,

and five friends, all of them up to their knees in surf,
started calling Orla! Orla!—that was my name.

Still in my clothes I joined them, and standing in the sea, I knew
that even if life stopped then, I'd been happy being Orla.

He considers his wife's new name, says, *Strange world, isn't it?*
and she says, *It is, but I'd like to stay around,*

and he wets her lips with a sponge, that much he can do,
then pictures her as a girl, as Orla, watches from a dune

as she and her friends run across the sand—it's low tide
and the beach reaches almost forever—he listens to their laughter

until they're so far off he can't hear them,
and there's only the larks and the far-off surf and their silhouettes,

the shadow play of happiness at the sea's edge.

Annie Deppe

Shelter

1.

In the harbour's new shop,
        a place geared
towards tourists, I find
        a crate of etchings

made by a woman
        from the next island.
In one, a small stone house
        hunkers

under a black onslaught
        of diagonal cuts.
This one interests me,
        I tell the girl

who minds shop. *The one*
        with the night? she asks.
But what I see is lashing rain.
        Is March storm. Is

shelter in a howler
        of a gale. I want
to show you
        but you are up the hill

trying to finish a poem
        of how we almost
lost each other
        in our own black spring.

2.

When we were twenty,
     to escape
our landlady's eyes
     we bicycled

out of Sligo and camped
     above Lough Gill.
We rigged a plastic sheet
     for shelter.

Two things I remember
     from that night:
the way we woke to find
     the full moon

beneath which we'd earlier
     made love
eclipsed
     to a rust red ring,

and how by morning
     our sleeping bags
were drenched
     despite the plastic sky.

3.

Something in me
     doesn't understand
why, instead of my friend, I'm here
     walking past his home.

The same March day I drifted
     on the operating table in Boston,
this island friend died.
     I'd been back on Cape Clear

almost a week
        before I felt ready to wander
through knee-high grass
        looking for his grave.

4.

Last year
        I couldn't comprehend
why every poem I wrote
        seemed ringed by death.

After our old dog Seamus
        died, I hoped
those poems would stop.
        Summer evenings

when our children were young
        we'd set up elaborate games
of croquet. Seamus
        would crouch on the sidelines

trembling with excitement
        until, no longer able to stand it,
he'd swoop through
        and make off

with someone's wooden ball.
        For the length of the game
we renamed Seamus *Fate*,
        and if he took a ball

and ran with it
        we had to play it where it lay.

Annie Deppe

Snapshot, Collioure

Late afternoon and the dirty
white walls of Collioure's back streets
are warmed to the same pink
as the flowers we've stolen
for Antonio Machado's grave.
An Andalusian in France, his boat
forever *tied to another shore.*

The elderly couple from Barcelona
we met earlier in the market
have brought their dog to Machado's grave.
They're taking turns
pushing a baby buggy
with the raggedy spaniel stretched out within.
He's on ice, they explain, as they flip back
the blanket. *His hips are shot,*
but he does so love to see the world.

Larry O. Dean

Top of the Morning

I'm running up Dolores Street
with Gabby, my dog –
up the hill that used to seem too steep,
now the halfway mark
of my morning jogs. It's early.
    I pass the tall
woman in black sweats,

her red hair and smile
a familiar sight
as she lopes by, heading
in the opposite direction.
We exchange hellos,
friends for an instant
otherwise caught up
in our individual
rituals. At the top

      of the hill, I turn
and start along 20th Street,
waiting for Gabby as she pees,
plays and rolls in the dewy grass,
a happy animal. Fog hangs
over the city, embracing
the bay bridge in the distance,
commuters' headlights needling
through what soon will evaporate
and let the sunshine in. I watch

my breath cloud before me,
thinking of the old lady
I soon will see and wave to

who hobbles along this street,
her German-accented greetings
and praise:
          "Exercise!
For you and your dog"; also
diligent paperboys delivering
the news by foot or by bike;
the homeless asleep in the park;
and those frail-looking Mexican
women placing flowers at the feet
of the Virgin Mary who stands
in stony silence at Mission Dolores.

          *   *   *

It feels good to be alive today –
outside, sweaty and breathless –
as I begin heading home
to shower and dress for work,
later on feeling the meaningful
ache in my calves

as I rise after squatting
thirty-two floors up,
rifling through boxes
of disorganised papers.

Alexander Hutchison

Mr Scales Walks His Dog

The dog is so old dust flies out from its arse as it runs;
the dog is so old its tongue rattles in its mouth, its eyes were changed
in the 17th century, its legs are borrowed from a Louis Fourteen
bedside cabinet.
The dog is barking with an antique excitement.
Scales dog is so old its barks hang in the air like old socks,
like faded paper flowers.
It is so old it played the doorman of the Atlantic Hotel in The Last Laugh,
so old it played the washroom attendant too.
Scales dog is so old he never learned to grow old gracefully.
Scales dog bites in stages.
Scales dog smells of naphtha.
Scales dog misjudges steps and trips.
Scales dog begs for scraps, licks plates.
Scales dog is seven times older than you think:
so he runs elliptically; so he cannot see spiders; so he is often distracted;
so he loses peanuts dropped at his feet; so he has suddenly
become diabetic and drinks from puddles; so there is bad wind
in his system that came over with the *Mayflower*; so he rolls on his back
only once a week.
Scales dog is Gormenghast, is Nanny Slagg.
Scales dog is Horus, is Solomon Grundy.
His body makes disconnected music.
He is so old his eyes are glazed with blood;
so old wonders have ceased; so old all his diseases are benign; so old
he disappoints instantly; so old his aim is bad.
Scales dog is so old each day Scales urges him to die.
Scales dog puts on a show like a bad magician.
Scales dog squats as if he was signing the Declaration of Independence.
Scales dog is so old worms tired of him.
So old his fleas have won prizes for longevity.
So old his dreams are on microfilm in the Museum of Modern Art.
So old he looks accusingly.
So old he scratches for fun.

Scales dog was buried with the Pharaohs, with the Aztecs; draws
social security from fourteen countries; travels with his blanket;
throws up on the rug; has a galaxy named after him; Scales dog
runs scared; would have each day the same, the same;
twitches in his sleep;
wheezes.

Judith Barrington

A True Dog Story

When Bradshaw's master listed him
in the telephone directory
the humans found it funny.
But Bradshaw went on hunting rats
in the barn, cheerful in his
brown and white terrier outfit.

Soon he had his choice of outfits
as catalogs from gentlemen's tailors
thumped through the mailslot:
"Brady Marsh Esquire," they said
on personalized address labels, but Bradshaw
gripped them in his teeth and shook hard.

The humans laughed themselves silly
when someone called wanting his opinion:
What was his favorite TV show?
What brand of toothpaste did he use?
"Brady can't come to the phone," they said,
"He's out in the grain bins chasing a rat."

They sent him Dutch bulb catalogs,
coupons for free pizzas,
and once even a special dogfood offer
but it wasn't a brand he liked
so he took the coupon instead and buried it
with some rabbit bones behind the shed.

"Play dead, Bradshaw," ordered the humans
as he rolled on his wide little back.
But when he got old, he refused
the trick and spent more time in the barn
dozing with the horses. He ignored his mail
with its ads for the finest funerals.

Judith Barrington

Beating the Dog

She lowered her belly into heather
and froze. Her nose explored
the breeze, sorted smells of weather
from what mattered. I saw how her eyes stared.

She was so young then, downwind
from two sheep on a hillside purple under blue;
there were farmers with guns in my mind
as I yelled NO. I was young too.

It was no use my yelling.
The sheep lifted their heads too high
and bolted, swerving, almost falling
over tussocks, while the sky

tilted and spun as I ran,
the dog ran, we barked and yelled
and the four of us alone up there
ploughed through bracken and harebells.

She heard me at last, left
the sheep heaving and bleating
by a gorse bush. Her eyes softened,
she crouched, and then I was beating

the dog with the leash,
farmers and guns in my mind
as rage washed over the hill
like a storm's hot wind.

I remember how she screamed twice
before I sank down in the heather.
It doesn't matter that she licked my face –
the sorry tears; it doesn't matter

that she barked and skipped through the stream
or that she never stared that way
at a sheep again. Ends and means.
How could things be simple after that day?

Eamonn Wall

A Life Of Pat The Scruff, Chapter 12

Somewhere on the road from St. Louis to Kansas City, my master, or that was how he saw it, keeled over.

He hit the ground with a dull thud that rose the dust into a light cloud, the sun high in the July sky. A goner!

We were on the Katy Trail, the quite interminable path that replaced a good Missouri railway line – designed for cyclists, walkers, the young and old. For dogs, recreational walking is a definite non-starter. We prefer to ride.

The trail we walked that day was criss-crossed by shadows cast from a long line of poplars, a legacy of Governor Ashcroft, the evangelist. Once, to an admiring crowd, we had heard the great man sing at an out-of-doors Springfield soiree. My master thought him an improvement on Andy Williams, a crooner he had lately heard in Branson, an evening I spent under a porch sheltering from driving rain and violent thunder. A man's life!

My name, they say, is Pat the Scruff or Scruff the Mutt. I eyed the heap in front of me. A light twig had blown into his pants' fold, his pack had rolled harmlessly to the path side. For once he did not jabber. On a fence post a blue jay stood, but I knew better than to bother with a bird. I took to pondering my situation.

Nearby, I heard a creek's flow though in no direction could I discern the voice of dog or man. For some, the middle of Missouri can feel like the middle of nowhere. For me, as I look back, it was heaven. To the best of my knowledge, I have never left the state. My master, he was fond of telling strangers, was a direct descendent of Mark Twain. I was on the verge of something great.

He had many sayings. His favourite was one attributed to Harry Truman. It goes, "If you want a friend in Washington, get yourself a dog." My master, or ex, would repeat this to me before beating me about the nose with the Kansas City Star. Who is a dog's best friend?

"Love the One You're With" is an old time song he liked to holler. That day, along the Katy Trail, I took that song's message to my heart. Moving on, certain I would be befriended along the way. In case my old man was merely sleeping, I stepped lively. A gentle breeze blew across the Katy Trail.

Who can resist a dog in uniform! To serve the Missouri Highway Patrol had for long been the most earnest of my desires. For many years I had dreamed of riding on a cruiser's soft leather as my partner at the wheel chased, in hot pursuit, packs of dirtbags and hardened criminals. In my heart, I have always felt the siren's wail. Little did I know, that day in mid-Missouri, that those dreams were about to be realised.

Biographical Notes

Scott Edward Anderson has been a Concordia Fellow at the Millay Colony for the Arts, and received both the Nebraska Review Award and the Aldrich Emerging Poets Award. His work has appeared in the *Alaska Quarterly Review, American Poetry Review, The Cortland Review, CrossConnect, Earth's Daughters, Isotope, Many Mountains Moving, Nebraska Review, Poetica, River Oak Review*, and *Terrain*, among other publications. He was a founding editor of Philadelphia's *Ducky Magazine* and writes the green skeptic blog (www.thegreenskeptic.com); his poetry website is: http://scottedwardanderson.com.

Renée Ashley is the author of four volumes of poetry – *Salt* (Brittingham Prize in Poetry, University of Wisconsin Press), *The Various Reasons of Light, The Revisionist's Dream*, and *Basic Heart* (X.J. Kennedy Prize, Texas Review Press) – as well as two chapbooks, *The Museum of Lost Wings* and *The Verbs of Desiring*, and a novel, *Someplace Like This*. She has been awarded fellowships from the National Endowment for the Arts and the New Jersey State Council on the Arts, and is on the core faculty of Fairleigh Dickinson University's MA in Creative Writing and Literature for Educators and the MFA Program in Creative Writing. She is a poetry editor for *The Literary Review*.

Neil Astley is editor of Bloodaxe Books, which he founded in 1978. His books include two poetry collections and several anthologies, including *Staying Alive: real poems from unreal times* (Bloodaxe, 2002), *Pleased to See Me: 69 very sexy poems* (Bloodaxe, 2002), *Do Not Go Gentle: poems for funerals* (Bloodaxe, 2003), *Being Alive: the sequel to Staying Alive* (Bloodaxe, 2004), *Passionfood: 100 Love Poems* (Bloodaxe, 2005), *Soul Food: nourishing poems for starved minds* [with Pamela Robertson-Pearce] (Bloodaxe, 2007), *Earth Shattering: ecopoems* (2007) and the DVD-book *In Person: 30 Poets* filmed by Pamela Robertson-Pearce (Bloodaxe, 2008). *Being Human*, the third anthology of the *Staying Alive* "trilogy", is due from Bloodaxe in 2011. He has published two novels, *The End of My Tether* (Flambard, 2002; Scribner, 2003), which was shortlisted for the Whitbread First Novel Award, and *The Sheep Who Changed the World* (Flambard, 2005). He received an Eric Gregory Award for his poetry and was given a D.Litt from Newcastle University for his work with Bloodaxe Books. He lives in Northumberland.

Celeste Augé is an Irish-Canadian writer who has lived in Ireland since she was twelve years old. Her poetry has been widely published in literary journals and anthologies, and she has published two chapbooks of poetry, *Tornadoes for the Weathergirl* and *Smoke & Skin*. In 2009, her poetry was short-listed for a Hennessy Literary Award and Salmon Poetry published her first full-length collection, *The Essential Guide to Flight*. She recently received an Irish Arts Council Literature Bursary to work on her second collection of poetry.

Michael Augustin, German poet and broadcaster, was born in Lübeck in 1953. He is the author of many volumes of poetry, drama, short prose and audio books. His work has been translated into many languages. He is an Honorary Fellow at the University of Iowa and at Dickinson College in the USA where he taught as a guest professor. He is co-directing the international festival Poetry on the Road in Bremen. In 2009 he was Writer-in-Residence in the Heinrich Boell Cottage on Achill Island, Co. Mayo. Two of his books were published in Ireland: *Ad infinitum*, a trilingual selection of his poems and epigrams in German, English, & Irish (Coiscéim 2001) and *Mickle Makes Muckle*, poems, mini-plays and short prose (Dedalus 2007). www.elektroschallarchiv.de

Paul Barclay is an ex-pat Canadian poet living permanently in Korea. His interests include storytelling, expressionism, and (Tuvan) throat singing. Some recent poetry can be found online in *ditch*, the *Atonal Poetry Review*, and *Feathertale*.

Judith Barrington has published three collections of poetry, most recently Horses and the Human Soul (Story Line Press, 2004). Previous titles include *History and Geography* and *Trying to be an Honest Woman*. Recent work includes two chapbooks: *Postcard from the Bottom of the Sea* and *Lost Lands* (winner of the Robin Becker Chapbook Award). Her *Lifesaving: A Memoir* won the 2000 Lambda Book Award and was a finalist for the PEN/Martha Albrand Award for the Art of the Memoir.

Eileen Battersby was born in California. She discovered reading - and dogs - at an early age. After taking an honours BA in English and History at University College Dublin followed by an honours MA on the American writer Thomas Wolfe, author of *Look Homeward, Angel* (1929) and *Of Time and the River* (1935), she became involved in journalism initially through book reviewing and sports writing. An Irish Times staff Arts Journalist and Literary Correspondent, she has written on all aspects of the arts including classical music, the visual arts, cinema and theatre as well as history, archaeology, architectural history, historical geography and horses. She has won the National Arts Journalist of the Year award four times. Her book, *Second Readings: From Beckett to Black Beauty*, a volume of literary criticism, was published in 2009 and subsequently reprinted.

Marck L. Beggs lives a in a cabin by a pond in Arkansas, sort of like Thoreau with technology and catfish. When he is not writing or singing his quasi-folk songs, he can sometimes be found watching the weeds proliferate in his garden as he daydreams of fresh tomatoes, cucumbers, and butternut squash. Needless to say, he cites Whitman as a major influence. He is the author of three collections of poetry: *Catastrophic Chords* (Salmon Poetry 2008), *Libido Café* (Salmon Poetry, 2004) and *Godworm* (1995). His folk-rock band, *dog gods*, released their debut CD in 2008, and he was named one of the "ten sexiest vegetarians over 50" by PETA in 2009.

Richard Berengarten is a poet who lives in Cambridge, Englans. His latest books are *For the Living*, *The Manager*, *The Blue Butterfly*, *In a Time of Drought* and *Under Balkan Light* (all from Salt Publishing, UK, 2008). Other collections include *Book With No Back Cover* (2005) and the ongoing *Manual* series. He has received many awards and his poetry has been translated into more than 90 languages (see http://interlitq.org/issue9/volta/job.php). The Salt *Critical Companion to Richard Berengarten* (2010) contains 33 essays on his work. Currently he is working on *Two to the Power of Six*, based on *Yi Jing (I Ching)*.

Drew Blanchard has worked in not-for-profit urban redevelopment and construction, as a journalist, and most recently as a teacher of literature and creative writing in Universities throughout the Midwest. He holds a BA in Journalism from the University of Iowa and an MFA in poetry from the Ohio State University. He is currently a PhD candidate in English at the University of Wisconsin-Milwaukee where he has twice been awarded The Academy of American Poets Prize. In January 2009 he received a university research grant to work with the Peruvian novelist, Iván Thays in Lima, Perú and in the Summer of 2010 he was a graduate student scholar at the National University of Ireland, Maynooth, a scholarship provided by the International Association for the Study of Irish Literatures. His writing has appeared in *Best New Poets*, *Notre Dame Review*, *Guernica – a magazine of art & politics*, *Blackbird*, *Meridian* and elsewhere.

Jane Blanchard earned degrees in English from Wake Forest and Rutgers. She resides with her family in Augusta, Georgia, and on St. Simon's Island, Georgia. Her poetry has appeared or is forthcoming in *Blue Unicorn*, *The Reach of Song*, *descant*, *Candelabrum Poetry Magazine*, *Common Ground Review*, *WestWard Quarterly*, *Time of Singing*, *Trinacria*, *Pearl*, *Light*, and *The Stray Branch*.

Pat Boran was born in Portlaoise, Ireland in 1963 and currently lives in Dublin. He has published four collections of poetry: *The Unwound Clock* (Dedalus, 1990), which won the Patrick Kavanagh Award, *Familiar Things* (Dedalus, 1993), *The Shape of Water* (Dedalus, 1996) and *As the Hand, the Glove* (Dedalus, 2001). His *New and Selected Poems* appeared from Salt Publishing in 2005 and was reissued, with minor revisions, by Dedalus in 2007. In addition to poetry he has published a collection of short stories, *Strange Bedfellows* (Salmon, 1991) and his short fiction title for children includes *All the Way from China* (Poolbeg, 1999) which was a finalist for the Bisto Book of the Year Award. His non-fiction titles include the writers' handbook *The Portable Creative Writing Workshop* (Salmon, 1999; revised and expanded, New Island, 2005) and *A Short History of Dublin* (Mercier, 2000). His memoir *The Invisible Prison: Scenes from an Irish Childhood*, was published by Dedalus in 2009. A former editor of *Poetry Ireland Review* and presenter of *The Poetry Programme* on RTÉ Radio 1, he has also edited *Wingspan: A Dedalus Sampler* (2006) and *Flowing, Still: Irish Poets on Irish Poetry* (Dedalus, 2009). In 2007 he was elected to the membership of Aosdána and in 2008 he received the Lawrence O'Shaughnessy Poetry Award of the University of St Thomas, St Paul, MN.

Eva Bourke was born in Germany and has long since lived in Galway. Among her poetry collections are *Gonella* (Salmon, 1985), with drawings by Jay Murphy, *Litany for the Pig* (Salmon, 1989), *Spring in Henry Street* (Dedalus, 1996), *Travels with Gandolpho* (Dedalus, 2000) and *The Latitude of Naples* (Dedalus, 2005). A teacher and translator, she is also the editor of a major dual language English / German anthology of Irish poetry entitled *In Green Ink / Mit Gruner Tinte* (1996) and, together with Eoin Bourke, she edited and translated the first major German anthology of Irish poetry *Hündrose* (Maroverlag, Augsburg, 1985). Her other translations include an English language verison of Elisabeth Borchers' *Winter on White Paper* (2002). She is co-editor, along with Borbála Faragó, of *Landing Places: Immigrant Poets in Ireland* (Dedalus, 2010). At present she is working on translations of contemporary German poets. Eva Bourke has received a number of awards and bursaries from the Arts Council and is a member of Aosdána, Ireland's academy of artists and writers. Her next collection *The Soul of the Piano* will be published by Dedalus in 2011.

Brian Brett, poet, fiction writer, critic, journalist, is the author of eleven books of poetry, fiction, and memoir – including *The Colour of Bones In A Stream, Tanganyika, The Fungus Garden, Coyote, Uproar's Your Only Music*, and the prize-winning best seller, *Trauma Farm*. As part of the Salt Spring Collective, he has also completed a CD of his 'Talking Songs' called *Night Directions for the Lost*, produced and arranged by Ramesh Meyers. He lives with his family on his farm on Salt Spring Island, British Columbia.

Megan Buckley was born in New York in 1977, and has lived in Ireland since 2004. Her poems have been published in the US, the UK, and Ireland, in publications such as *The Ledge* (US), *The Pedestal* (US), *eclectica.org* (US); the 'Dazzle and Attract' Project in Newcastle-on-Tyne (UK), in which one of her poems was projected onto the wall of a building (UK); *Crannóg* (IRL), and others. She presented her work at the Over The Edge Showcase at the Cúirt International Festival of Literature in April 2008, and was a judge for the Cúirt Poetry Grand Slam in 2009. Buckley is currently a PhD candidate in the English Department at NUI, Galway, where she teaches seminars on nineteenth-century women's poetry.

Simmons B. Buntin is the author of two books of poems, *Riverfall* (Salmon Poetry, 2005) and *Bloom* (Salmon Poetry, 2010). His award-winning poetry and prose have appeared in numerous North American and European journals and anthologies. He is the founding editor of the acclaimed international journal *Terrain.org: A Journal of the Built & Natural Environments*, for which he also writes a regular editorial. He is the recipient of the Colorado Artists Fellowship for Poetry, an Academy of American Poets prize, and grants by the Arizona Commission on the Arts and Tucson Pima Arts Council. He is an avid photographer, website designer, and all-around rabble-rouser who lives with his wife and two daughters in the Sonoran desert of southern Arizona. Catch up with him at www.simmonsbuntin.com.

Sandra Bunting is from Canada and has lived in Galway for more than 20 years. She is on the editorial board of Crannóg Magazine and her poetry collection, *Identified in Trees*, was published in 2006 by Marram Press. Sandra gives poetry tutorials at NUI Galway and has set up the Academic Writing Centre there.

Louise C. Callaghan was born in 1948 and brought up in County Dublin, Ireland. She still lives in Dublin, close to her four children and many grandchildren. Her poetry collections are *The Puzzle-Heart* (Salmon, 1999), *Remember The Birds* (Salmon, 2005) and *In The Ninth House* (Salmon, 2010). She compiled and edited *Forgotten Light: An Anthology of Memory Poems* (A & A Farmar, 2003). Her poetry, which is widely anthologised in Ireland and England, is included in the *Field Day Anthology: Vols IV & V*. She completed an M.Litt in Creative Writing at St. Andrews University in Scotland (2007), receiving a First Class Honours in her poetry dissertation.

Hélène Cardona is a poet and actor and a citizen of the U.S., France and Spain. She is the author of the bilingual poetry collections *The Astonished Universe*, forthcoming from Tupelo Press, and *Breeze Rider*, forthcoming from Salmon Poetry. She has translated the Lawrence Bridges film "Muse of Fire" for the NEA, the poetry of Dorianne Laux, her father José Manuel Cardona and many others.

Seamus Cashman – poet, editor, teacher and publisher – taught in Tanzania and in Ireland before joining Irish University Press as editor. In 1974, he founded and developed Wolfhound Press into a leading literary and cultural publishing house, remaining its publisher until 2001. Cashman's most recent collection *That Morning will Come: New and Selected Poems* (Salmon Poetry, 2007) includes 'Secrets', poem responses to issues of justice in Palestine. Previous books include *Carnival* (1988); *Clowns & Acrobats* (2000), and anthologies, *Irish Poems for Young People*, and the award winning *Something Beginning with P: New Poems from Irish Poets*. He has given poetry readings in Ireland, in the US across Iowa and Nebraska & Wisconsin, in Brussels, at London's Southbank – and at Bangor's POETica in Wales. Cashman also works as an independent editorial advisor and creative writing facilitator. He is a Fellow of The Black Earth Institute, Wisconsin. He lives in Portmarnock, County Dublin.

Ann Fox Chandonnet was born and bred in Massachusetts. She earned a master's degree in English literature from the University of Wisconsin. She won the Wisconsin Union prize for a sequence of seven sonnets. She and her husband Fernand lived in Alaska from 1973 to 2006. Her poetry collections include *The Wife and Other Poems* (1978), *Ptarmigan Valley* (1980), *Auras, Tendrils* (1984) and *Canoeing in the Rain* (1990). Chandonnet's poems have appeared in magazines such as *permafrost, The Fiddlehead, harpoon, The Buffalo News, The Kansas Quarterly, Hard Row to Hoe, Hyperion: Black Sun, New Moon, Kalliope, Midatlantic Review, Mr. Cogito, Northeast Journal, Ploughshares, Maize, New Kauri, Northward Journal* and *Plains Poetry Journal*. She wrote the words for the musical work about the Exxon Valdez oil spill, *Shadows* (music by Philip Munger). Her work appears in anthologies including *Last New Land* (1996), *Merrimack* (1992), *In the Dreamlight: 21 Alaskan Writers* (Copper Canyon Press, 1984), and *Whispered Secrets*, as well as in an anti-war archive in Italy. In autumn 2006, Chandonnet retired to North Carolina where she weeds, reads, listens to owls and raises tomatoes. Her most recent book is a history, *"Write Quick": War and a Woman's Life in Letters, 1835-1867* (Winoca Press, 2010).

Patrick Chapman was born in 1968. *The Darwin Vampires*, his fifth collection of poetry was published by Salmon in 2010, following *Jazztown* (Raven Arts Press, Dublin, 1991), *The New Pornography* (Salmon Poetry, 1996), *Breaking Hearts and Traffic Lights* (Salmon Poetry, 2007) and *A Shopping Mall on Mars* (BlazeVOX Books, Buffalo, N.Y., 2008). His book of short stories is *The Wow Signal* (Bluechrome, UK, 2007). Also a scriptwriter, he adapted his own published story for *Burning the Bed* (2003). Directed by Denis McArdle, this award-winning film stars Gina McKee and Aidan Gillen. Chapman has written several episodes of the Cbeebies and RTÉ series *Garth & Bev* (Kavaleer, 2009/10). His audio play, *Doctor Who: Fear of the Daleks* (Big Finish, UK, 2007), was directed by Mark J. Thompson. With Philip Casey, he founded the Irish Literary Revival website in 2006. His story 'A Ghost' won first prize in the Cinescape Genre Literary Competition in L.A. The title poem of *The Darwin Vampires* was nominated for a Pushcart Prize.

Kelly Cherry has published twenty books and eight chapbooks of fiction (long and short), poetry, memoir, criticism, and essay, as well as translations of two classical plays. Her most recent titles are *The Woman Who*, a collection of stories, *Girl in a Library: On Women Writers & the Writing Life*, and *The Retreats of Thought: Poems*. She has received fellowships from the National Endowment for the Arts, the Rockefeller Foundation, and the Institute for Advanced Study. Her numerous prizes include the Hanes Prize from the Fellowship of Southern Writers for a body of work and the Dictionary of Literary Biography Yearbook Award for the best volume of stories in 1999. She is currently completing a new book of short stories and carrying out research for a book-length poem.

Sarah Clancy is from Salthill, Galway and is a participant in the Galway Arts Centre Poetry Workshops facilitated by Kevin Higgins. She has previously read her poetry at North Beach Poetry Nights, The Cúirt Grand Slam and the Over The Edge Poetry Readings in Galway Library. In 2010 Sarah was shortlisted in the poetry section of the WOW awards; the Listowel Writers' Week Poetry Competition; and the Over the Edge New Writer of the Year Competition. Her poems feature in *Behind the Masks* from the advanced poetry workshop at Galway Arts Centre. A short collection of her poetic oddities, *Stacey and the Mechanical Bull*, will be published in 2010 by Lapwing Press, Belfast, Northern Ireland.

Jennifer Clark's poetry, short stories and articles have been published in *Editions Bibliotekos, the Pittsburgh Post-Gazette, In Pittsburgh Magazine, Port Austin (Michigan) Times*, and in the anthology, *Lessons from Dad*, by Joan Aho Ryan. Her play *Father's Not There* was featured at the U.S. National Conference on Child Abuse and Neglect. Her poem "Breakfast Mourning" was nominated for a Pushcart Prize in 2009. She has work forthcoming in Raven Chronicles. Clark lives and writes in Kalamazoo, Michigan where she serve as director of school and community relations for Kalamazoo Communities In Schools.

Thomas Cochran is a native of Haynesville, Louisiana, who currently lives in rural northwest Arkansas, where he trades the rigours of being a schoolteacher for the time the job allows him to read and write. His work includes the novels *Roughnecks* (Harcourt) and *Running the Dogs* (FSG). Poetry and nonfiction under his name have appeared or are forthcoming in various print and online journals.

Andrea Cohen's poems and stories have appeared in *The Atlantic Monthly, Poetry, The Threepenny Review, Glimmertrain, The Hudson Review* and elsewhere. Her poetry collections include *The Cartographer's Vacation*, winner of the Owl Creek Poetry Prize, *Long Division* (Salmon Poetry, 2009) and *Kentucky Derby* (Salmon Poetry, 2011). She has received a PEN Discovery Award, Glimmertrain's Short Fiction Award, and several residencies at The MacDowell Colony. She directs the Blacksmith House Poetry Series in Cambridge, MA.

Susan Cohen is a journalist and former professor of journalism in Berkeley, California. She's the author of two poetry chapbooks: *Backstroking*, which won the Acorn-Rukeyser Chapbook award, and *Finding the Sweet Spot* from Finishing Line Press. Her poems appear or are forthcoming in many places, including *Atlanta Review, Poet Lore, Poetry East, Poetry International, Puerto del Sol, Southern Poetry Review*, and *Verse Daily*. Poetry honours include a Pushcart Prize nomination and a Best Poem Award from *New Millennium Writings*. She's also the co-author of *Normal at Any Cost; Tall Girls, Short Boys, and the Medical Industry's Quest to Manipulate Height* (Tarcher/Penguin;2009). Although she doesn't own a dog, she keeps thinking about getting one.

Nahshon Cook's poems have appeared in literary publications which have included *The Houston Literary Review* and *Post Poetry Magazine*. His first collection of poetry *A New Beginning* was published in January 2010 by Paper Flower Press. He lives in Denver, Colorado.

The Irish poet **Patrick Cotter** was born in 1963 and educated at University College, Cork. After leaving college in the mid 80s, Cotter worked as Literature Officer at the Triskel Arts Centre before embarking on a career as a bookseller which ended in 2002. He continues to live and work in Cork as director of the Munster Literature Centre. His poems have been translated into Estonian, Italian, Norse, Norwegian, Russian, Spanish and Swedish and he's given readings of his work in Ireland, California, Germany, Estonia, Norway, Italy and India. He's been shortlisted for both the Hennessy Award and the Patrick Kavanagh Award. Today's selection is from his first full-length collection of poems, *Perplexed Skin*, which was published by Arlen House in 2008.

Dallas Crow's poems have appeared in a number of publications in the U.S., including *Arion, Cairn, English Journal, Minnetonka Review, Poet Lore*, and *Red Rock Review*, and – as part of a public art project – in the sidewalks of St. Paul, Minnesota. "Regret" and "Separated" are his first poems to appear outside the U.S. He lives in Minnesota where he is a high school English teacher. His website is http://corvus-at-large.blogspot.com.

Eleanor Cummins grew up in Co.Carlow. She survived the 1980's trawling to festivals fuelled by porter and a love of music and theatre. She joined the Macnas street theatre company in 1989 and toured Scotland and England. She played Lucky in *Waiting for Godot*, directed by Nora Connolly. She was in the ground-breaking play *Eclipsed*, by Patricia Burke Brogan (Salmon) which won a Fringe First Award at the Edinburgh Festival. She received an Honours Degree in English and Philosophy from the National University of Ireland, Galway (NUIG) in 1996. With the poet Rab Fulton, she founded The Global Music Project for Asylum Seekers to express poetry and music. In 2008 her play *The Sacred Sow* was produced by the Prague Playhouse. The director was Brian Caspe, with Eileen Pollock in the lead road. It was one of the top three plays at The Prague Fringe Festival.

Jack Brae Curtingstall is a blog-poet and situationist. His blog-poetry can be found in the archives of *The Guardian*'s Poster Poems blog and on the blog known as *Politely Homicidal*. His translations have appeared on *Perp Walk*. He is also a minimalist and is interested in the areas of haiku practice that pertain to gendai, ultraist and martianistic approaches. He abides in North Kerry, Ireland, in the region of Sliabh Luachra with his dogg (a muse-familiar that, ironically, resembles a cat). He is the changeling-other of another.

Gill Dalley originally from Leeds, England, retired to Phuket, Thailand, with husband John in 2003. Determined to do something to alleviate the appalling suffering endured by the countless street dogs there, together with husband John and a Dutch ex patriot Margot Homburg she established the Soi Dog Foundation. In 2004 she became critically ill after rescuing a dog from a flooded water buffalo field. A rare life threatening bacteria entered her system. After three months intensive care she survived but lost both her lower legs and suffered damage to her arms. Three days after her release from hospital, the Asian tsunami struck and Gill immediately went to the aid of bereaved and injured survivors, counselling them in the local hospitals despite at that time being wheelchair bound. Following this she continued to work with the dogs as she does to this day regularly working twelve hours a day, seven days a week as Director of Field Operations. In 2008 Gill was named an Asian of the Year (the first Non Asian by birth to be so recognised) by the Singaporean news channel CNA.

J.P. Dancing Bear is the author of *Inner Cities of Gulls* (Salmon Poetry, 2010), *Conflicted Light* (Salmon Poetry, 2008), *Gacela of Narcissus City* (Main Street Rag, 2006), *Billy Last Crow* (Turning Point, 2004) and *What Language* (Slipstream, 2002), winner of the 2001 Slipstream Prize. His poems have been published in *New Orleans Review, National Poetry Review, Knockout, Bateau, diode, DIAGRAM, Verse Daily* and many others. His work has been ten times nominated for a Puschart Prize and once for a Forward Prize. He has been working with Nicaraguan poet Blanca Castellon on translating of her poetry into English, the first will appear in *Redactions, Marlboro Review, International Poetry Review, iconoclast* and *The Bitter Oleander*. He has also been working with Mexican poet Oscar Wong to translate his work into English. He is the editor of the *American Poetry Journal* and Dream Horse Press and the host of "Out of Our Minds" a weekly poetry program on public radio station KKUP.

Larry O. Dean was born and raised in Flint, Michigan. He attended the University of Michigan, during which time he won three Hopwood Awards in Creative Writing, an honour shared with fellow poets Robert Hayden, Jane Kenyon, and Frank O'Hara, among others; and Murray State University's low-residency MFA program. He is author of numerous chapbooks, including *I Am Spam* (2004), a series of poems "inspired" by junk email; his poetry has also been internationally translated and anthologised. In addition, he is a singer-songwriter, performing solo as well as with his current band, The Injured Parties; he has released many critically-acclaimed CDs, including *Fables in Slang* (2001) with Post Office, *Gentrification Is Theft* (2002) with The Me Decade, and *Fun with a Purpose* (2009). Dean was a 2004 recipient of the Gwendolyn Brooks Award, presented by the Poetry Centre of Chicago. www.larryodean.com.

Susie DeFord studied poetry at Florida State University, and received her MFA from the New School University. She writes *subTEXT*, a poetry column for *BOMB* magazine. Her work has appeared recently in *Poets & Artists, Work Magazine*, and *Dog Fancy*. She has taught writing at Brooklyn Friends School, Berkeley Carroll, and the College of New Rochelle. Also a musician, she fronted the bands *Terset* and *Wu Wei*. She lives in Brooklyn, where she runs Susie's Pet Care, a dog walking and training business and writes the blog *Dog Poet Laureate*. She is currently seeking a publisher for her first book of poems and photographs called *The Dogs of Brooklyn* (c.2007-2009). www.susiedeford.com

Annie Deppe is the author of two collections of poetry, *Sitting in the Sky* (Summer Palace Press, 2003) and *Wren Cantata* (Summer Palace Press, 2009.) Her work has been anthologised in the *Forward Book of Poetry* 2004. Born in Hartford, Connecticut, Deppe has made her home on the west coast of Ireland since 2000.

Theodore Deppe is the author of four books of poems, including *Orpheus on the Red Line* (Tupelo, 2009) and *Cape Clear: New and Selected Poems* (Salmon, 2002). In the U.S., he was awarded two fellowships from the National Endowment for the Arts and a Pushcart Prize. He has been the writer in residence for Phillips Academy in Andover, Massachusetts and the James Merrill House in Stonington, Connecticut. He has lived in Ireland since 2000 and presently lives in Galway. He directs a programme that brings writing students from the Stonecoast Masters in Fine Arts programme to study in Ireland.

Stephen Dobyns' most recent book of poems *Winter's Journey* was published in 2010 by Copper Canyon. His most recent work of fiction is a book of short stories *Eating Naked* (Holt, 2000). His other work includes *Best Words, Best Order* (Palgrave, 2003), which is a book of essays on poetry, and *Velocities* (Penguin, 1994) a volume of new and selected poems. He has also published eleven other books of poetry and twenty novels. Two of his novels and two of his short stories have been made into films. Since 1995, Dobyns has been a feature writer for the *San Diego Reader*. He has received a Guggenheim fellowship, three fellowships from the National Endowment of the Arts and numerous prizes for his poetry and fiction. His novel *The Church of Dead Girls* (Holt, 1997) was translated into twenty languages. Dobyns teaches in the MFA Program of Warren Wilson College, and also at Sarah Lawrence College. In the past he has taught at Emerson College, Syracuse University, Boston University, University of Iowa and half a dozen other colleges and universities. He was born in New Jersey in 1941. He lives with his wife in Westerly, RI.

Theo Dorgan is a poet, prose writer, documentary scriptwriter and editor. His latest collection of poems, *Greek*, was published in early 2010 by Dedalus and his prose narrative *Time On The Ocean*, a Voyage from Cape Horn to Cape Town, appeared in October of this year from New Island. He is the 2010 recipient of the O'Shaughnessy Award for Irish poetry, and a member of Aosdána.

Amy Dryansky's first book, *How I Got Lost So Close To Home*, was published by Alice James Books and individual poems have appeared in a variety of journals and anthologies. She's been nominated for several Pushcart Prizes and awarded fellowships to the MacDowell Colony, Vermont Studio Center, Villa Montalvo and the Bread Loaf Writers' Conference. She's also a former Associate at the Five College Women's Studies Research Center at Mt. Holyoke College, where she looked at the impact of motherhood on the work of women poets. She writes about what it's like to navigate the territory of mother/artist/poet at her blog, *Pokey Mama*. She lives with her family, including one dog and one cat, in western Massachusetts.

Susan Millar DuMars was born in Philadelphia in 1966. Her poetry collections to date are *Big Pink Umbrella* (Salmon Poetry, 2008) and Dreams for Breakfast (Salmon Poetry, 2010). Her work appears in *The Best of Irish Poetry 2010* and *Landing Places: Immigrant Poets in Ireland* (Dedalus, 2010). A fiction writer as well, she published a collection of short stories, *American Girls*, with Lapwing in 2007, and is at work on a further story collection. Susan has been the recipient of an Arts Council Literature Bursary. She lives in Galway, where she works as a creative writing teacher. Susan and her husband, Kevin Higgins, have run Galway's Over the Edge readings series since its inception in 2003.

Cynthia Schwartzberg Edlow's poetry has appeared widely in numerous journals, including *The American Poetry Review, ACM, Cimarron Review, Gulf Coast, American Literary Review, Jewish Women's Literary Annual, Barrow Street, The Chiron Review, Diner, Smartish Pace, The Tusculum Review* and *Galatea Resurrects*. A recipient of the Willow Review Prize for Poetry, a Beullah Rose Poetry Prize, and an award from the Chester H. Jones Foundation National Poetry Competition (selected by Robert Creeley, Diane Wakoski and Charles Wright), her poems have also been featured in the anthologies *Not A Muse* (Haven Books), *In the Eye* (Thunder Rain Publishers), and *The Emily Dickinson Awards Anthology* (Universities West Press). A 2011 Pushcart Prize nominee, Cynthia Schwartzberg Edlow's debut poetry collection, *The Day Judge Spencer Learned the Power of Metaphor*, is forthcoming from Salmon Poetry in 2011.

Peter Fallon farmed for many years in Loughcrew in County Meath where he still lives. He is editor and publisher of The Gallery Press which he started in 1970.

His recent publications include *The Georgics of Virgil* (2004, reprinted by OUP in its World Classics Series) and *The Company of Horses* (poems, 2007). *Works and Their Days* (after Hesiod) is forthcoming.

Elaine Feeney was born in Galway in 1979. She studied English and History at University College Galway and completed post graduate study in University College Cork and University of Limerick. In 2006 she won the North Beach Nights Grand Slam and in 2008 won the Cúirt Festival's Poetry Grand Slam. Elaine has performed at many venues including The Edinburgh Fringe Festival, The Electric Picnic, The Vilenica Festival and The Cúirt International Literature Festival. She was the chosen writer on a One Sheet collaboration in 2010 with an artist and a graphic designer and this work is currently on exhibit across Dublin. Her work has been translated into Slovene. Her debut collection, *Where's Katie?*, was published by Salmon in 2010.

John Fitzgerald is an attorney for the disabled. He has been Development Director for Red Hen Press and Associate Book Editor for Cider Press Review. His three books of poetry are *Spring Water* (Turning Point, 2005), *Telling Time by the Shadows* (Turning Point, 2008), and *The Mind* (Salmon Poetry, 2011).

Gabriel Fitzmaurice was born, in 1952, in the village of Moyvane, Co. Kerry where he still lives. For over thirty years he taught in the local primary school from which he retired as principal in 2007. He is author of more than forty books including collections of poetry in English and Irish as well as several collections of verse for children. He has translated extensively from the Irish and has edited a number of anthologies of poetry in English and Irish. He has published two volumes of essays and collections of songs and ballads. He has been described as "the best contemporary, traditional, popular poet in English" in *Booklist* (US), "a wonderful poet" in the *Guardian*, "one of Ireland's favourite poets" in *Books Ireland*, "Ireland's favourite poet for children" in *Best Books!* and "the Irish A.A. Milne" by Declan Kiberd in the *Sunday Tribune*.

Janice Fitzpatrick Simmons has five collections of poems: *Leaving America* (Lapwing Press, 1992); *Settler* (Salmon Poetry, 1996); *Starting At Purgatory* (Salmon Poetry, 1999); *The Bowsprit* (Lagan Press, 2005); *Saint Michael In Peril Of The Sea* (Salmon Poetry, 2009). A part of her memoir was published by Salmon in *Poetry: Reading It Writing It, Publishing It* (2009). In 2009 she received the Patrick and Katherine Kavanagh Fellowship and The Royal Literary Fund Grant.

Lisa Frank was born and raised in Los Angeles but has spent most of the past ten years living in the Pacific Northwest before moving to the west of Ireland in 2007. She received her MFA in Creative Writing from Eastern Washington University and has had fiction, poetry, nonfiction and screenwriting published in both the US and Ireland. Her most recent publication is in the anthology *Landing Places: Immigrant Poets in Ireland* (Dedalus Press, 2010). She currently works as a freelance literary editor and is the editor/layout designer for Doire Press in Connemara.

Philip Fried is a New York-based poet and little-magazine editor. His poems have been widely published in journals and have appeared in many anthologies, including *Salmon: A Journey in Poetry, Poems 1981-2007* and *Poetry After 9/11: An Anthology of New York Poets*. His poetry collections include *Big Men Speaking to Little Men* (Salmon Poetry, 2006) and *Cohort* (Salmon Poetry, 2009). *Early/Late: New & Selected Poems* will appear from Salmon in 2011. In addition to being a poet, Fried is the founding editor of *The Manhattan Review*, an international poetry journal that critics have called "excellent" and "lively." He collaborated with his wife, the fine-art photographer Lynn Saville, on a volume combining her nocturnal photographs with poetry from around the world: *Acquainted with the Night* (Rizzoli, 1997).

Paul Genega is the author of four full-length volumes of poetry, including *That Fall* (Salmon) and *At The Tone* (Three Mile Harbor Press, New York). Highly awarded, his honours include the "Discovery", the Nation Award and a fellowship from the National Endowment for the Arts, the Charles Angoff Award from the *Literary Review*, and the Lucille Medick Award from *New York Quarterly*. He teaches creative writing at Bloomfield College where he also serves as coordinator of English and Chair of the Faculty.

Peter Joseph Gloviczki lives in Minneapolis, where he is a PhD student in Mass Communication at the University of Minnesota. His poems have appeared in *The Christian Science Monitor, Modern Haiku, Frogpond: The Journal of the Haiku Society of America, Margie, New Orleans Review* and elsewhere. *Kicking Gravity*, his first full-length collection of poetry, is currently seeking a publisher.

Desmond Gough was born in Surrey, England, and educated by the Christian Brothers in Tipperary. While living in Galway, bhí mé i mo bhall den na Fánaithe Amharclann Gaeilge, and Flying Pig Comedy Troupé with whom he co-wrote street and pub theatre and 'Peig the Musical'. His work has been published by the *Cúirt Journal, Force 10, Tuar Ceatha* and broadcast by @ last TV on Network 2 (RTE). He has performed his poetry at various events including Earth Song Harvest Camp 2010. He has spent the last decade studying Gelugpa Tibetan Buddhism under The Venerable Panchen Ötrul Rinpoche at Jampa Ling Buddhist Centre in Cavan.

Julian Gough was born in London, to Tipperary parents. When he was seven, the family returned to Tipperary. At university in Galway, he began writing and singing with the underground literary rock band Toasted Heretic. They released four albums, and had a top ten hit in Ireland in 1991 with 'Galway and Los Angeles'. His first novel, *Juno & Juliet,* was published in 2001. His second, *Jude: Level 1*, came six years later. *Jude: Level 1* was described by the Sunday Tribune as possibly "the finest comic novel since Flann O'Brien's *The Third Policeman*". In the UK, it was shortlisted for the Everyman Wodehouse Prize for Comic Fiction. In 2007, his story 'The Orphan and the Mob' won the BBC National Short Story Prize. He also wrote the first short story ever printed in the Financial Times, 'The Great Hargeisa Goat Bubble'. In 2009, 'The Great Hargeisa Goat Bubble' was broadcast as a radio play on BBC Radio 4. In early 2010, the Sunday Tribune chose *Jude: Level 1* as their Irish Novel of the Decade. His book of poems and song lyrics, *Free Sex Chocolate: Poems & Songs*, was published by Salmon in 2010. His third novel, *Jude in London*, will be published by Old Street in September 2011.

Laura-Gray Street is co-editor of *Ecopoetry: A Contemporary American Anthology*, forthcoming from Trinity University Press. Her work has appeared in *Many Mountains Moving, Gargoyle, From the Fishouse, ISLE, Shenandoah, Meridian, Blackbird, Poetry Daily, The Notre Dame Review*, and elsewhere. She has been awarded a fellowship from the Virginia Commission for the Arts, the inaugural poetry contest award from *Terrain.org*, the Editors' Prize in Poetry from *Isotope*, the Emerging Writer in Poetry Award for the Southern Women Writers Conference, the Dana Award in Poetry, and *The Greensboro Review's* Annual Literary Award in Poetry. Street holds an MA in English from the University of Virginia and an MFA in poetry from the Warren Wilson Program for Writers. She is an Assistant Professor of English at Randolph College in Lynchburg, Virginia.

Richard W. Halperin's poems are widely published in journals and anthologies. His first collection *Anniversary* (Salmon Poetry) appeared in June 2010, and a second collection *The Crepuscular Theory of Light* is scheduled for 2012 with Salmon. Mr Halperin submits the present poems while thinking of Buffy, part-spitz part-springer spaniel, born 20 November 1955.

Gerard Hanberry has published three collections of poetry: *Rough Night* (2002), *Something Like Lovers* (2005), and *At Grattan Road* (Salmon Poetry, 2009) and is widely published in literary journals and newspapers in Ireland and abroad. He won the Brendan Kennelly/ Sunday Tribune Poetry Award, the Galway County and City Council Poetry Prize, has been shortlisted for many poetry awards, and won the Originals Short Story Prize at Listowel Writers' Festival 2000. His biography of Oscar Wilde and his family *More Lives Than One* is to be published by The Collins Press in 2011. As well as delivering various courses on creative writing and poetry at NUI Galway he teaches English at St. Endas College, Salthill. He holds an MA in Writing from NUI, Galway.

Noël Hanlon began writing seriously in 1994 when she attended the Flight of the Mind workshop on the McKenzie River in Oregon. Her poems have been published in the US and Ireland. She is a member of a small poetry group which includes several inspirational writers, including Ursula Le Guin and Molly Gloss. She has served on the board of Soapstone, an Oregon residency that provides women writers with a stretch of uninterrupted time for their creative work, and the opportunity to live in semi-solitude in the natural world. Noël herself lives this dream; her own poetry is born out of her relationships with the people, landscapes and animals, tame and wild, of her native Oregon. Her collection, *Blue Abundance*, appeared from Salmon in 2010.

Maurice Harmon, in addition to being a poet, is the leading scholar-critic of his generation in the field of Anglo-Irish Literature. He pioneered its development as an academic discipline and is the author of a number of significant works, from a basic bibliographical guide to headline studies of Seán O'Faoláin, Austin Clarke, Thomas Kinsella, and others. His publications include *Seán O'Faoláin. A Life* (1994), *Selected Essays* (2006), and *Thomas Kinsella. Designing for the Exact Needs* (2008). He edited the definitive anthology *Irish Poetry after Yeats* (1978, 1998) and published *The Dialogue of the Ancients of Ireland* (2009), a new translation of Acallam na Senórach. His poetry collections include *The Last Regatta* (Salmon, 2000), *The Doll with Two Backs and other poems* (Salmon, 2004), *The Mischievous Boy and other poems* (Salmon, 2008) and *When Love Is Not Enough: New & Selected Poems* (Salmon, 2010). In 2010, Salmon published a tribute book celebrating Harmon's 80th year, *Honouring The Word: Poetry and Prose, Celebrating Maurice Harmon on his 80th birthday*, compiled and edited by Barbara Brown.

Anne Le Marquand Hartigan is a prize-winning poet, playwright and painter. She trained as a painter at Reading University, England. She returned to Co. Louth, Ireland, in 1962 with her husband Tim Hartigan where they farmed and reared their six children. She now lives in Dublin. She has published six collections of poetry: *To Keep The Light Burning: Reflections in times of loss* (Salmon, 2008); *Nourishment* (Salmon, 2005); *Immortal Sins* (Salmon, 1993); the award winning long poem with Anne's drawings, *Now is a Moveable Feast* (Salmon, 1991); *Return Single* (Beaver Row Press, 1986); and *Long Tongue* (Beaver Row Press, 1982). Her prose work includes *Clearing The Space: A Way of Writing* (Salmon, 1996). Hartigan won the Mobil Prize for Playwriting for her play *The Secret Game* in 1995. *In Other Worlds* (2003) was commissioned and performed by Ohio University, USA, then performed at the Edinburgh Fringe Festival and Otago Dunedin New Zealand. *Jersey Lilies* was performed at the Samuel Beckett Theatre Dublin 1996, where Anne acted with Robert Gordon in this two hander. *La Corbiere* was performed at the Project Theatre during the Dublin Theatre Festival 1989, and has since been performed in Beirut 2004 and by Solas Nua Theatre Company in Washington DC July 2006.

Michael Heffernan was born in 1942 in Detroit. He studied at the University of Detroit (A.B.) and the University of Massachusetts (Ph.D.). Since then he has resided mainly in Michigan, Kansas and Arkansas. He has taught the study and practice of poetry at the University of Arkansas (Fayetteville) since 1986. He began writing poems in 1958. His books include *The Cry of Oliver Hardy* (1979), *To the Wreakers of Havoc* (1984), both recently reissued by the University of Georgia Press; *The Man at Home* (Arkansas, 1988); *Love's Answer* (Iowa Poetry Prize, 1994); *The Night Breeze Off the Ocean* (Eastern

Washington University Press, 2005), along with three books from Salmon, *The Back Road to Arcadia* (1994), *Another Part of the Island* (1999) and *The Odor of Sanctity* (2008). His work has earned three fellowships from the National Endowment for the Arts (US), two Pushcart Prizes, and the Porter Prize for Literary Excellence. He and his wife, Ann, have four grown children, three sons and a daughter.

Patrick Hicks is a dual citizen of Ireland and the United States, as well as Writer-in-Residence at Augustana College. He is the author of several poetry collections, including *This London* (Salmon, 2010), and his work has appeared in scores of journals such as *Ploughshares, Tar River Poetry, Glimmer Train, Virginia Quarterly Review, Natural Bridge, Indiana Review, Nimrod*, and many others. Aside from being a Visiting Fellow at Oxford, he has been nominated several times for the Pushcart Prize and he is the recipient of a number of grants, including one from the Bush Foundation to support his first novel, which is about Auschwitz. After living in Europe for many years, he now enjoys thunderstorms rolling across Midwest America.

Kevin Higgins is co-organiser of Over The Edge literary events in Galway, Ireland. He facilitates poetry workshops at Galway Arts Centre; teaches creative writing at Galway Technical Institute and on the Brothers of Charity Away With Words programme. He is also Writer-in-Residence at Merlin Park Hospital and the poetry critic of the *Galway Advertiser*. His first collection of poems *The Boy With No Face* was published by Salmon in February 2005 and was short-listed for the 2006 Strong Award. His second collection, *Time Gentlemen, Please*, was published in March 2008 by Salmon. One of the poems from *Time Gentlemen, Please*, 'My Militant Tendency', features in the *Forward Book of Poetry 2009*. His most recent collection, *Frightening New Furniture*, appeared from Salmon in 2010. One of the poems in that collection, 'Ourselves Again', appeared in *Best of Irish Poetry 2009* (Southword Editions). His work also features in the *The Watchful Heart – A New Generation of Irish Poets* (Ed Joan McBreen, Salmon Poetry, 2009) & in *Identity Parade – New British and Irish Poets* (Ed Roddy Lumsden, Bloodaxe, 2010).

Rita Ann Higgins was born in 1955 in Galway, Ireland. She is one of thirteen children. Her first five poetry collections were published by Salmon: *Goddess on the Mervue Bus* (1986); *Witch in the Bushes* (1988); *Goddess and Witch* (1990); *Philomena's Revenge* (1992); and, *Higher Purchase* (1996). Bloodaxe Books published her next three collections: *Sunny Side Plucked* (1996); *An Awful Racket* (2001); and *Throw in the Vowels: New & Selected Poems* in May 2005 to mark her 50th birthday. *Throw in the Vowels* was reissued in 2010 by Bloodaxe with an accompanying CD of poems read by Rita Ann Higgins. Her plays include: *Face Licker Come Home* (Salmon 1991); *God of the Hatch Man* (1992), *Colie Lally Doesn't Live in a Bucket* (1993); and *Down All the Roundabouts* (1999). She was Galway County's Writer-in-Residence in 1987, Writer-in-Residence at the National University of Ireland, Galway, in 1994-95, and Writer-in-Residence for Offaly County Council in 1998-99. Her collection *Sunny Side Plucked* was a Poetry Book Society Recommendation. She divides her time between Galway City and Spiddal, County Galway. Her book of poems and essays, *Hurting God - Part Essay Part Rhyme*, was published by Salmon in 2010. Bloodaxe will publish a new collection of her poetry, *Ireland Is Changing Mother*, in 2011.

John Hildebidle has been a teacher for nearly forty years, from public secondary school, to Harvard, and the Massachusetts Institute of Technology (MIT) where he teaches English, Irish, and American literature. He writes poetry and fiction. He has published four collections of poetry, most recently *Signs, Translations* (Salmon Poetry, 2008).

Amy Holman is the author of the poetry collections, *Wrens Fly Through This Opened Window* (Somondoco Press, 2010) and *Wait For Me, I'm Gone* (Dream Horse Press, 2005), and works as a literary consultant and teacher. She also writes prose, and maintains a blog, *Lending Whale*, at WordPress. Her work has been nominated for Pushcart Prizes and selected for the Best American Poetry 1999. The golden retriever in her poems also stars in the essay, "Lounge Act," published online at Connotations Press. Currently, she is delighted by a nine-year old Glen of Imaal terrier named Dolly, who was her mother's dog, first, with a backyard in northwestern New Mexico, and now engages the myriad canines and humans on the streets of south Brooklyn, New York.

Ron Houchin a retired public school teacher in the Appalachian region of southernmost Ohio, taught for thirty years. Though raised on the remote banks of the Ohio River in Huntington, West Virginia, he has travelled throughout Europe, Canada, and the U.S. His work has appeared in *Poetry Ireland Review, The Stinging Fly, The Southwest Review, Appalachian Heritage, The New Orleans Review*, and over two hundred other venues. He has been awarded an Ohio Arts Council Grant for teachers of the arts, a tutorial fellowship to teach in a Dublin writing workshop, a poetry prize from Indiana University, as well as a book of the year award from the Appalachian Writers' Association. His poems have been featured on *Verse Daily*. He has published three collections with Salmon Poetry, most recently *Museum Crows* (2009).

Adam Houle was born in Green Bay, Wisconsin, and is currently a PhD student at Texas Tech University. His poetry has appeared or is forthcoming in *AGNI* online, *Southeast Review, Apalachee Review*, the anthology, *Red, White, and Blues*, and elsewhere. He is an associate editor for *Iron Horse Literary Review* and *32 Poems*.

Ben Howard is a native of eastern Iowa and the author of *The Pressed Melodeon: Essays on Modern Irish Writing* (Story Line Press, 1996), the verse novella *Midcentury* (Salmon, 1997), and four previous collections of poems, most recently *Dark Pool* (Salmon, 2004) & *Leaf, Sunlight, Asphalt* (Salmon, 2009). He has received numerous awards, including the Milton Dorfman Prize in Poetry and a fellowship from the National Endowment for the Arts. He is Professor of English Emeritus at Alfred University, New York.

Holly J. Hughes is the editor of *Beyond Forgetting: Poetry and Prose* about Alzheimer's Disease, published by Kent State University Press as part of their Literature and Medicine series in spring 2009. Her award-winning chapbook *Boxing the Compass* was published by Floating Bridge Press in 2007. Her poems have appeared in a number of literary journals and anthologies, among them: *Dancing with Joy: 99 Poems* and more recently, *Working the Woods, Working the Sea* and *The Poet's Guide to Birds*. She has spent the last thirty summers working on the sea in Alaska, most recently as a naturalist. A graduate of the Rainier Writing Workshop low-residency MFA program, she teaches writing at Edmonds Community College, Washington, where she co-directs the Convergence Writers Series and the Sustainability Initiative. She lives in a log cabin built in the 1930s in Indianola, Washington. She lives in a log cabin built in the 1930s in Indianola, Washington.

Alexander Hutchison was born and brought up in Buckie, a fishing town on the north-east coast of Scotland. He has worked on and off in universities, including eighteen years in Canada and the USA, though he gave up being a literary academic some time ago. As a poet (and occasional translator) he writes in Scots and English. Currently he lives in Glasgow. Based on recent experience he has decided that while wishful thinking doesn't do it, a proper determination can make the cosmos perk up and take a bit of notice. "Mr Scales Walks His Dog," an underground perennial, was composed in the early seventies and drew praise from Lawrence Ferlinghetti and Michael Ondaatje.

Sabine Huynh is a poet, novelist and literary translator. She holds a Ph.D. in Linguistics from the Hebrew University of Jerusalem, where she taught from 2002 to 2008, and has done post-doctorate studies in Sociolinguistics at the University of Ottawa. She was born in Saigon in 1972, grew up in France, and worked and studied in England, the USA, Israel and Canada. She now lives in Tel Aviv. She writes mainly in English and French, and translates from English and Hebrew into French and Vietnamese. Her poems have appeared in literary journals in the USA, Quebec, Israel, and Italy, including the *Dudley Review, Poetica Magazine, Cyclamens* and *Swords, Voices Israel, arc, Art Le Sabord, Danse Macabre, Terres de Femmes, Traduzionetradizione,* and *Continuum.* Her short stories have been published in *The Jerusalem Post* (French edition), *Zinc, Virages* and *Art Le Sabord.* Her first novel, *La Mer et l'enfant,* has been accepted for publication in France by Galaade Editions (2011).

Brad Johnson has two chapbooks *Void Where Prohibited* and *The Happiness Theory* available at puddinghouse.com. Work of his has recently been accepted by *The Jabberwock Review, The Madison Review, Steam Ticket, Willow Springs* and others. He currently serves as Poetry Editor of *Magnolia: A Florida Journal of Literary and Fine Arts* (www.magnoliafloridajournal.com).

Fred Johnston was born in Belfast, Northern Ireland, in 1951. A journalist for some years, he founded Galway's annual *Cúirt* Literature Festival in 1986 and is now director of the Western Writers' Centre, Galway. In 2004 he was writer in residence to the Princess Grace Irish Library at Monaco. A new collection of stories in French translation by Kristian Le Braz is due from *Terre de Brume* this year, and a collection of stories in English from Parthian Books (UK) in May 2011. He now writes and publishes poetry only in French and has had work in journals in France such as *Le Grognard, Verso, Hopala* and elsewhere. He lives in Galway.

Thomas Kabdebo was born in Budapest, and attended university courses in Budapest, Cardiff, Rome and London, pursuing degrees in Hungarian Literature, English and European History, History of Art and Librarianship. He has a PhD in History and taught Military History in Manchester for six years. He was the library director in the University of Guyana, Georgetown; in Westminster University London; and in the combined universities of St. Patrick's College and the National University of Ireland Maynooth, between 1983-2000. In Maynooth he was responsible for setting up the John Paul II University Library. Since his retirement, he has been busy writing and translating books, such as the Danube trilogy and the Dictionary of Dictionaries. He has written a scholarly book, entitled *Ireland and Hungary,* and a travel book in Hungarian, entitled *Irorszag ket arca* (*The Two Faces of Ireland*), and translated the selected poems of several Irish poets including Eiléan Ní Chuilleanáįn, Michael Longley and Peter Fallon. He has edited two anthologies of contemporary Irish poetry. He has won ten literary prizes for his own writing.

Conor Mark Kavanagh has been a journalist with RTE News, working on Television and Radio, after joining the national broadcaster straight from college, becoming RTE's youngest news reader at the age of 19. He is an accomplished songwriter – two of his co-writes appear on Charlie McGettigan's album *Stolen Moments* and his songs have been short listed twice in public competitions for Ireland's entry in the Eurovision song contest. He also worked as a freelance reporter for Mike Murphy's Arts Show on Radio 1 and compiled and presented a documentary about the rehearsals and performance of Yeats's "Cuchulainn cycle" at the Abbey Theatre: *Player and painted stage.* He was invited back to the Arts Show as a guest some years later to read his poem "Homecoming", which was published in the Sligo Arts Festival poetry broadsheet. His interest in writing poetry was rekindled after watching an Arts Lives documentary about the work of Thomas Kinsella. His first poetry collection will be published by Salmon Poetry in 2011.

Jean Kavanagh was born in Dublin, and is now living in Lahinch, Co.Clare. She studied Irish Folklore and English Literature at University College, Dublin. In 2001 she co-founded The Cascades writing group in Ennistymon, and is now participating in the Advanced Poetry Workshop in The Galway Arts Centre. Her work has been published in their showcase anthologies, *Lady Gregory's Townhouse* and *Behind the Masks*. She has read her poetry at Clifden Arts Week, the Salthill Arts Festival, and 2009's National Poetry Day event for County Clare. In 2010 she was a featured reader in the Over the Edge Reading Series in Galway, and was shortlisted for Over the Edge New Writer of the Year. She has recently spent time with the Oglala Lakota Sioux tribe on Pine Ridge Indian Reservation, South Dakota. She would love a puppy, but her cats have told her that as long as she lives under their roof she can't have one.

Deirdre Kearney is originally from Omagh, Co. Tyrone and has lived in Galway since 1983. She has been a featured reader in the Over the Edge readings in Galway City Library. She has read her work at Clifden Arts Week, in Westside Library, Galway, and The Galway Arts Centre Studio, in Nuns' Island, Poets for Oxfam launch in Galway in 2006 and at Ái, An Taibhdhearc showcase for Galway Arts Festival. Her poetry has been published in: *The Shop, ROPES, West 47 Online, Cúirt New Writing 2007, The Ulster Herald, Crannóg, Words on the Web, Tinteán, Treóir, Over the Edge* and *Galway Exposed*. Her first collection *Spiddal Pier* was published in 2009 by Lapwing Press. She was short-listed for 2009 Cúirt/Over The Edge showcase reading.

Anne Kennedy, poet, writer, photographer and broadcaster, came from Orcas Island, off the coast of Washington state, to live in Galway, Ireland in 1977. Her first book *Buck Mountain Poems*, published by Salmon in 1989, is based on her Orcas experiences. *The Dog Kubla Dreams My Life* was published in 1994. A keen documentor of history, in 1993 she contributed an oral history project to the Duke Ellington archive in the Smithsonian Museum of American History. Anne Kennedy died on 29th September 1998.

Noel King is a writer, actor and musician, native of Tralee, Co. Kerry. His poetry, haiku, short stories, articles and reviews have appeared in publications in over thirty countries, the poetry in journals as diverse as *Poetry Ireland Review, The Sunday Tribune, Bongos of the World* (Japan), *The Dalhousie University Review* (Canada), *Kotaz* (South Africa), *Poetry Salzburg Review* (Austria) and *Quadrant* (Australia). Along the way he has been a singer with the famous Bunratty Castle Entertainers and has worked as an arts administrator and poetry editor. His debut collection, *Prophesying the Past*, was published by Salmon in 2010.

Philip Kingston moved to Dublin from Manchester in 2006. Nowadays he works mainly as an actor and teacher of Shakespeare while slowly writing plays for love not money.

Jacqueline Kolosov's poetry collections are *Modigliani's Muse* (TurningPoint, 2009) and *Vago* (Lewis-Clark, 2007). Her poems have recently appeared in *Orion, The Southern Review*, and *Cave Wall*. Also a fiction writer, she has published several novels for young adults and coedited two anthologies of women's prose. She lives with her family and two dogs in West Texas.

Ted Kooser served two terms as U. S. Poet Laureate and during those years he won the Pulitzer Prize in poetry for his book, *Delights & Shadows*, published by Copper Canyon Press. His most recent book is for children, *Bag in the Wind*, published by Candlewick Press. Kooser lives in rural Nebraska with his wife, Kathleen Rutledge, the retired editor of *The Lincoln Journal Star*, and is Presidential Professor of English at the University of Nebraska-Lincoln.

Danuta E. Kosk-Kosicka writes and translates poetry in two languages, Polish and English. Born and raised in Poland, she has lived in the USA for the past 30 years. For the first two decades English was the language in which she wrote her grant proposals and scientific publications as a biochemist. In 1997 she turned to poetry, and began creative writing in English. Her poems, written respectively in English or Polish, have been published in both the USA and Poland, including *Ellipsis: Literature and Art*; *Baltimore Review*; *Passager*; *Pivot*; *Loch Raven Review*; *Little Patuxent Review*; *Weavings 2000: Maryland Millennial Anthology*; *Thy Mother's Glass*; *Stranger at Home: Anthology of American Poetry with an Accent*; *Little Patuxent Review*; *Akcent*; *Więź*. She is the translator of two bilingual books of poems by Lidia Kosk, *Słodka woda, słona woda/ Sweet Water, Salt Water* and *niedosyt/ reshapings*. Her translations of poems by Lucille Clifton, Josephine Jacobsen, and Linda Pastan have appeared in Poland. She is the translator for two bilingual books of poems by Lidia Kosk, *niedosyt/ reshapings* and *Słodka woda, słona woda/ Sweet Water, Salt Water*, the latter of which she has also edited.

Anatoly (Anthony) Kudryavitsky is a Russian/Irish poet and novelist living in South Co. Dublin and working as editor of *Shamrock Haiku Journal* (www.shamrockhaiku.webs.com). In 2005, Goldsmith Press published his first collection entitled *Shadow of Time*. His second collection, a book of his English haiku titled *Morning at Mount Ring* (Doghouse Books), appeared in 2007. He also edited an anthology of contemporary Russian poetry in English translation entitled *A Night in the Nabokov Hotel* (Dedalus Press, 2006). Among his other publications are seven collections of his Russian poems, a novel, two novellas and a number of short stories. He was a recipient of several of international literary awards including the Capoliveri Premio Internazionale di Poesia (Italy, 2007) and the Suruga Baika Haiku Prize of Excellence (Japan, 2008). His poems have appeared in magazines nationally and internationally, and have been translated into twelve languages.

Maxine Kumin's 17th poetry collection, *Where I Live: New and Selected Poems 1990-2010*, was published by Norton. Northwestern University Press published her new essay collection, *The Roots of Things*, and Candlewick Press, a children's book about a black-and-white dog with an identity crisis, *What Color Is Caesar?* Her awards include the Pulitzer and Ruth Lilly Poetry Prizes, the Aiken Taylor Award, the Poets' Prize, and the Harvard Arts and Robert Frost Medals. She and her husband live on a farm in central New Hampshire with three rescued dogs and two very old horses.

Yahia Lababidi is the author of *Signposts to Elsewhere* (Jane Street Press) which was selected as a 2008 Book of the Year by The Independent, UK. His latest book is the critically-acclaimed, *Trial by Ink: From Nietzsche to Belly Dancing* (Common Ground Publishing). Lababidi is also an internationally-published aphorist, poet, and essayist with selected works translated into Arabic, Slovak, Swedish, Turkish, and Italian. He is the only contemporary Arab writer featured in the encylopedia: *Geary's Guide to the World's Great Aphorists*, and the youngest poet included in the best-selling US college textbook, *Literature: an Introduction to Reading and Writing* (10th edition).

Jessie Lendennie's prose poem *Daughter* was first published in 1988 (reissued in 1991 as *Daughter and other poems)*. It was followed in 1990 by *The Salmon Guide to Poetry Publishing* and in 1992 by *The Salmon Guide to Creative Writing in Ireland*. Her poetry has been anthologised in *Irish Poetry Now: Other Voices*, *Unveiling Treasures: The Attic Guide To The Published Works of Irish Women Literary Writers* and *The White Page/An Bhileog Bhan: Twentieth-Century Irish Women Poets*, among others. She is the co-founder and Managing Director of Salmon Poetry. In 2008, she edited *Salmon: A Journey in Poetry, 1981-2007*, an anthology of Salmon Poetry. In 2009 she compiled and edited *Poetry: Reading it, Writing it, Publishing it*. In 2010, she compiled & edited this book, *Dogs Singing: A Tribute Anthology*, a long-planned project dear to her heart.

Dave Lordan was born in Derby, England, in 1975, and grew up in Clonakilty in West Cork. In 2004 he was awarded an Arts Council bursary and in 2005 he won the Patrick Kavanagh Award for Poetry. His collections are *The Boy in The Ring* (Cliffs of Moher, Salmon Poetry, 2007), which won the Strong Award for best first collection by an Irish writer and was shortlisted for the Irish Times poetry prize; and *Invitation to a Sacrifice* (Salmon Poetry, 2010). Eigse Riada theatre company produced his first play, *Jo Bangles*, at the Mill Theatre, Dundrum in 2010. He has lived in Holland, Greece and Italy, and now resides in Greystones, Co Wicklow. He can be contacted at dlordan@hotmail.com.

Caroline Lynch lives in Galway. She grew up in Cork and studied law at UCC. While there, she won the inaugural Sean Dunne Memorial Poetry Competition. She then trained as an actor and worked in the theatre for a number of years before returning to law and qualifying as a solicitor. She obtained an MA in Writing from NUIG. She won the Listowel Writers' Week poetry collection competition in 2007 and Salmon Poetry published her first collection *Lost in the Gaeltacht* in 2008. She is the recipient of an Arts Council Literature Bursary. She is a founding member of Galway-based Mephisto Theatre Company.

Thomas Lynch is the author of four collections of poems, three books of essays and a book of stories, *Apparition & Late Fictions*. *The Undertaking* won the American Book Award and was a finalist for the National Book Award. His work has been the subject of two documentary films, *Learning Gravity* by Cathal Black and PBS Frontline's *The Undertaking*. His work has appeared in *The Atlantic* and *Granta*, *The New Yorker* and *Esquire*, *Poetry* and *The Paris Review*, also *The Times* (of New York, Los Angelus, London and Ireland). He lives in Milford, Michigan and Moveen, West Clare.

Bette Lynch Husted lives in rural Oregon. Her first full-length poetry collection is forthcoming from Wordcraft of Oregon this year, and a chapbook was published by Pudding House in 2002. A collection of memoir essays, *Above the Clearwater: Living on Stolen Land* (Oregon State U Press, 2004) was a finalist for the Oregon Book Award and the WILLA Award in creative nonfiction, and a second collection is forthcoming from Plain View Press. In 2007 she received an Oregon Arts Commission Award.

John MacKenna is the author of fourteen books – poetry, short-stories, novels, biography and memoir – and a number of stage and radio plays. He is a winner of the Hennessy Literary Award; the C Day Lewis Award and the Irish Times Fiction Award. His radio documentary – "How the Heart Approaches What It Yearns" – on the work of Leonard Cohen – won a Jacobs' Radio Award. He lives in Co. Kildare. He is, more or less, owned by his mutt Dogger.

Mary Madec was born and raised in the west of Ireland. She received her early education at NUI, Galway, obtaining her B.A. in French and English, and her M.A in Old English; in 2002 she received her doctorate in Linguistics from the University of Pennsylvania, USA. She has taught courses for NUI, Galway, UPenn, and Open University and is currently Director of the Villanova Study Abroad Program in Galway. She has received awards and accolades for her work in the Raftery Competition 2007, the WINDOWS Showcase and Anthology 2007 and the Maria Edgeworth Competition 2008. In April 2008 she was also the recipient of the Hennessy XO Award for Emerging Poetry. With her husband Claude Madec of the LIFE programme (Brothers of Charity Services) she started up a community-writing project, Away with Words, now in its third year. Her debut collection, *In Other Words*, was published by Salmon in 2010.

Tom Mathews was born in Dublin in 1952. After working in advertising he studied Fine Art at the National College of Art and Design in Dublin. He has been a freelance cartoonist, writer and critic since 1975. His work appears weekly in *The Irish Times* and *Sunday Independent*. He has had thirty one-man shows and his paintings have been exhibited in Living Art, the National Portrait Show and at the RHA. He has illustrated a dozen books, written a novel and published three volumes of cartoons. His last book,

The New Adventures of Keats and Chapman, was published in 2008. Best known as one of Ireland's most popular cartoonists, Tom Mathews has for many years contributed poems to a number of small magazines and journals. His most recent collection of poetry, *The Owl and the Pussycat and other poems*, was published by Dedalus Press in 2009.

Sebastian Matthews is the author of the poetry collection *We Generous* (Red Hen Press, 2007) & the memoir, *In My Father's Footsteps* (W.W. Norton, 2004). He co-edited, with Stanley Plumly, *Search Party: Collected Poems of William Matthews* (Houghton Mifflin, 2004) and *New Hope from the Dead: Uncollected Matthews* (Red Hen Press, 2010). Matthews teaches at Warren Wilson College in Asheville, North Carolina, for the Great Smokies Writing Program & serves on the faculty at Queens College Low-Residency MFA in Creative Writing. His poetry & prose has appeared in many journals, including most recently *Pisgah Review, 32 Poems, American Poetry Review* & *Georgia Review*. He serves on the board of Q Ave Press, creators of handmade chapbooks & broadsides. Check out his collages and snapshots at 3bythefire.blogspot.com & merzpictures.blogspot.com.

William Matthews won the National Book Critics Circle Award in 1995 and the Ruth Lilly Award of the Modern Poetry Association in 1997. Born in Cincinnati in 1942, and educated at Yale University and the University of North Carolina. Matthews taught and lectured all over the United States. At of the time of his death in 1997, he was a professor of English and Director of the writing program at the City University of New York. In his lifetime, Matthews authored over a dozen books of poetry and prose, including *Search Party: Collected Poems of William Matthews* (Houghton Mifflin).

Afric McGlinchey spent her childhood and early adult years between Ireland and various countries in Africa. She has also lived in Spain, London and Paris. She returned to Ireland for good in 1999. Dogs have been a significant feature of her life, most of them rescued, the first from the Zambian bush when she was five years old. She hid him in the empty house next door and stole food to feed him. A freelance book reviewer, editor and workshop facilitator, Afric's poetry has appeared in a number of journals in Ireland and abroad, including *Southword, Poetry Ireland Review, the SHOp, Revival, Tear in the Fence, Scottish Poetry Review* and *Acumen*. She lives in Kinsale, Co. Cork and is currently working towards her first collection.

Cecilia McGovern was born in Co. Mayo and has lived in Dublin since becoming a teacher. Her poetry has featured in *The Sunday Tribune, Poetry Ireland Review* and various anthologies, the most recent being *The Thornfield Poets: Poems by the Thornfield Poets* (Salmon Poetry, 2008). She was a prizewinner in *Féile Filíochta* (Poetry Now, Dun Laoghaire International Poetry Competition) and in the National Womens' Poetry Competition. In 2007, she obtained an M.A. in Creative Writing from the School of English, Drama and Film, U.C.D. A collection of her work *Polishing The Evidence* was published by Salmon Poetry in 2008.

Iggy McGovern was born in Coleraine and lives in Dublin, where he is Associate Professor of Physics at Trinity College. His poems have appeared widely in both journal and anthology formats, as well as in the "Poetry In Motion" series on DART trains. Awards include the Ireland Chair of Poetry Bursary and the Hennessy Literary Award for Poetry. A first collection, *The King of Suburbia*, published by Dedalus Press in 2005, received the inaugural Glen Dimplex New Writers Award for Poetry. A second collection *Safe House* is published by Dedalus Press in 2010.

Irene McKinney has five books of poetry, including *Six O'Clock Mine Report*, which was reissued in the Carnegie Mellon Contemporary Classics series in 2009, and *Unthinkable: Selected Poems* (Red Hen Press, 2009). She is the West Virginia State Poet

Laureate, and the director of the Low Residency MFA Program at West Virginia Wesleyan.

Kevin McLellan is the author of the chapbook *Round Trip* (Seven Kitchens, 2010), a collaborative series with numerous women poets. He has recent or forthcoming poems in journals including: *Barrow Street, Colorado Review, Drunken Boat, Hunger Mountain, Interim, Southern Humanities Review, Sugar House Review, Versal* and several others. Even though he lives in Cambridge, Massachusetts, a rural sensibility lives in him. Currently, Kevin teaches creative writing at the University of Rhode Island in Providence.

Devon McNamara's poems, essays, interviews and reviews have appeared in *The Christian Science Monitor, The Hiram Poetry Review, The Laurel Review,* and *Wild Sweet Notes: Fifty Years of West Virginia Poetry*, among other publications. She has taught writing in schools, prisons, summer camps, and reform facilities in Appalachian and Midwestern states and originated the West Virginia Public Radio course "Women and Literature." Her poems have been performed in collaboration with dancers from The Dayton Ballet and The Dayton Contemporary Dance Company. She was the recipient of a YADDO fellowship. She is Professor of English, Irish Literature, and Creative Writing at West Virginia Wesleyan College where she directs the Honors Program.

Máighréad Medbh was born in County Limerick. She has four published poetry collections: *The Making of a Pagan* (Blackstaff Press, 1990); *Tenant* (Salmon Publishing, 1999); *Split* (¡Divas!, Arlen House, 2003); and *When the Air Inhales You* (Arlen House, 2008). She produced a CD, *Out of My Skin*, in 2002, and her work has been included in a wide range of anthologies and journals. A new collection, *Twelve Beds for the Dreamer*, will be published in 2010, and Salmon will be publishing a new edition of *Tenant*. Widely known as a performance poet, Máighréad continues to perform at a large variety of venues in Ireland and abroad. Each of the two significant dogs in her life were coloured black and amber. The first, instantly forgiven, accidentally left her with a permanent scar. With natal Mercury in Aries, she probably has canine features herself, though her bark etc.

Paula Meehan was born in Dublin where she still lives. Her most recent collections of poetry are *Dharmakaya* and *Painting Rain*, available from Carcanet Press and Wake Forest University Press. Her poem here is inspired by her dog Bella, who had a collie mother and a lab/retriever father and who would be running for public office if she had an opposable thumb.

John Menaghan, born in New Jersey, has lived in Boston, Berkeley, Vancouver, Syracuse, London, Dublin, Belfast, Galway, Gortahork, and Dingle, & presently makes his home in Venice, CA. Winner of an Academy of American Poets Prize and other awards, he has published poems and articles in various journals and given readings in Ireland, England, France, Hungary, and the U.S. He has also had several short plays produced in Los Angeles and one in Omaha. Menaghan teaches at Loyola Marymount University in Los Angeles, where he also serves as Director of both the Irish Studies and Summer in Ireland programs and runs the LMU Irish Cultural Festival. His poetry collections are *All the Money in the World* (Salmon, 1999), *She Alone* (Salmon, 2006) and *What Vanishes* (Salmon, 2009).

Alexa Mergen has worked as a florist, pet sitter, dishwasher, gardener, humane educator, editor, and English and Journalism teacher. She has taught poetry to adults and children in diverse settings and was a fellow of the Writing Project at the University of California-Davis. She's the author of *From Bison to Biopark: 100 Years of the National Zoo*, a chapbook, *We Have Trees*, and co-editor of the 45th anniversary anthology for California Poets in the Schools, *What the World Hears*. Born in Iowa in 1967, she grew up in Washington, DC and Nevada, and lives in California where she writes essays and book reviews as well as poetry.

Karla Linn Merrifield is a four-time Pushcart Prize nominee, one-time "Best of the Net" nominee, and 2009 Everglades National Park Artist-in-Residence. Her poetry has appeared in dozens of publications as well as in many anthologies. She has published five books, including *Godwit: Poems of Canada*, which received the 2009 Andrew Eiseman Writers Award for Poetry. *The Urn*, a chapbook, is forthcoming from Finishing Line Press, and her full-length collection *Athabaskan Fractal and Other Poems of the Far North* will appear from Salmon Poetry. She was founding poetry editor of *Sea Stories* (www.seastories.org), and is now book reviewer and assistant editor for *The Centrifugal Eye* (www.centrifugaleye.com) and moderator of the poetry blog, *Smothered Air* (smotheredair.yuku.com/). She teaches at Writers & Books, Rochester, NY. You can read more about her and sample her poems and photographs at http://karlalinn.blogspot.com.

Agi Mishol is one of Israel's most popular contemporary poets. Her latest volume of poems, *House Call* – whose title poem deals at length with her experience as the daughter of Holocaust survivors – follows on a dozen earlier ones, including her bestselling *Collected Poems*. Mishol's next book will be a selection of essays on writing and literature, including the figure of the muse. A version of "The Ascension" appeared in *Look There*, a selection of her poems in English (translated by Lisa Katz), published by Graywolf Press in 2006. Born in a Hungarian-speaking area of Romania, Mishol came to Israel as a child. She lives on a pomegranate, peach and pecan farm near Gedera, and teaches literature at Alma College for Jewish Culture in Tel Aviv. Translator and poet **Lisa Katz** teaches at Hebrew University and writes book reviews for the English edition of *Haaretz*. She is the author of *Reconstruction*, a book of her poems translated into Hebrew.

Noel Monahan has published five collections of poetry with Salmon: *Opposite Wall* (1991), *Snowfire* (1995), *Curse of The Birds* (2000), *The Funeral Game* (2004) and *Curve of the Moon* (2010). He is Co-Editor of Windows Publications. Noel has won numerous literary awards including: Poetry Ireland's Seacat National Award, The RTE PJ O'Connor Drama Award, The Hiberno-English Poetry Award, The Irish Writers Union Award for poetry. His play, *The Children of Lir*, was performed by Livin Dred Theatre in 2007 and his most recent play *Lovely Husbands* was premiered in 2010. His poetry is prescribed text for The Leaving Certificate English Course for examination in 2011 & 2012. Noel Monahan holds an MA in Creative Writing.

John Montague was born in Brooklyn, NY, in 1929, and reared on the family farm in County Tyrone. He now lives in County Cork. He has taught in France, Canada and the US, where he was Poet-in-Residence at the NY State Writers' Institute. For much of his career he taught at University College Cork. His major publications include *The Rough Field*, *The Great Cloak*, *The Dead Kingdom*, *Mount Eagle* and *Smashing the Piano*. His collections of stories include *Death of a Chieftain*. *Collected Poems* appeared in 1995 from the Gallery Press, the year he received the America Ireland Fund Literary Award. In 1998 he became first Ireland Professor of Poetry.

Alan Jude Moore is from Dublin. His poetry collections – *Black State Cars* (2004), *Lost Republics* (2008) and *Strasbourg* (2010) – are all published by Salmon. His poetry is also widely published, in Ireland and abroad, and his fiction has been twice short-listed for the Hennessy Literary Award for New Irish Writing. Translations of his work have been published in Italy, Russia and Turkey. He lives in Dublin. (www.alanjudemoore.com)

Susan Moorhead's writing has been published in a variety of places including *The Comstock Review, Goblin Fruit, Bayou, Mothering, Feile-Festa*, among others. Currently poems online can be viewed at Anderbo.com and at *Alice Blue Review* (.org) and a poetry book review is forthcoming from *The Chattahoochee Review*. An essay in *Brain, Child* was nominated for a Pushcart Prize. She is a librarian by trade.

Mary Mullen's poems and non-fiction work have been published in *The Stinging Fly, Crannóg, West47online, The Cúirt Annual, Landing Places: An Anthology of Irish Immigrant Poets, The Cork Literary Review, We Alaskans, The Irish Times, Peninsula Clarion, Anchorage Daily News* and RTÉ Radio's *Sunday Miscellany*. She was awarded an MA in Writing from the National University of Ireland, Galway, in 2006. A savant of memoir, she taught memoir writing at Galway Arts Centre, and now tutors writers privately. Mary was born in Anchorage, and raised on her parent's homestead in Soldotna, Alaska. She moved to Ballinderreen, Co. Galway, Ireland in 1996, where she still lives with her daughter Lily, a sparkly Galway girl who was born with Down syndrome. Her debut collection, *Zephyr*, was published by Salmon in 2010.

Pete Mullineaux lives in Galway, Ireland, where he teaches drama and creative writing. He is also resident MC for the Cúirt International Festival of Literature poetry slam. His publications are: *Zen Traffic Lights* (Lapwing 2005) *A Father's Day* (Salmon 2008.) A new collection is forthcoming from Salmon in 2011.

The poet **Richard Murphy** celebrated his eightieth birthday with a visit to Inishbofin on the 6th August 2007. He first came to the island in 1952, in a pookhaun (púcán) from Rosroe, a trip described in the title poem of *Sailing to an Island* (Faber, 1963). His poetry has most recently been anthologised in *The Penguin Book of Irish Verse*. Born at Milford House on the Mayo-Galway border near Kilmaine, Richard spent some of his early child-hood in Ceylon and his later at boarding schools in England before taking a degree at Oxford, where his tutor was C.S. Lewis. But his preferred abode was the north-west coastal area of Connemara and adjacent islands, which inspired much of his poetry. Even after he moved to Dublin in 1980, and subsequently to post-apartheid South Africa, he continued to write about the west. He now lives in the ancient cultural heartland of Sri Lanka. Richard's daughter, Emily Avis Riordan, for whom he wrote the Doggerel, lives with her husband and two children in Knysna, South Africa. Emily came first to Inishbofin at the age of three in 1956; and most recently in May 2008, when she celebrated her fifty-second birthday by running the Half-Marathon.

Les Murray is an Australian poet, anthologist and critic. His career spans over forty years, and he has published nearly thirty volumes of poetry, as well as two verse novels and collections of his prose writings. His poetry has won many awards and he is regard-ed as one of the leading poets of his generation. He lives in the trees between Forster and Gloucester in New South Wales.

Joan Newmann has published several books of poetry, the most recent, *Prone*, a poetic narrative of her hospitalisation after a serious car accident. She is the recipient, along with Francis Harvey, of the Criobh na Eigse Award. She has read her work in Russia, America and Mexico and has taught creative writing all over Ireland, including writer-in-resi-dencies at Belfast City Hospital; Waterside Hospital, Derry, and for the Verbal Arts Centre and the Arts Council.

Kate Newmann compiled the *Dictionary of Ulster Biography* (published by Queen's University, Belfast) and has two books of poetry. Her new collection, *I Am a Horse* (Arlen Press) will be launched at Stuttgart Book Festival in 2010. She has been writer-in-resi-dence for the Down Lisburn Health Trust, and for the Arts Council, in Ballycastle, Mayogall, Buncrana and most recently in Carrickfergus for the Louis MacNeice Centenary Celebrations. She has collaborated on community projects with composers, dancers and artists, and produced a CD, *How Well Did You Love?*, of some of her own poems set to music.

Sheila Nickerson lives in Bellingham, Washington, with her husband Martin and her two dogs, Gus, a Weimaraner, and Copper, a Lhasa apso-terrier cross. A former Poet Laureate of Alaska, she has published widely in chapbooks, magazines, and anthologies and won two Pushcart Prizes for poetry. Her most recent poetry title is *Along the Alaska Highway* (Sheltering Pines Press, 2009); Her nonfiction includes *Disappearance: A Map* and *Midnight to the North*. She is presently at work on a history of sledge dogs in the Arctic in the mid-Nineteenth century.

Tommy Frank O'Connor lives in Tralee, Co. Kerry, Ireland. A novelist, poet, dramatist and story writer, his published works include a novel *The Poacher's Apprentice* (Marino Books, 1997); a novel for children *Kee Kee, Cup & Tok* (Wynkin de Worde, 2004); a collection of stories *Loose Head* (Doghouse, 2004), his award winning collection *Attic Warpipes* (Bradshaw Books, 2005) and his philosophical work *Pulse* (Doghouse, 2006). He is regularly published in literary presses and anthologies worldwide. His work has been performed on RTE Radio and on BBC Radio 4. He conducts Creative Writing Residencies in Schools, Libraries, Prisons and Colleges. He has had two terms as Writer in Residence for Co. Kerry, 2007 and 2008. He is *Clan File* of the O'Connor Kerry Clan.

Mary O'Donnell's first three poetry collections (*Reading the Sunflowers in September*, *Spiderwoman's Third Avenue Rhapsody*, and *Unlegendary Heroes*) were published by Salmon Poetry. The 2003 collection *September Elegies* was published by Lapwing Press, Belfast and her selected poems, *The Place of Miracles* was published in 2006 by New Island. A sixth collection, *The Ark Builders*, appeared from Arc Publications UK in autumn 2009. She has written three novels and two collections of short fiction. A member of Aosdána, she is on the faculty of a Carlow University Pittsburgh's MFA Creative Writing programme and teaches poetry part-time at NUI Maynooth. Interests include photography, future-oriented fiction and new models of pastoral poetry in the contemporary world. www.maryodonnell.com

Gréagóir Ó Dúill divides his time between Dublin and Gortahork, Co. Donegal. Eight collections in Irish published by Coiscéim were followed by his selected poems, *Rogha Dánta*. Selections were translated as *Traverse* (Lapwing,) and by Bernie Kenny as *Gone to Earth* (Black Mountain Press). Two influential anthologies were *Filíocht Uladh 1960 – 1985* and *Fearann Pinn 1900-1999*. Short stories, *Mar Atá*, followed biography *Samuel Ferguson, beatha agus saothar*. His first collection of original English poetry, *New Room Windows*, was published by Doghouse, Tralee, 2008. He continues to publish in Irish – his new collection *Dán Nollag faoin Samhradh* won the Oireachtas prize for best collection, 2010. His translations from the Scottish Gaelic of Crisdean MacIllebhain appeared as *Dealbh Athar*, Coiscéim in 2009. Educated in Queen's University, Belfast and University College, Dublin, Gréagóir took a Ph.D. in English in Maynooth and has taught in the Poets' House, Falcarragh and in Queen's University.

James Desmond O'Hara is a dual Irish and US citizen. O'Hara has been published by Nimrod International Poetry Journal, has read on National Public Radio in the US, and was sponsored as an Ireland poet representative by the Irish Arts Foundation. His first collection *Petition for Our Birthright* will be published by Salmon Poetry in 2011.

Chris Oke spent several years writing for the *Yukon News* in Whitehorse, Canada. During this time, he helped a friend tend to her eighteen geriatric sled dogs. This involved spending time with the hounds, feeding and scooping a staggering amount of poo. Sadly, an affectionate dog named Eastwood developed glaucoma in his one remaining eye. He was in pain and the eye had to be removed. Defying the pessimism of this poem, Eastwood recovered quickly from the operation and continues to run with the team every winter. Oke is currently living in Paris, where he is completing a Master's in Creative Writing through the University of British Columbia.

Michael O'Loughlin was born in Dublin in 1958 and educated at Trinity College, Dublin. He lived in Amsterdam for twenty years, and is now based in Dublin again. He has published four collections of poetry, including a Selected Poems, *Another Nation*, and many essays and translations. He worked for many years as a screenwriter, with four feature films to his credit. In recent years he has been Writer in Residence in Galway City and County, and Writer Fellow in Trinity College, Dublin. A new collection of poetry, *In This Life*, will be appearing soon from New Island Books.

Nessa O'Mahony was born in Dublin and lives in Rathfarnham where she works as a freelance teacher and writer. Her poetry has appeared in a number of Irish, UK, and North American periodicals and has been translated into several European languages. She won the National Women's Poetry Competition in 1997 and was shortlisted for the Patrick Kavanagh Prize and Hennessy Literature Awards. She was awarded an Arts Council of Ireland literature bursary in 2004, a Simba Gill Fellowship in 2005 and an artists' bursary from South Dublin County Council in 2007. She has published three books – her first collection, *Bar Talk*, appeared in 1999. Her second, *Trapping a Ghost*, was published in 2005. A verse novel, *In Sight of Home*, was published by Salmon in 2009.

Mary O'Malley was born in Connemara in 1954 and educated at University College, Galway. She travels and lectures widely in Europe and America, has written for both radio and television and is a frequent broadcaster. Her poems have been translated into several languages. She is a member of the Poetry Council for Ireland. She teaches on the MA in Writing at the National University of Ireland, Galway. Her collections are: *The Boning Hall* (Carcanet, 2002), *A Perfect V* (Carcanet, 2006), *Asylum Road* (Salmon, 2001), *The Knife in the Wave* (Salmon, 1997), and *Where the Rocks Float* (Salmon, 1993).

Padraig O'Morain's first full collection will be published by Salmon in 2011. His pamphlet of 20 poems, *You've Been Great* (Smith/Doorstop 2008), was a winner of the Poetry Business Pamphlet Competition 2007 and he was shortlisted in the top three for the Cinnamon Poetry Publications Award 2010. His poems have been published in *Poetry Ireland Review, Cyphers, Ambit, The Rialto, Stand, Magma* and *The North*. He has an MA in Creative Writing from Lancaster University.

Born in Dublin, **Micheal O'Siadhail** was educated at Clongowes Wood College, Trinity College Dublin and the University of Oslo. He has published thirteen collections, his most recent *Tongues* was published by Bloodaxe this Autumn (2010). Previous collections include *Our Double Time* (1998), *The Gossamer Wall* (2002), *Love Life* (2005) and *Globe* (2007). O'Siadhail was awarded an American Cultural Institute Prize (1982) and the Marten Toonder Prize for Literature (1998). O'Siadhail's poem suites *The Naked Flame, Summerfest, Crosslight, Dublin Spring* and *At Night A Song Is With Me* were commissioned and set to music for performance and broadcasting. O'Siadhail has been a lecturer at Trinity College Dublin, a professor at the Dublin Institute for Advanced Studies and poet in residence at the Yeats Summer School, UBC Vancouver and the University of West Chester. His work is translated into several languages including Japanese and German.

Alicia Ostriker as twice nominated for a National Book Award, she is author of twelve volumes of poetry, most recently *The Book of Seventy* (2009), which won the Jewish Book Award for Poetry. As a critic Ostriker is the author of two pathbreaking volumes on women's poetry, *Writing Like a Woman and Stealing the Language: The Emergence of Women's Poetry in America*. She has also published three books on the Bible, *Feminist Revision and the Bible*, the controversial *The Nakedness of the Fathers*; *Biblical Visions and Revisions*, a combination of prose and poetry that re-imagines the Bible from the perspective of a contemporary Jewish woman, and a set of essays, *For the Love of God: The Bible as an Open Book*. Her most recent book of criticism is *Dancing at the Devil's Party: Essays on Poetry, Politics and the Erotic*.

Her poems have appeared in *The New Yorker, The Paris Review, Antaeus, The Nation, Poetry, American Poetry Review, Kenyon Review, The Atlantic, MS, Tikkun,* and many other journals, and have been widely anthologised. Her poetry and essays have been translated into French, German, Italian, Chinese, Japanese, Hebrew and Arabic. She has lectured and given performances of her work throughout the USA, as well as in Europe, Australia, Israel, Japan and China.

She has received awards from the National Endowment for the Arts, the Poetry Society of America, the San Francisco State Poetry Centre, the Judah Magnes Museum, the New Jersey Arts Council, the Rockefeller Foundation, and the Guggenheim Foundation. She lives in Princeton, NJ with her husband. She is Professor Emerita of Rutgers University and is a faculty member of the New England College Low-Residency Poetry MFA Program. Ostriker has taught in the Princeton University Creative Writing Program and in Toni Morrison's Atelier Program. She has taught midrash writing workshops in the USA, Israel, England and Australia.

Katie O'Sullivan is a native Californian. She attended UCLA (Uni. of Calif at Los Angeles) but graduated from the American University of Beirut after the birth of her seventh child. Her husband's career led the family to Lebanon where they lived for fifteen years despite crisis and evacuations. The family's dogs travelled with them. The first, a Spaniel, lived for seventeen years, followed by German Shepherds and, last and least in size but grand in heart, their toy poodle, Eddy. Katie's poems, essays, memoirs, fiction and a short play have appeared in print and on-line journals, including *Damazine, Noble Generation ll, Dana Literary Society, Knoxville Writers Guild, Cup of Comfort, Inscribed, Texas Poetry Calendar* 2004, 2005, 2011 and she has received a First Prize for Flash Fiction in the anthology *Ascent Aspirations* (Spring Issue, 2009). She resides in Houston, Texas.

Harry Owen, the inaugural Poet Laureate for Cheshire (UK), moved to South Africa's Eastern Cape in January 2008. His work is widely published in literary journals and anthologies in the UK, USA and South Africa. He is the author of four poetry collections: *Searching for Machynlleth* (2000), *The Music of Ourselves* (2004), *Five Books of Marriage* (2008) and *Non-Dog* (2010). He is a widely experienced performer and workshop facilitator and also hosts the hugely popular monthly open-floor poetry event called *Poetry @ Reddits* in Grahamstown, where he lives. Further details can be found on his website: www.harry-owen.co.uk

Richard Peabody, a prolific poet, fiction writer and editor, is an experienced teacher and important activist in the Washington D.C. community of letters. He is editor of *Gargoyle Magazine* (founded in 1976), and has published a novella, two books of short stories, six books of poems, plus an e-book, and edited (or co-edited) nineteen anthologies including: *Mondo Barbie, Mondo Elvis, Conversations with Gore Vidal, A Different Beat: Writings by Women of the Beat Generation,* and *Kiss the Sky: Fiction and Poetry Starring Jimi Hendrix.* Peabody teaches fiction writing for the Johns Hopkins Advanced Studies Program. You can find out more about him at: www.gargoylemagazine.com, www.gargoylemagazine.com or www.wikipedia.org.

Gary Percesepe is Associate Editor at the *Mississippi Review* and serves on the Board of Advisors at *Fictionaut.* His short stories, poems, essays, book reviews, interviews, literary and film criticism, and articles in philosophy and religion have been published in *Salon, Mississippi Review, Antioch Review, Review of Metaphysics, Christian Scholar's Review, New Ohio Review, Enterzone, Intertext, Luna Park, Istanbul Literary Review, Pank, elimae, Wigleaf, Prick of the Spindle, Metazen, Stymie,* and other places. A former philosophy professor, he is the author of four books in philosophy published by Macmillan and Prentice Hall, including *Future(s) of Philosophy: The Marginal Thinking of Jacques Derrida.* He has studied with William H. Gass and T.C. Boyle, and just completed his second novel, *Leaving*

Telluride. His first novel, an epistolary novel written with Susan Tepper, is called *What May Have Been: Letters of Jackson Pollock and Dori G*, and is forthcoming from Cervena Barva Press in the fall of 2010.

John Perrault is the author of *Jefferson's Dream*, *The Ballad of the Declaration of Independence* (Hobblebush Books, 2009); *The Ballad of Louis Wagner and other New England Stories in Verse* (Peter Randall Publisher, 2003); and *Here Comes the Old Man Now* (Oyster River Press, 2005). He is an independent scholar with the New Hampshire Humanities Council, and a touring artist with the NH State Council on the Arts and the New England Foundation for the Arts. He was a co-recipient of the Rosalie Boyle/Norma Farber Award, 2008, from the New England Poetry Club; a finalist in the 2007 Comstock Review Poetry Contest; and a past recipient of the Virginia Prize from Lyric Magazine. His poetry has appeared in The Café Review, The Christian Science Monitor, Commonweal, Poet Lore and elsewhere. He was poet laureate of Portsmouth, New Hampshire, 2003-2005. Some of his poems and songs can be found at www.johnperrault.com.

George Petty has been an insurance underwriter, airplane mechanic, airline flight engineer, union president, newspaper reporter, college teacher, tennis coach, racing sailor, and an author and editor of books on hiking for the New York - New Jersey Trail Conference. His poems have been prize-winners in national contests and have aired on National Public Radio. Through his varied career he has always thought of himself as a poet, even when the world required him to appear otherwise. His working life has taken him all over the world, but he has alway returned to New Jersey, where he lives and writes today.

Susan Pilewski was born and raised in New York City and is a graduate of the MFA program at Sarah Lawrence College. Her first book, *Fetish*, was published in 2007 by Writers Ink Press. Her second collection, *Bones of True Believers*, is forthcoming from Salmon Poetry. Ms. Pilewski's three cats Bella, Squeaky, and Lucyfur Connick Jr. tolerate her efforts to support organizations that help dogs worldwide, but draw the line at actually allowing her to bring one home.

Alexis Quinlan is a teacher and writer living in New York City. Her poems have appeared in journals ranging from Denver Quarterly to Paris Review and on websites including Drunken Boat. Her 2008 chapbook, *Landloper*, was published by Finishing Line Press.

Jacob Rakovan has been described as sociopathic show pony. He has been writing since the age of nine, winning his first writing award in sixth grade for an essay on patriotism that he even he knew was bullshit. He served as editor to the arts magazine *Bacchus* and the Portsmouth Free Press and was a founding member of the now defunct Southern Ohio Underground Poetry and Spoken Word Collective. He has been published in many print and web journals including *My Favorite Bullet, The Dead Mule School of Southern Literature, the Deep Cleveland Junkmail Oracle, San Francisco's Other Magazine, Ghoti* and *Anemone Sidecar*. Rakovan has had two of his poems adapted into screenplays. His first, "My Electric Bill" won Outstanding Screenplay in Texas' 2006 24PS film festival. He was recently anthologized in Arsenic Lobster's 2010 anthology. He currently resides in Rochester New York and is a father of five.

Barbara Regenspan has taught social justice-focused education in a liberal arts context her whole life, encouraging her students to seek multiple perspectives on history and literature. Her book, *Parallel Practices,* (Peter Lang Publishing, 2002) represents autobiographical narrative research, a genre that offers useful background for writing poetry. In the past year, she has participated in craft workshops with Tony Hoagland, Patricia Lewis, Marie

Howe, and, most recently, Peter Balakian at the annual summer writing conference at Colgate University, where she teaches in the educational studies department. Her poem, "Introduction to Teaching Nietszche", was written for a particular group of students in a course called "The Challenges of Modernity" who were having difficulty understanding Nietszche's problems with history.

C. R. Resetarits' work has appeared in numerous journals including *Kenyon Review, Gender Studies, Fabula, Parameters*, and *Dalhousie Review*. Her most recent work will appear in the Native American writing issue of *The Florida Review*. She recently moved to Washington after three years in the tiny village of Hursley, Hants, UK.

Billy Reynolds was born and raised in Huntsville, Alabama ("The Rocket City"). His awards include the Tennessee Williams scholarship in poetry from the Sewanee Writers' Conference and an Emerging Artist grant from the Greater Kalamazoo Arts Council. In 2007, he received the John Ciardi scholar in poetry from Bread Loaf Writers' Conference. His poems have been published in *Hunger Mountain, Sewanee Theological Review*, and *Third Coast*, among others. Currently, he lives in Tifton, Georgia, where he serves as the interim head of the Department of Literature and Language at Abraham Baldwin College.

Moira Rhoarke is a retired award-winning journalist and photographer who lives with her family in a rural area of Arkansas. She writes a weekly column for a daily newspaper and has published one novel.

Patricia Robertson's most recent book is *The Goldfish Dancer: Stories and Novellas*. Born in the UK, she grew up in Canada and received her MA in Creative Writing from Boston University. Her work has been nominated for the B.C. Book Prizes, the Journey Prize, the Pushcart Prize, and the Canadian National Magazine Awards (three times). She travelled to the Yukon, where she now lives, with a Lakeland terrier named Lacey. A very talkative husky-lab cross, Freya, is currently the *genius loci* of the household. This winter Robertson will be writer-in-residence at the Roderick Haig-Brown House in Campbell River on Vancouver Island, British Columbia.

Bertha Rogers's poems appear in journals and anthologies and in the collections *Even the Hemlock: Poems, Illuminations, and Reliquaries* (poetry and visual art, Six Swans Artists Editions, NY, 2005); *The Fourth Beast* (chapbook, Snark Publishing, IL, 2004); *A House of Corners* (Three Conditions Press, Baltimore, MD, 2000); and *Sleeper, You Wake* (Mellen Press, NY, 1991). Her translation of *Beowulf*, the Anglo-Saxon epic poem, was published in 2000 (Birch Brook Press, NY); and her translation of the Anglo-Saxon riddle-poems from the Exeter Book, *Uncommon Creatures, Singing Things*, will be published in 2010. In 2006, Rogers received an A. E. Ventures Foundation Grant for excellence in writing and visual arts and for contributions to the field. In 2003 she received a Ludwig Vogelstein grant. In 1992, she founded Bright Hill Press, Inc. with her husband, Ernest M. Fishman. Her collection *Heart Turned Back* was published by Salmon in 2010. Her website is bertharogers.com.

James Silas Rogers is editor of *New Hibernia Review*, a journal of Irish Studies published by the University of St Thomas in Minnesota. His poems have appeared in such journals as *Poetry East, Nimrod*, and *Natural Bridge*, and his chapbook *Sundogs* was published by Parallel Press, an imprint of the University of Wisconsin Libraries, in 2006. In 2011, Blueroad Press will publish his mixed-genre book (chiefly literary nonfiction) on cemeteries and sacred space. Rogers is also the co-editor of *After the Flood: Irish America, 1945-1960*, published by Irish Academic Press in 2009, and is active in the American Conference for Irish Studies.

William Pitt Root's prize-winning work, published in *Poetry, New Yorker, Nation, Harpers, APR* and nine collections, has been translated into 20 languages, broadcast over Voice Of America, and funded by the Guggenheim and Rockefeller Foundations, National Endowment for the Arts, Stanford University, and US/UK Exchange Artists program. Joseph Brodsky wrote of *The Unbroken Diamond: Nightletter to the Mujahedeen* "Your lines may not much help those poor people, but they surely redeem this nation." *White Boots: New & Selected Poems of the West* is Root's most recent collection. *Welcome, Traveler: Selected Early Odes of Pablo Neruda* is forthcoming. He's taught throughout the country (Hunter College, University of Montana, Interlochen, NYU, Amherst, etc), read and photographed throughout the world.

Gabriel Rosenstock is the author/translator of over one hundred books, including thirteen volumes of poetry in Irish. A member of Aosdána (the Irish Academy of Arts and Letters), he has given readings in Europe, the US, India, Australia, Japan and has been published in various leading international journals including *Akzente, Neue Rundschau,* and *die horen* (Germany), *Poetry* (Chicago) and *World Haiku Review*. He has given readings at major festivals, including Berlin, Vilenica and Medellín. His selected poems (from the Irish) have appeared in German, English and Hungarian. He has translated into Irish the selected poems of, among others, Francisco X. Alarcón, Seamus Heaney, G. Grass, W M Roggeman, Said, Zhāng Ye, Michele Ranchetti, Michael Augustin, Peter Huchel, Georg Trakl, Georg Heym, H. Schertenleib, H. Domin, J P Tammen, Munir Niazi, G. Kunert, Michael Krüger, Muhammad Iqbal and his Irish-language versions of haiku masters Issa, Buson, Shiki, Santōka, J W Hackett and others are much loved in his native country. Rosenstock is the Irish language advisor for the poetry journal *THE SHOp*. His *Selected Poems/ Rogha Dánta* (Cló Iar-Chonnachta) appeared in 2005 and the bilingual volume *Bliain an Bhandé/ Year of the Goddess* came out in 2007 (Dedalus Press). In 2009 he was awarded the Tamgha-I-Khidmat medal by the President of the Islamic Republic of Pakistan. His debut volume in English, *Uttering Her Name*, was published by Salmon in 2010.

Gibbons Ruark was born in Raleigh, North Carolina, in 1941, and grew up in various Methodist parsonages in the eastern part of the state. Educated at the Universities of North Carolina and Massachusetts, he taught English largely at the University of Delaware until his retirement in 2005. He has published his poems widely for over forty years. Among his eight collections are *Keeping Company* (1983), *Passing Through Customs: New and Selected Poems* (1999) and *Staying Blue*, a 2008 chapbook. The recipient of many awards, including three NEA Poetry Fellowships, a Pushcart Prize and the 1984 Saxifrage Prize for *Keeping Company*, he lives with his wife Kay in Raleigh.

Lex Runciman, born and raised in Portland, has lived most of his life in Oregon's Willamette Valley. *Starting from Anywhere* is his fourth collection of poetry was published by Salmon in 2009, following *Luck* (1981), *The Admirations* (1989) which won the Oregon Book Award, and *Out of Town* (2004). He holds graduate degrees from the writing programs at the University of Montana and the University of Utah. A co-editor of two anthologies, *Northwest Variety: Personal Essays by 14 Regional Authors* and *Where We Are: The Montana Poets Anthology*, his own work has appeared in several anthologies including, *From Here We Speak, Portland Lights* and *O Poetry, O Poesia*. He was adopted at birth. He and Deborah Jane Berry Runciman have been married thirty-seven years and are the parents of two grown daughters. He taught for eleven years at Oregon State University and is now Professor of English at Linfield College, where he received the Edith Green Award in teaching in 1997.

Layne Russell has published poetry and haiku in journals, books, and anthologies for many years and has actively given readings, sometimes with live music, since 1996. She received her degree in English in 1969 from California State University, Chico, where she studied poetry and creative writing with poet George Keithley. She did post graduate work in Religious Studies at CSU, Chico, and in the Arts and Buddhist Studies at Naropa University, Boulder, Colorado. Layne is also a photographer and a guitarist and songwriter with many years of performance behind her and is currently making a guitar and preparing to record a CD of the newest of her songs. Poetry website: http://whiteowlweb.com

Breda Wall Ryan lives in Co. Wicklow. Her work has been shortlisted for a Hennessy Literary Award for Fiction, The Davy Byrnes Irish Writing Award, The Francis MacManus Short Story Award the Fish Poetry Prize and Mslexia Poetry Prize, and is published in literary journals and anthologies including *The Stinging Fly, The New Hennessy Book of Irish Fiction, The Faber Book of Best New Irish Short Stories* 2007, *Let's be Alone Together, Fish Anthology 2010, The Workshop Anthology, Mslexia* and *The Stony Thursday Book.* She has completed a novel, *Nightshade and Rue;* a short story collection, *The Hardest Winter and Other Stories;* and a poetry collection, *The Woman who Toasted the Owl.* Porter, the dog remembered in "Meanwhile…", was a gentle, clever and handsome Rottweiler with a strong herding instinct, who was part of the family throughout the Cork childhood of her now grown-up children.

C.J. Sage's poems appear nationally and internationally in publications such as *The Antioch Review, Black Warrior Review, Boston Review, Ploughshares, Shenandoah, The Threepenny Review,* et cetera. Her most recently collection, *The San Simeon Zebras,* was published by Salmon in 2010. Previous books are *Let's Not Sleep* (poems), *And We The Creatures* (anthology), *Field Notes in Contemporary Literature* (textbook/anthology), and *Odyssea* (poems). After taking her M. F. A. in Creative Writing/Poetry, she taught poetry, writing, and literature for many years. A native of California, she now edits *The National Poetry Review* and Press and works as a Realtor in Santa Cruz and surrounding counties. Sage resides in Rio Del Mar, California, a coastal town on the Monterey Bay.

Aimée Sands is the co-director of the Brookline Poetry Series. Her work has appeared in *FIELD, Poet Lore, Measure, Salamander, Lyric Poetry Review, Beloit Poetry Journal, Poetry Ireland Review,* and elsewhere. Her first book of poems is forthcoming from Salmon Poetry in 2012. She is the director of the independent documentary short *What Makes Me White?* which is currently in use as a tool for anti-racism work in two-hundred colleges, churches, and nonprofits in the US and Canada. In her twenty plus years as a public radio and television producer, Aimée has received eighteen awards for her work, including an Emmy, a Peabody Award, and a San Francisco Film Festival Golden Gate Award. She teaches at Babson College, and is currently raising major funds to expand *What Makes Me White?* to a full hour.

John W. Sexton was born in 1958 and is the author of four previous poetry collections: *The Prince's Brief Career,* Foreword by Nuala Ní Dhomhnaill, (Cairn Mountain Press, 1995), *Shadows Bloom / Scáthanna Faoi Bhláth,* a book of haiku with translations into Irish by Gabriel Rosenstock (Doghouse, 2004), *Vortex* (Doghouse, 2005), and *Petit Mal* (Revival Press 2009). Under the ironic pseudonym of Sex W. Johnston he has recorded an album with legendary Stranglers frontman, Hugh Cornwell, entitled *Sons of Shiva,* which has been released on Track Records. He is a past nominee for The Hennessy Literary Award and his poem "The Green Owl" won the Listowel Poetry Prize 2007. In 2007 he was awarded a Patrick and Katherine Kavanagh Fellowship in Poetry.

Anne Shaw is the author of *Undertow* (Persea Books), winner of the Lexi Rudnitsky Poetry Prize. Her work has appeared or is forthcoming in *Black Warrior Review, Beloit Poetry Journal, Barrow Street, Drunken Boat, Green Mountains Review,* and *New American Writing.* She has been featured in Poetry Daily and From the Fishouse. Her extended poetry project can be found on Twitter at twitter.com/anneshaw. She and her pitbull live in Providence, Rhode Island, where they enjoy running, leaping, bouncing, and eating bones from under picnic tables.

Glenn Shea was born and has lived most of his life in Connecticut. He has worked in the library of a cancer clinic and in the French department of a foreign-language bookshop, washed dishes in the Scottish Highlands, gone to pilgrim's mass in Santiago and eaten really good Tex-Mex in Chengdu. He has read his poetry in venues ranging from the Harvard Divinity School to Shakespeare and Company in Paris. He is living for the moment in an old farmhouse in Uncasville and works with a group of illuminati in a huge used-book shop in Niantic, Connecticut. He has published two chapbooks. *Find A Place That Could Pass For Home*, his first full-length collection, was published by Salmon in 2010.

Eileen Sheehan is originally from Scartaglin, Co Kerry, now living in Killarney. Her first collection, *Song Of The Midnight Fox* (Doghouse Books) was published in 2004. Anthology publications include *The Watchful Heart: A New Generation of Irish Poets* (Salmon Poetry, 2009); *TEXT – A Transition Year English Reader* (Ed Niall MacMonagle, The Celtic Press); *The Open Door Book of Poetry* (Ed Niall MacMonagle); *Winter Blessings* by Patricia Scanlan; *Our Shared Japan* (Dedalus Press). Her second collection, *Down the Sunlit Hall*, was launched in 2008. She has just completed a second term as Poet in Residence with Limerick Co Council Arts Office.

Joan I. Siegel's poetry has appeared in more than fifty journals including *The Atlantic Monthly*, *The American Scholar*, The Gettysburg Review and in numerous antthologies. She is recipient of poetry prizes including the New Letters Poetry Award and the Anna Davidson Rosenberg Award. Her recent book, Hyacinth for the Soul (Deerbrook Editions, 2009) was highly praised by former US Poet Laureate, Maxine Kumin.

Scot Siegel is an urban planner and poet from Oregon. He serves on the board of trustees of the Friends of William Stafford. His books include *Some Weather* (Plain View Press, 2008) and two chapbooks, *Untitled Country* (Pudding House Publications, 2009) and *Skeleton Says* (forthcoming from Finishing Line Press). Siegel's second full-length collection is due out from Salmon Poetry in early 2012.

Kevin Simmonds is a writer and musician originally from New Orleans. His writing appears in *Asia Literary Review, Chroma, FIELD, Fuselit, jubilat, Kyoto Journal, Massachusetts Review, Poetry* and elsewhere. His debut poetry collection, *Mad for Meat*, is forthcoming from Salmon Poetry in 2011. He wrote the musical score for the documentary *Hope: Living and Loving with HIV in Jamaica* which won a 2009 Emmy Award, and *Wisteria: Twilight Songs for the Swamp Country*, which opened Poetry International at London's Royal Festival Hall and was the subject of a 2007 BBC radio documentary. He has received fellowships from the Atlantic Center for the Arts, Cave Canem, Fulbright, Jack Straw, Community of Writers at Squaw Valley, Napa Valley Writers' Conference and the San Francisco Arts Commission. He lives in San Francisco.

Ben Simmons began writing in his early teens. He joined a weekend poetry group for young writers, which published two small collections of local young writer called *Open Up*. In 2007 he started at NUIGalway, where he continued to write and work with the university drama society and Mephisto theatre company. Having returned from a Erasmus programme in Malta, Ben is now commencing the final year of his B.A. in English and Classics and returning to work at Trench productions in Galway.

James Simmons was born in Londonderry in 1933. He published volumes of poems regularly since his first book came out from The Bodley Head in 1967 with a welcome from Graham Greene on the cover. He won the Gregory and Cholmondeley Awards for poetry. He was founder editor of *The Honest Ulsterman*. Four collections of his songs have been issued, much praised by Paul Durcan. His critical biography of Sean O'Casey (Macmillan) is a standard text. He read and sang all over the world from Tokyo to Los Angeles to Belfast. He was co-director of The Poets' House, which was situated in its formative years in County Antrim and is now in Donegal. He was a member of Aosdána. He was writer in residence at Queens University Belfast. He lectured from 1968 to 1984 at The University of Ulster. James Simmons passed away at home on June 20th, 2001.

Siobhán of Carna was a participant in a writing workshop given by Gabriel Fitzmaurice at Clifden Arts Festival, 2007. She lives in the Connemara Gaeltacht.

Knute Skinner was born in St. Louis, Missouri. He has had a home in Ireland since 1964. He has taught at the University of Iowa and at Western Washington University, where he was a Professor of English. Retired from teaching, he lives in Killaspuglonane, County Clare with his spouse, Edna Faye Kiel. His most recent book of poetry, *Fifty Years: Poems 1957-2007* (Salmon, 2007), collects fifty years of published work, beginning with poems which first saw serial publication in 1957 and continuing through thirteen books. In 2010, Salmon published *Help Me To A Getaway*, a memoir of Skinner's time spent in Europe in the late 1950s.

J.D. Smith was awarded a 2007 Fellowship in Poetry from the National Endowment for the Arts. He has published two collections of poetry, *The Hypothetical Landscape* (Quarterly Review of Literature Poetry Series, 1999) and *Settling for Beauty* (Cherry Grove Collections, 2005). His first children's book, *The Best Mariachi in the World*, was published in bilingual, Spanish and English editions in 2008 by Raven Tree Press. Smith's one-act play *Dig*, currently being adapted for film, was produced by CurvingRoad at London's Old Red Lion Theatre in June 2010. His first collection of essays, *Dowsing and Science*, will be published by Texas Review Press in 2011. Smith lives near the Southwest Waterfront in Washington, DC with his wife Paula Van Lare and their rescue dog Roo, a beagle mix, and he is at work on projects in several genres. Additional information is available at http://jdsmithwriter.blogspot.com.

Laura Lundgren Smith, a native of Texas, lives in Fort Worth with her husband Ben and daughter India Samhaoir. She holds a Bachelor of Arts with Honors in Theatre and English and a Master of Arts in Theatre from Texas A&M University at Commerce. She was awarded an Arts Council of Ireland Commissions Grant in 2004 for playwriting. Her plays *Sending Down the Sparrows* (Salmon, 2001), *Digging up the Boys* (Salmon, 2007), and *The Shape of the Grave* have been produced many times across the United States. In 2007, her play *Seamless* was chosen by Dallas' Kitchen Dog Theatre to be part of their renowned New Works Festival.

Steven Ray Smith has published work in *The Kenyon Review, The Raintown Review, Lucid Rhythms, The Concho River Review, The Alembic, SN Review, storySouth, Orbis*, and others. He is the former editor of *Texas Poetry Journal*. He was raised in Texas, attended the University of Texas and Yale University. He is currently the president of a culinary school and lives in Austin, Texas with his wife, two children, two dogs, two cats, and a gerbil. Their dog Olive Oyl is a mix Afghan and Doberman, very sweet, sleek, and always on patrol. Their dog Sunny is an affable Golden Doodle who follows along and is always content.

Costa Rican-American author **Mark Smith-Soto** is professor of Romance Languages, editor of *International Poetry Review* and Director of the Center for Creative Writing in the Arts at the University of North Carolina at Greensboro. Winner of a 2005 National

Endowment for the Arts fellowship in creative writing, he has published two full-length poetry collections to date, *Our Lives Are Rivers* (University Press of Florida, 2003), and *Any Second Now* (Main Street Rag Publishing Co., 2006). His poetry has appeared in *Antioch Review, Kenyon Review, Literary Review, Nimrod, Poetry East, Quarterly West, Rosebud Magazine, The Sun* and numerous other publications. His manuscript *Waiting Room* was published in December, 2008, as the winner of Red Mountain Review's annual chapbook competition, and his bilingual edition of the selected poetry of Costa Rican writer Ana Istarú, *Fever Season*, was published this spring by Unicorn Press.

Gerard Smyth was born in Dublin where he still lives and works as Managing Editor with The Irish Times newspaper. His poetry has appeared widely in publications in Ireland, Britain, and America, as well as in translation, since the late 1960s. His seven collections include *Daytime Sleeper* (2002), *A New Tenancy* (2004), and *The Mirror Tent* (2007) and most recently *The Fullness of Time, New and Selected Poems* (Dedalus Press, 2010). He is a member of Aosdana.

Joel R. Solonche has been contributing poems to magazines, journals and anthologies in the U.S. since the early 70s. These include *The American Scholar, The New Criterion, The Progressive, The Journal of the American Medical Association, The North American Review, The Literary Review, Salmagundi, the Anthology of Magazine Verse* and many others. He is co-author (with wife Joan I. Siegel) of *Peach Girl: Poems for a Chinese Daughter* (Grayson Books).

Julian Stannard lectures at the University of Winchester and is the author of *Rina's War* and *The Red Zone* (Peterloo Poets, UK) and a third volume - *The Parrots of Villa Gruber Discover Lapis Lazuli* – will be published by Salmon in 2011. His work has appeared in the *TLS, Spectator, Poetry Review, Ambit, Poetry Ireland, Poetry Wales, PN Review* and he reviews for the Guardian and Nouva Corrente (Italy). He was awarded second prize in the Strokestown International Poetry Competition 2010.

Scott T. Starbuck is a Creative Writing Coordinator at San Diego Mesa College. You can see his fossil art at The Spirit of the Salmon Fund (www.critfc.org/Gala/07starbuck.html) and hear him read two poems at Fogged Clarity (foggedclarity.com/2010/01/january-2010). His recent chapbook, *The Warrior Poems*, was one of six finalists of over 500 entries at the 2009 Pudding House National Chapbook Contest, featuring protest poems about human rights, animal rights, media distortions, Iraq War, sour economy, and the G.W. Bush presidency. His "Wild Salmon" creative nonfiction essay will appear in the 2011/12 issue of *The Trumpeter Journal of Ecosophy* (http://trumpeter.athabascau.ca/index.php/trumpet) at Athabasca University regarding the theme of deep ecology across generations.

Matthew Sweeney was born in Donegal in 1952. He is currently based in Cork, having previously been resident in Berlin, Timişoara and, for a long time, London. His latest book is a retrospective selection *The Night Post* (Salt, 2010). Previous books include *Black Moon* (2007), *Sanctuary* (2004) and *Selected Poems* (2002). He has also written books of poetry for children, including *Up on the Roof* (2001). Bilingual collections came out in Germany and Holland in 2008. Earlier translations appeared in Mexico, Romania, Latvia and Slovakia. He is a member of Aosdána.

Adam Tavel won the 2010 Robert Frost Award from the Robert Frost Foundation and was also a finalist for the 2010 Intro Prize with Four Way Books. His poems have appeared or are forthcoming in *Indiana Review, Redivider, Portland Review, South Carolina Review, Poet Lore, Apalachee Review, New South, Clarion, Georgetown Review*, and *Cave Wall*, among others. He lives and teaches on Maryland's Eastern Shore.

Jordan Taylor is a self-proclaimed binge writer and an expert on dogs in film. Her collection of canine movie memorabilia includes over 400 pieces dating from the 1920s to current releases. She has been volunteer, dog trainer, foster home, and permanent home for animal shelters and private rescue groups alike. Author of fiction and nonfiction, including Wonder Dogs: 101 German Shepherd Dog Films, she lives on an island in the Pacific Northwest where she trains dogs for film and print media as well as producing her own short films. You can find Jordan on her dog blog at reeldogs.blogspot.com or her website: www.jordantaylorbooks.com

Ilsa Thielan's love of dogs began in early childhood curled up with big dogs and when barely six years old she was determined to free a grey wolf in the zoo to bring him back to the forest. Her grandparents who she lived with and who nurtured her love for nature, had a hard time convincing her that it was impossible. This wolf became Ilsa's imaginary companion throughout her childhood. Ever since she has lived with big dogs. After studying Art and Literature in Germany, Ilsa settled down in Clare. She works with photography, tapestry and words. Her poetry and short stories have appeared in many anthologies. Her debut collection, *Night Horses*, is forthcoming from Salmon.

A New York native, **Nancy J. Thompson**'s work has appeared in the U.S. and abroad, including in *Harpur Palate, Iodine, CQ, The MacGuffin, Atom Mind, Sojourner, The Humanist, Adirondac, The Christian Science Monitor, The Chronicle of Higher Education* and many other publications. She is professor of English at Clark College in Washington and teaches writing for Community College of Vermont and Johnson State College. Her book, *Killing the Buddha*, a collection of poetry related to Buddhism, came out in 2008. She currently lives in Portland, Oregon with her daughter, two cats, and of course, Sally the schnauzer.

Wendy Thornton is a writer in Gainesville, Florida, and a graduate of the University of Florida. She has been published in such journals as *The Literary Review, Riverteeth*, the *MacGuffin* and others. She was nominated for a Pushcart Prize and has been an editors' pick multiple times on salon.com. She is the president of the Writers Alliance of Gainesville. www.writersalliance.org.

Diana Thurbon is old enough to know better. Her adult children are more grown up than she is, and her delightful grandchildren are more grown up than their parents. She lives in Melbourne, Australia, with her flying instructor/pilot/writer husband, their cranky cocker spaniel, Anakin, and two rescue hens. Diana used to be a librarian but became a medical herbalist after a serious bout with lymphoma and a bone marrow transplant. She is also a writer. She tries out her work by reading aloud to the resident spaniel. Mostly he falls asleep. An avid supporter of Soi Dog in Thailand, she is also a committee member of Soi Dog Australia. Writing is part of who she is, and oddly a number of her essays, stories and poems are about dogs. Despite an idiosyncratic approach to punctuation, a number of her stories and poems have been published in Australia and overseas. She is a keen literary contest writer and has won firsts in a number of competitions. Her writing is mostly suitable for Human Beings to read. When she finishes a story and reads it, she likes to enjoy it. She always hopes her readers will respond the same way.

Pam Uschuk is the author of five books of poems, including the award-winning *Finding Peaches in the Desert*, and, her latest, *Crazy Love* (Wings Press, 2009), nominated for the National Book Award, a Tufts Kingsley Award, and winner of the American Book Award 2010. She is also the author of several chapbooks of poems, including *Pam Uschuk's Greatest Hits* (Pudding House Press, 2009). Uschuk's work has been translated into nearly a dozen languages and has appeared in over three hundred journals and anthologies worldwide, including *Best of the Web 2010, Poetry, Parnassus Review, Agni Review,*

Ploughshares, and *Beloit Poetry Journal*. Her literary prizes include the 2010 *New Millenium Poetry Prize*, Struga International Prize for a single poem, the Dorothy Daniels Writing Award from the National League of American PEN Women, the 2001 Literature Award from the Tucson/Pima Arts Council, The King's English Prize as well as awards from the Chester H. Jones Foundation, *Iris, Ascent, Sandhills Review*, and *Amnesty International*. Nearly 30 individual poems have been nominated for Pushcart Prizes. She has been a featured writer at Prague Summer Workshops, University of Pisa, International Poetry Festivals in Malmo Sweden and Struga, Macedonia, the British School in Pisa, Italy, Vilenica in Slovenia, the Scandinavian Book Fair, the Deep South Writers Conference, and many universities and book stores. Pam Uschuk is a Professor of Creative Writing at Fort Lewis College, where she teaches creative writing and environmental literature. She is also Director of the Southwest Writers Institute at FLC. In Spring 2011, she will hold the Hodges Chair as Visiting Writer at University of Tennessee, Knoxville. Editor-In-Chief of the literary magazine, *Cutthroat, A Journal of the Arts*, Uschuk lives in Bayfield, Colorado.

Michelle Valois lives in Western Massachusetts, USA, with her partner, three children, and a very dog-like cat. Her beloved beagle, Daisy, passed away two summers ago; no new canine has yet to capture her heart. She teaches at a community college. Her writing has appeared or is forthcoming in TriQuarterly, Fourth Genre, Brevity, the North American Review, the Florida Review, Pank, and others. She blogs at http://www.readmelikeabook.net/.

Peter van de Kamp was born in The Hague, The Netherlands in 1956. He taught English and Anglo-Irish Literature, Rhetoric and Stylistics at the University of Leiden and University College, Dublin, where he was a Newman Scholar. He now teaches at the Institute of Technology, Tralee. A poet, translator, critic, anthologist and scholar, he has published extensively in Ireland, England, Europe and the States. He co-authored a biography of Flann O'Brien with Peter Costello, edited, with Jacques Chuto et al., *The Collected Works of James Clarence Mangan*, with Frank van Meurs the most comprehensive bilingual anthology of Dutch poetry in English (*Turning Tides*), and with A. Norman Jeffares the recent series of anthologies, *Irish Literature: The Eighteenth Century* and *Irish Literature: The Nineteenth Century*. In all, he has published eighteen books. Salmon published two of his books of poems – *Notes* (1999) and *In Train* (2008). His most recent poetry collection is *Scratch & Sniff* (2010). He was the founder of K.I.S.S., the Kerry International Summer School of Living Irish Authors. Peter lives in Tralee, with his wife Caroline and his dog Mickey.

Michèle Vassal is French but her years in Ireland have given her an unconditional love for Irish Literature. She started writing in English in the late nineties, going on to receive the first prize for a new poetry collection at Listowel Writers Week (*Sandgames*, Salmon Poetry, 2000). She has been widely published internationally, in both French and English. She currently lives and writes in France where she shares her keyboard and her bed with some out of control felines and a gigantic but slightly confused dog, Dougal, who thinks he is a cat.

Jeanne Wagner is the recipient of several awards including Writers-at-Work, the Frances Locke Award, the MacGuffin Poet Hunt, Ann Stanford Prize and the 2009 Briar Cliff Review Award. Her poems have appeared in *The Southern Poetry Review, Mississippi Review* and *Spoon River* among others. She has four poetry collections, including *The Zen Piano-Mover*, winner of the 2004 Stevens Manuscript Prize. A new book of poems, *In the Body of Our Lives*, is forthcoming from Sixteen Rivers Press.

Drucilla Wall grew up in Philadelphia. Her fist collection of poetry, *The Geese at the Gates*, will be published by Salmon Poetry in January. 2011. Her poetry engages her mixed heritage of Creek/Muscogee American Indian, Irish, and Jewish identity. Individual poems and essays appear in *Cream City Review, Kalliope, The Red River Review*, and *Eighteenth Century Life*; and in anthologies such as: *The People Who Stayed: Southeastern Indian Writing After Removal*; *Eating Fire, Tasting Blood: Breaking the Great Silence of the American Indian Holocaust*; *Times of Sorrow/Times of Grace: Writing by Women of the Great Plains/High Plains*; and *True West: Authenticity and the American West*. She teaches at the University of Missouri-St.Louis.

Eamonn Wall is a native of Enniscorthy, Co. Wexford, who now lives in Missouri. He has the author of five poetry collections, most recently *A Tour of Your Country* (Salmon, 2008), with a sixth collection, *Sailing Lake Mareotis*, due from Salmon in 2011. His essays and articles are collected in *From the Sin-é Café to the Black Hills* (University of Wisconsin Press). He teaches at the University of Missouri-St. Louis.

Emily Wall is an Assistant Professor of Creative Writing at the University of Alaska Southeast. She has been published in a number of literary journals in the U.S. and Canada. Her first book, *Freshly Rooted*, came out in 2007 from Salmon Poetry. She lives in Douglas, Alaska.

William Wall is the author of two collections of poetry (and a third to be published by Salmon in 2011) a collection of short fiction and four novels, the latest of which was nominated for the 2005 Man Booker Prize. He lives in Cork where he and his wife are owned by a dog.

Gordon Walmsley grew up in easy New Orleans in a time of forced-segregation and the grey fifties. In the post-Beatles era, he attended Princeton, where he majored in German Literature, returning to New Orleans to acquire a, more or less, useless Law Degree. "It has been useful in the sense that you develop a feeling of how an unfriendly eye might misinterpret what you have written. You thus become more circumspect in your writing." Among his various projects, is the online literary magazine, *The Copenhagen Review* (www.copenhagenreview.com), which he edits. The magazine takes place in five languages, Norwegian, Swedish, Danish, German and English. His next book of poems, *Echoes of a River, Poems of New Orleans and Beyond*, will be published by Salmon Poetry in 2011. A poetically constructed novella, *Daisy, The Alchemical Adventures of a New Orleans Hermaphrodite*, has now reached completion.

John Walsh was born in Derry in 1950. After sixteen years teaching English in Germany, in 1989 he returned to live in Connemara. His first collection *Johnny tell Them* was published by Guildhall Press (Derry) in October 2006. In 2007 he received a Publication Award from Galway County Council to publish his second collection *Love's Enterprise Zone* (Doire Press, Connemara). His poems have been published in Ireland, the UK and Austria and he has read and performed his poems at events in Ireland, the UK, Germany, Sweden and most recently the USA. He is organizer and MC of the successful performance poetry event North Beach Poetry Nights in the Crane Bar, Galway. He has also been known to show up with his guitar and deliver one or two of his own songs. *Chopping Wood with T.S. Eliot*, a collection of sixty new poems to celebrate his reaching the mature age of sixty, was published by Salmon in 2010.

David Wheatley is the author of four collections of poetry with Gallery Press: *Thirst, Misery Hill, Mocker* and *A Nest on the Waves*. He has edited the work of James Clarence Mangan, also for Gallery, and Samuel Beckett's *Selected Poems* for Faber and Faber. His reviews appear widely. He lives in Hull.

Laurelyn Whitt's poems have appeared in various journals in Canada and the United States, including *The Malahat Review, PRISM International, The Fiddlehead, The Tampa Review, Puerto Del Sol*, and *The Spoon River Poetry Review*. Her recent collection of poetry, *Interstices*, won the Holland Prize and was published by Logan House Press in 2006. She lives in Minnedosa, Manitoba and is a Professor of Native Studies at Brandon University.

C. K. Williams was born in Newark, New Jersey, in 1936. His books of poetry include *The Singing* (Farrar, Straus, and Giroux, 2003), which won the National Book Award; *Repair* (1999), winner of a Pulitzer Prize; *The Vigil* (1997); *A Dream of Mind* (1992); *Flesh and Blood* (1987), which won the National Book Critics Circle Award; *Tar* (1983); *With Ignorance* (1997); *I Am the Bitter Name* (1992); and *Lies* (1969). Among his many awards and honours are an American Academy of Arts and Letters Award, a Guggenheim Fellowship, the Lila Wallace-Reader's Digest Award, the PEN/Voelcker Award for Poetry, a Pushcart Prize, and the Ruth Lilly Poetry Prize. Williams teaches in the creative writing program at Princeton University and lives part of each year in Paris.

Christopher Woods is a writer, teacher and photographer who lives in Houston and in Chappell Hill, Texas.

Joseph Woods is a poet and Director of Poetry Ireland. A winner of the Patrick Kavanagh Award, *Cargo* (Dedalus Press, 2010) gathers his first two books in a single volume and Dedalus will publish a third collection in 2011. He has co-edited *Our Shared Japan* (Dedalus Press, 2007), an anthology of contemporary Irish poetry concerning Japan.

Adam Wyeth was born in 1978. He was a prize winner of The Fish International Poetry Competition, 2009 and a runner-up of The Arvon International Poetry Competition, 2006. His poems have been published in numerous literary journals and anthologised in *The Best of Irish Poetry* anthology 2010, *Landing Places* (2010), *Something Beginning with P*, *The Arvon 25th Anniversary Anthology* and *The Fish Anthology*. His first collection, *Silent Music*, is forthcoming from Salmon in 2011.

Sharon Young has won awards for her carved stone animal sculptures, created and sold finely tooled leather art, played banjo with Drowsy Maggie, an Irish trad band, and has had dozens of her photographs published in newspapers and magazines. Six years ago she and her three dogs took on the logistic and bureaucratic challenges of moving from the United States to County Clare, where she lives today, spending her time teaching piano, writing a piano method book based on traditional Irish music, creating a unique form of textile art she calls "Fabrication," and now and then writing a poem.

Acknowledgements

Special thanks to Des Kenny, finder of lost books.

All poems in this anthology are copyright their authors. Salmon Poetry also wishes to thank the following publishers and journals where some of the poems in this anthology were first published:

RENEE ASHLEY: "The Dogs" from *Basic Heart* (X. J. Kennedy Poetry Prize, Texas Review Press, 2009). "I Am Still Here" from *Basic Heart* (X. J. Kennedy Poetry Prize, Texas Review Press, 2009).

NEIL ASTLEY: "The Hound of the Baskervilles" was runner-up in the Arvon Poetry Competition and was subsequently published, under a pseudonym, in *The Observer* and *The Arvon Anthology*.

MICHAEL AUGUSTIN: "Dog" and "In a Pavement Café" from *Mickle Makes Muckle* (Dedalus Press, Dublin, 2007). Translated from the German by Sujata Bhatt.

JUDITH BARRINGTON: "A True Dog Story" and "Beating the Dog" from *Horses and the Human Soul* (Story Line Press, 2004).

RICHARD BERENGARTEN: Excerpt from "The Manager" first appeared in *The Manager* (Salt Publishing, Cambridge, 2008)

MARCK L. BEGGS: "Kilty Sue" has also appeared in the anthologies *Dog Music* (St. Martin's Press, 1996) and *Bark* (Bulfinch Press, 2000) and in the collection *Libido Café* (Salmon, 2004).

DREW BLANCHARD: "Winter Dogs," *Blue Canary*, Issue #16, Spring 2008

PAT BORAN: "A Man is Only as Good ..." and "Fetch" from *New and Selected Poems* (Dedalus Press, 2007).

EVA BOURKE: "In Duiche Iar" from *Travels with Gandolpho* (Dedalus Press, Dublin, 2000)

MEGAN BUCKLEY: "Seventh son of a seventh son" first appeared in *Landing Places: Immigrant Poets in Ireland*, edited by Eva Bourke and Borbála Faragó (Dedalus Press, Dublin, 2010).

SIMMONS B. BUNTIN: "Coyote" originally appeared in *Sou'wester* and in the collection *Riverfall* (Salmon Poetry, 2005).

LOUISE C. CALLAGHAN: "Death of a Dog" first appeared in *In The Ninth House* (Salmon Poetry, 2010)

ANDREA COHEN: "Seven Dogs" from *Kentucky Derby* (Salmon Poetry, 2011). "Eureka" and "A Coonhound on Lieutenant's Island" from *Long Division* (Salmon Poetry, 2009).

SUSAN COHEN: "Yowl" first appeared as "Dog Years" in the *Seattle Review*, 2002. (Vol. XXIV, No. 2.). It also appeared in the chapbook *Backstroking* (Unfinished Monument Press; 2005).

PATRICK COTTER: "The Singing Bichon" from *Perplexed Skin* (Arlen House, 2008).

DALLAS CROW: "Regret" has also appeared in *Red Rock Review*, College of Southern Nevada.

LARRY O. DEAN: "Lutherans" was previously published in *Renovated Lighthouse* #48. "To My Dog, with a Broken Leg" was previously published in the chapbook, *Eyes, Ears, Nose & Throat* (Zenith Beast Books, 1990). "Top of the Morning" was previously published in the chapbook, *QWERTYUIOP* (Zenith Beast Books, 1989).

ANNIE DEPPE: "Snapshot, Collioure" and "Shelter" from *Wren Cantata* (Summer Palace Press, 2009). "Shelter" also appeared in *The Stinging Fly* (Issue 10/volume two, Summer 2008).

THEODORE DEPPE: "Orla" was first published in *Orpheus on the Red Line* (Tupelo Press, 2009).

STEPHEN DOBYNS: "How to Like It" from *Cemetery Nights* (Viking, 1987) and *Velocities* (Penguin, 1994).

AMY DRYANSKY: "The Space on the Floor..." and "Dog on Hind Legs" from *How I Got Lost So Close to Home* (Alice James Books, 1999).

PETER FALLON: "Collie" from *The Speaking Stones* (1978) by permission of the author. "Own" from *News of the World: Selected and New Poems* (1998) by permission of the author and The Gallery Press.

JOHN FITZGERALD: "Seven" will appear in the forthcoming collection *The Mind* (Salmon Poetry, 2011)

GABRIEL FITZMAURICE: "Lassie" from Twenty-One Sonnets (Salmon, 2007).

JANICE FITZPATRICK SIMMONS: "Cocoon" first appeared in *The Bowsprit*, Lagan Press, Belfast, 2005

PHILIP FRIED: "Theogony" first appeared in *Quantum Genesis* ((Zohar, 1997) and also appears in *Early/Late: New & Selected Poems* (Salmon Poetry, 2011).

PETER JOSEPH GLOVICZKI: This poem first appeared in *Modern Haiku*.

LAURA-GRAY STREET: "Goya's Dog" won the poetry prize at *Terrain.org: A Journal of the Built and Natural Environments* and was published in issue #26, Fall/Winter 2010.

RICHARD W. HALPERIN: "I didn't think I could be this happy, my dear, ever again" from *Anniversary* (Salmon, 2010). It also appeared in *Obsessed with Pipework* No.47, Summer 2009 (Flarestack Publishing, Pilton, Somerset).

ANNE LE MARQUAND HARTIGAN: "Dark Goddess" from *Long Tongue* (Beaver Row Press, Dublin, 1982).

KEVIN HIGGINS: "Regime Change" also appeared in *A Menu of Poems on All Ireland Poetry Day*, Thursday, 7th October, 2010.

RITA ANN HIGGINS: "Dog is Dog is Dog" from *Witch in the Bushes* (Salmon Publishing, 1988); also appeared in *The Salmon International Literary Journal*. "Rat-Like Dogs and Tattooed Men" from *Philomena's Revenge* (Salmon Publishing, 1992) and *Throw in the Vowels: New & Selected Poems* (Bloodaxe, 2005).

AMY HOLMAN: "Drawing Near" and "Or, Something" from *Wrens Fly Through This Opened Window* (Somondoco Press, 2010).

ADAM HOULE: "Begging Home a Stray" first appeared in *MARGIE / The American Journal of Poetry*.

BEN HOWARD: "Greta" first appeared in *Dark Pool* (Salmon, 2004)

HOLLY J. HUGHES: "The Wounded Dog Theory: My Dog Responds" appeared in *Boxing the Compass* (Floating Bridge Press, 2007).

ALEXANDER HUTCHISON: "Mr Scales Walks His Dog" from *Scales Dog* (Salt Publishing, 2007).

ANNE KENNEDY: "The Dog Kubla Dreams My Life" first appeared in *The Dog Kubla Dreams My Life* (Salmon Publishing, 1994)

JACQUELINE KOLOSOV: "Guidance" and "Refrain" were first published in the collection, *VAGO* (Lewis-Clark, 2007).

TED KOOSER: "January 19, Still Thawing, Breezy" from *Winter Morning: 100 Postcards to Jim Harrison* (Carnegie Mellon University Press, 2001).

DANUTA E. KOSK-KOSICKA: "In Salamanca: Sinbad, the Dog" first appeared in the chapbook of Mexican poems and photographs *On the Verge of Light and Shadow*.

ANATOLY KUDRYADIVSKY: "beach at sunrise..." first appeared in *Notes from the Gean* (Vol. 2, Issue 3, 2010). "first snow..." first appeared in *World Haiku Review* (August 2010, No 1).

MAXINE KUMIN: "Seven Caveats in May", "Widow and Dog", "Xochi's Tale" and "The Apparition" from *Where I Live: New & Selected Poems 1990-2010* (W. W. Norton & Co.)

THOMAS LYNCH: "The Blood We Paid For" from *Skating with Heather Grace* (Knopf, 1987) and

Grimalkin & Other Poems (Ireland/UK: Jonathan Cape, 1994) – reprinted by permission of The Random House Group Ltd.

JOHN MACKENNA: "Dog Soul" was broadcast on RTE Radio 1, 'A Living Word' 2nd November, 2010.

TOM MATHEWS: "False Start" from *The Owl and the Pussycat and other poems* (Dedalus Press, Dublin, 2009).

SEBASTIAN MATTHEWS: "Night Pee" first appeared in *The Bark*, Winter 2000

WILLIAM MATTHEWS: "Above the Aquarius Mine, Ward, Colorado" from *New Hope for the Dead: Uncollected Matthews* (Red Hen Press, 2010).

DEVON MCNAMARA: An earlier version of "Spring Lament" first appeared in *Vandalia*, Volume 10, Spring 2010 (West Virginia Wesleyan College, Buckhannon, West Virginia)

PAULA MEEHAN: "Who'd Be A Dog?" from *Painting Rain* (Carcanet Press, Manchester, 2009).

ALEXA MERGEN: "Yet" appeared in a slightly different version on the blog *Medusa's Kitchen* in 2009).

AGI MISHOL: A version of "I. The Ascension" first appeared in *Look There* (Graywolf Press, 2006).

JOHN MONTAGUE: "Walking the Dog" from *Poisoned Lands* (McGibbon & Kee, London, 1961).

ALAN JUDE MOORE: "Magione Umbria" from *Strasbourg* (Salmon Poetry, 2010).

PETE MULLINEAUX: "Salty Dog" was first published in *Crannóg* (Issue 17, Spring 2008).

RICHARD MURPHY: "Doggerel for Emily" first appeared in *Something Beginning with P: New Poems from Irish Poets* (edited by Seamus Cashman, The O'Brien Press). Poem copyright © Dennis O'Driscoll.

LES MURRAY: "Two Dogs" is part of a sequence of poems titled *Translations from the Natural World*. "Trees register the dog" is part of a sequence of poems titled *Nostril Songs*. Both poems from *Collected Poems* (Carcanet Press, U.K. and Black Inc., Melbourne, Australia).

MARY O'DONNELL: "Wilderness Legacy" from *The Place of Miracles: New & Selected Poems* (New Island Books, 2005).

GREAGOIR Ó DUILL: "Cu na gCleas" from *Saothrú an Ghoirt* (Coisceim, Dublin, 1994). Translated by the author and published in the collection *Traverse* (Lapwing, Belfast, 1998). Copyright in both cases Gréagóir Ó Dúill

MICHAEL O'LOUGHLIN: "Elegy For A Basset Hound" previously appeared in *Poetry Ireland Review* 85.

MARY O'MALLEY: "Anubis in Oghery" and "Cleo" from *Asylum Road* (Salmon Publishing, 1991).

Harry Owen: "The Language of Hooligans" and "Non Dog" from *Non-Dog* (The Poets Printery, East London, South Africa).

JACOB RAKOVAN: "In the Northern Country" first appeared in *ghoti magazine*.

C. R. RESETARITS: "Dog Gone" first appeared in *Parameter Magazine*, Issue 2 (March 2006.)

JAMES SILAS ROGERS: "Past Guessing" from *Sundogs* (Madison, Wisconsin: Parallel Press, 2006). "Dogs in Passing Cars" appeared in *Emprise Review* (2009).

WILLIAM PITT ROOT: "Elegy for Apu" from *The Storm and Other Poems* (Atheneum, 1969; reprinted by Carnegie Mellon Univ Press, 2005) and *Trace Elements from a Recurring Kingdom* (Confluence Press, 1986).

GABRIEL ROSENSTOCK: "Koan" from *Portrait of the Artist as an Abominable Snowman, Selected Poems of Gabriel Rosenstock* (Forest Books, 1989). The Irish translation of "Koan" by Michael Hartnett is reproduced by kind permission of the Estate of Michael Hartnett c/o The Gallery Press.

GIBBONS RUARK: "Wallace Stevens Welcomes John Crowe Ransom to Hartford" from *Staying Blue* (Lost Hills Books in Duluth, Minnesota, 2008).

C.J. SAGE: "How to Keep a Setter" from *The San Simeon Zebras* (Salmon Poetry, 2010).

GLENN SHEA: "The Moon" from *Find A Place That Could Pass For Home* (Salmon, 2010).

JOAN I. SIEGEL: "Dog Outside a Grocery on Broadway" first appeared in *Dog Blessings* (New World Library, 2008) edited by June Cotner.

SCOT SIEGEL: "Thermodynamics" from *Haggard & Halloo* (February, 2010); also appears in *Skeleton Says*, forthcoming from Finishing Line Press. "Fire Poker" first appeared in *Front Porch Journal*, Issue 13, 2010; it also appears in *Skeleton Says*, forthcoming from Finishing Line Press.

KEVIN SIMMONDS: "Seeing Eye" from *Fogged Clarity* (May 2010).

JAMES SIMMONS: "Charlie" from *Mainstream* (Salmon, 1995)

KNUTE SKINNER: "For Rimbaud" from *Fifty Years: Poems 1957-2007* (Salmon, 2007)

J.D. SMITH: "Policy" from *The Hypothetical Landscape* (Quarterly Review of Literature Poetry Series, 1999). "Aubade" first appeared in the September-October 2006 issue of *The Bark*.

MARK SMITH-SOTO: "Night Watch" has also appeared in *Poetry East* Nos. 64 and 65 and online at Ted Kooser's *American Life in Poetry* (www.americanlifeinpoetry.org).

JULIAN STANNARD: "Oliver" first appeared in *Ambit*.

SCOTT T. STARBUCK: "Warrior Says People on 17th Street in Portland, Oregon, Are Dreaming of Dogs" first appeared in *Hubbub* (Reed College, Portland, Oregon) and in the chapbook *The Warrior Poems* (Pudding House, 2010).

MATTHEW SWEENEY: "Dog on a Chain" from *Blue Shoes* (Secker & Warburg, 1989). Included in forthcoming Salt retrospective selection, *The Night Post* (2010). "The Dog" from *The Bridal Suite* (Cape, 1997). Included in forthcoming Salt retrospective selection, *The Night Post* (2010). "His Dog" from *Cacti* (Secker & Warburg, 1992). Also included in *Selected Poems* (Jonathan Cape, 2002). Reprinted by permission of The Random House Group Ltd. "Bones" from *Fatso in the Red Suit* (Faber, 1995). Also included in *Selected Poems* (Jonathan Cape, 2002). Reprinted by permission of The Random House Group Ltd.

ILSA THIELAN: "My Brother" from *Night Horses* (forthcoming, Salmon Poetry). Previously appeared in *Viewpoints*, Vol. 7 (a North Clare Writers' Workshop anthology).

PAM USCHUK: "Walking In Snow On A Full Moon Night" from *Crazy Love* (Wings Press, 2009).

PETER VAN DE KAMP: "Mickey" from *Notes* (Salmon, 1999). "Bark" and "Dear Mickey" from *In Train* (Salmon, 2008)

JEANNE WAGNER: "Conversation and Its Discontents" first appeared in *Marin Poetry Centre Anthology* Volume XI.

DRUCILLA WALL: "Bullet Dog" from *The Geese at the Gates* (Salmon Poetry, 2011).

JOHN WALSH: "Tranquillity" from *Chopping Wood with T.S. Eliot* (Salmon Poetry, 2010).

DAVID WHEATLEY: "Three Legged Dog" from *Three-Legged Dog* (with Caitríona O'Reilly, Wild Honey Press, 2002).

C.K. WILLIAMS: "The Dog" from *Collected Poems by C.K. Williams* (Bloodaxe, 2006) and *Collected Poems by C.K. Williams* (Farrar, Straus & Giroux, 2007).

JOSEPH WOODS: "Kerry Blue" from *Bearings* (Worple Press, Kent, 2005).

Index of Authors

Scott Edward Anderson 41, 394
Renée Ashley 241, 242
Neil Astley 30
Celeste Augé 198
Michael Augustin 392, 393
Paul Barclay 391
Judith Barrington 413, 414
Marck L. Beggs 197, 388, 390
Richard Berengarten 386
Drew Blanchard 384
Jane Blanchard 395
Pat Boran 196, 258
Eva Bourke 382
Brian Brett 195
Megan Buckley 381
Simmons B. Buntin 399
Sandra Bunting 193, 194, 380
Louise C. Callaghan 192
Hélène Cardona 33
Seamus Cashman 130
Ann Fox Chandonnet 83
Patrick Chapman 88
Kelly Cherry 190
Sarah Clancy 188
Jennifer Clark 379
Thomas Cochran 187
Andrea Cohen 215, 216, 218
Susan Cohen 378
Nahshon Cook 185, 376
Patrick Cotter 244
Dallas Crow 374, 375
Eleanor Cummins 66
Jack Brae Curtingstall 184
Gill Dalley vii
J.P. Dancing Bear 371, 372, 373
Larry O. Dean 53, 54, 409
Susie DeFord 178, 180, 182
Annie Deppe 405, 408

Theodore Deppe 404
Stephen Dobyns 220
Theo Dorgan 323
Amy Dryansky 251, 252, 253
Susan Millar DuMars 259
Cynthia Schwartzberg Edlow 34
Peter Fallon 79, 80
Elaine Feeney 174
John Fitzgerald 370
Gabriel Fitzmaurice 173
Janice Fitzpatrick Simmons . . 369
Lisa Frank 172
Philip Fried 368
Paul Genega 60
Peter Joseph Gloviczki 367
Desmond Gough 61, 365, 366
Julian Gough 36
Richard W. Halperin 363, 364
Gerard Hanberry 170
Noel Hanlon 167, 169
Maurice Harmon 73, 75
Anne Le Marquand Hartigan 265
Michael Hartnett 301
Michael Heffernan 49
Patrick Hicks 362
Kevin Higgins 361
Rita Ann Higgins 238, 240
John Hildebidle 56
Amy Holman 358, 359
Ron Houchin 318, 319, 320
Adam Houle 352, 353, 354
Ben Howard 72
Holly J. Hughes 351
Bette Lynch Husted 44, 156
Alexander Hutchison 411
Sabine Huynh 165
Brad Johnson 164
Fred Johnston 348

Thomas Kabdebo 212
Conor Mark Kavanagh 163
Jean Kavanagh 227
Deirdre Kearney 162
Anne Kennedy 203
Noel King 346, 347
Philip Kingston 161
Jacqueline Kolosov 159, 345, 401
Ted Kooser 51
Danuta E. Kosk-Kosicka 157, 158
Anatoly Kudryadivsky 400
Maxine Kumin 31, 222, 224, 225
Yahia Lababidi 342
Jessie Lendennie 58, 59
Dave Lordan 289
Caroline Lynch 338, 339
Thomas Lynch 50
John MacKenna ix
Mary Madec 153
Sebastian Matthews 254, 256
Tom Mathews 337
William Matthews 209
Afric McGlinchey 155, 336
Cecilia McGovern 154
Iggy McGovern 335
Irene McKinney 128
Kevin McLellan 334
Devon McNamara 62, 64
Máighréad Medbh 150
Paula Meehan 29
John Menaghan 332, 333
Alexa Mergen 148, 149
Karla Linn Merrifield 147
Agi Mishol 330
Patricia Monaghan 207
Noel Monahan 146
John Montague 213
Alan Jude Moore 329
Susan Moorhead 326, 327, 328
Mary Mullen 145
Pete Mullineaux 143, 144, 324, 325
Richard Murphy 103

Les Murray 321, 322
Kate Newmann 67
Joan Newmann 68
Sheila Nickerson 141, 142
Tommy Frank O'Connor 139
Mary O'Donnell 248, 249
Gréagóir Ó Dúill 70
James Desmond O'Hara 138, 317
Michael O'Loughlin 106
Nessa O'Mahony 105
Mary O'Malley 135. 136
Padraig O'Morain 275
Micheal O'Siadhail 274
Alicia Ostriker 210, 211
Katie O'Sullivan 99
Chris Oke 137
Harry Owen 134, 316
Richard Peabody 315
Gary Percesepe 231, 232
John Perrault 133
George Petty 132
Susan Pilewski 314
Alexis Quinlan 313
Jacob Rakovan 126, 310
Barbara Regenspan 309
C. R. Resetarits 306
Billy Reynolds 305
Moira Rhoarke 311, 312
Patricia Robertson 113
Bertha Rogers 32, 307, 308
James Silas Rogers 302, 303, 304
William Pitt Root 108, 110, 112
Gabriel Rosenstock 301
Gibbons Ruark 300
Lex Runciman 125
Layne Russell 124
Breda Wall Ryan 122, 298
C.J. Sage 291
Aimée Sands 397
John W. Sexton 295, 297
Anne Shaw 121
Glenn Shea 230

Eileen Sheehan 292, 294
Joan I. Siegel 199, 200, 201, 202
Scot Siegel 261, 262
Kevin Simmonds 263
Ben Simmons 119
James Simmons 116
Siobhán of Carna 246
Knute Skinner 114, 288
J.D. Smith 52, 287
Laura Lundgren Smith 76
Mark Smith-Soto 104
Steven Ray Smith 250
Gerard Smyth 78
Joel R. Solonche 286
Scott T. Starbuck 283
Julian Stannard 100, 284
Laura-Gray Street 233
Matthew Sweeney 279, 280, 281, 282
Jordan Taylor 39
Adam Tavel 94, 95
Ilsa Thielan 398
Nancy J. Thompson 98
Wendy Thornton 93, 278
Diana Thurbon 355, 357
Pam Uschuk 81, 82
Peter van de Kamp 89, 90, 92
Michelle Valois 101
Michèle Vassal 86
Jeanne Wagner 403
Drucilla Wall 276
Eamonn Wall 416
Emily Wall 264
William Wall 69
Gordon Walmsley 273
John Walsh 45, 272
David Wheatley 270, 271
Laurelyn Whitt 269
C.K. Williams 228
Christopher Woods 267, 268
Joseph Woods 260
Adam Wyeth 219
Sharon Young 57

Royalties from the sale of this book go to the following dog welfare charities:

The Soi Dog Foundation
Web: www.soidog.org

The Soi Dog Foundation (SDF) is a fully registered charity in Thailand, The Netherlands, and Australia. Established in late 2003 on Phuket by Margot Homburg (now retired) and husband and wife John and Gill Dalley, SDF is dedicated to reducing the suffering of the street dogs and cats of Thailand and setting an example to the rest of the region on how to humanely control a stray population through mass sterilization. SDF treats hundreds of animals every year for injuries and disease and runs a shelter that houses over 300 animals that have been the victims of cruelty or abuse. SDF also educates local children about responsible pet ownership, and runs an active international adoption program. The result is that the stray population of Phuket has been significantly reduced and the remaining animals are in far better condition. As a result of their efforts Phuket has been named Thailand's first rabies free province. Its long term aim is to spread SDF throughout Thailand.

(Charity registration number Thailand: Phor.Gor. 39/2548. Charity registration number Australia: 58982568831. Charity registration number in Holland: 37120202).

MADRA – Mutts Anonymous Dog Rescue & Adoption
Web: www.madra.ie

MADRA is a volunteer-run organisation under the management of registered dog trainers Marina Fiddler and Tara Nic Dhiarmada. It is dedicated to finding new homes for unwanted, neglected, abused and abandoned dogs. MADRA actively searches for permanent, quality homes for their dogs through advertisements in local newspapers, veterinary clinics, pet shops, and special events that provide exposure. The MADRA website and Facebook page provides current, up-to-date information on all our dogs and information on all our work. MADRA actively support, encourage and promote neutering of pet dogs as an ethical solution to the over-population and killing of dogs in Ireland. We also wish to improve the welfare of dogs through general education of the public and through the running of education programmes for children. MADRA's ultimate and overall aim is that all dogs have permanent, loving homes. It wishes to educate members of the general public to have a responsible attitude towards dogs and their welfare and to help create a world where no healthy, good-natured dogs are killed merely because they are considered to be a surplus number.

(Charity registration number: chy18782).

ABOUT THE EDITOR

Jessie Lendennie's prose poem *Daughter* was first published in 1988 (reissued in 1991 as *Daughter and other poems*). It was followed in 1990 by *The Salmon Guide to Poetry Publishing* and in 1992 by *The Salmon Guide to Creative Writing in Ireland*. Her poetry has been anthologised in I*rish Poetry Now: Other Voices, Unveiling Treasures: The Attic Guide To The Published Works of Irish Women Literary Writers* and *The White Page/ An Bhileog Bhan: Twentieth-Century Irish Women Poets*, among others. In 2008, she edited *Salmon: A Journey in Poetry, 1981-2007*, an anthology of Salmon Poetry. In 2009 she compiled and edited *Poetry: Reading it, Writing it, Publishing it*. In 2010, she compiled & edited this book, *Dogs Singing: A Tribute Anthology*, a long-planned project dear to her heart. She is currently working on a memoir for the University of Arkansas Press. She is the co-founder and Managing Director of Salmon Poetry.

ABOUT THE COVER ARTIST

Margaret Nolan attended Art College in Dublin and Galway in the 1980s and returned in 2000 to receive her degree in Fine Art in Galway. She has exhibited her work over many years. Margaret is currently Artist in Residence for Galway City Council. Margaret paints people, animals and places in the urban landscape – ordinary things we walk by every day and not notice – as she believes they hold their own beauty. The painting "blue", used on the cover of this book, is such an example. She can be contacted at: margaretnolangraffiti@gmail.com